BRICKS AND TORTURE

BY

ALAN NEALE

Authors On Line

Visit us online at www.authorsonline.co.uk

An AuthorsOnLine Book

Copyright © Authors OnLine Ltd 2004

Text Copyright © Alan Neale 2004

Cover design by Sandra Davis ©

All rights reserved. No part of this publication may be reproduced, stored in a retrieval system, or transmitted in any form or by any means, electronic, mechanical, photocopy, recording or otherwise, without prior written permission of the copyright owner. Nor can it be circulated in any form of binding or cover other than that in which it is published and without similar condition including this condition being imposed on a subsequent purchaser.

ISBN 0 7552 0120 5

Authors OnLine Ltd
40 Castle Street
Hertford SG14 1HR
England

This book is also available in e-book format, details of which are available at
www.authorsonline.co.uk

Alan Neale – who, what, where (and indeed, why)

Of course it would be much more entertaining if I said I was the 17th son of an Albanian immigrant elephant trainer who, legend has it, worked with Walt Disney on the creation of Dumbo after they met by chance at a New York underground station, but I think that may be construed as stretching the truth somewhat – well, lying, actually.

'Middle' is a word I hate, as it tends more often than not to mean neither here nor there/neither one thing or the other/can't make up your bloody mind, although come to think of it, that seems too often to define my thought process. Nevertheless, I suppose middle-class-middle-England is a recognised term for someone who generally gets on with things, minds their own business, suffers persistent poor service with the odd moan and gripe, has a well-worn Tesco club card, likes a drop of red wine (but never more than £4 a bottle),and thinks that if Linda Barker pops up on the telly one more time, human cloning of the worst kind has truly arrived.

After the almost obligatory degree (about which I will not be disparaging and to this day am justifiably proud that I managed an Upper Second *with* honours, despite a range of extra curricular activities, which included significant alcohol consumption, a laughably failed attempt to kidnap a nurse and the rather brainless stunt of lying down in the middle of the A4) I landed the one job that seemed to be available following more than 70 hand written applications – perhaps they took pity on me.

Ever since this fateful first step, I have been largely involved in the property industry, but it has been a journey which has encountered more unexpected diversions and direction changes than a bank holiday drive around the M25. This has included buying and selling houses, land, shops, offices and anything else generally immovable, managing experienced professionals who had 20 years expertise while I had the grand total of 20 weeks, procuring planning consent for anything from change of use of a shop to a Chinese takeaway, to hundreds of houses on otherwise pristine farmland (and then watching the developer put up something rather less imaginative than my youngest daughter with her favourite lego) valuing industrial units, pubs, care homes and houses for Council Tax (yes, I am sorry, I have helped to implement this fleecing of the public) right through to helping to manage the establishment, development and often precarious teetering of a telecoms' consultancy business – don't ask about the last one, even I don't know how I managed to get there.

Having moved around various parts of the south and east of England, we have been 'settled' in East Herts now for more than 12 years, and since I was born in Hertfordshire more years ago than I am prepared to reveal, it has been a homecoming of sorts. I have a wife who tells me she loves me, but then I have yet to send her for any psychiatric assessment. Her tolerance level has to be of monumental proportions, as she not only has to put up with me, but also two individual and independent children of the female variety, whilst also managing part-time the vagaries of a dental practice nearby, and most particularly a range of patient demands (and frequent abuse) that sometimes beggar belief. The girls are (thank god) happy, lively and healthy and, given that, one should not wish for any more. However, the female obsession in the household is with dancing, all I can say is this has absolutely nothing to do with any genes on my side (foot tapping is probably about as energetic as it gets in my bloodline).

I have never contributed to *The Sunday Times*, had anything published in *Esquire*, or created even the grubbiest footnote in *Rubber Monthly* (and of course, would have no idea where to find the latter publication on the shelves of WH Smith). I did once pen a couple of articles for the sadly now defunct magazine of the East Herts MG Owners Club, and have on occasion foisted some material on the Editors of *Autosport*, but to no-ones great surprise, they failed to take up the offer.

Today, I allegedly hold a 'management' position (Tip: read *'The Little Book of Management Bollocks'* by Alistair Beaton to find out what this term really entails), work too many hours, see too little of my family, have more grey hairs, mortgage payments and credit card bills than is healthy and love motor racing (but despite some illicit prayers, have not received a call from Bernie Ecclestone to be his right-hand man). My ultimate ambition is utterly unattainable – to relax and enjoy life more. In the meantime, if I get my book published, it will at least give me the satisfaction of knowing that one particularly one-dimensional English teacher at Richard Hale School in the 1970's knew nothing of value about me, or indeed, English.

Acknowledgements

In order to avoid being hailed as an ungrateful sod, but more particularly because they deserve it, I should acknowledge the contribution and fortitude of a number of human beings. Firstly, my fellow sufferers Sharon, Sian and Cara, whose general good humour was frequently in contrast to my own dark demeanour, but whose presence was a lifeline; My parents, Joyce and Gerry, whose experience of World War II must at times have seemed strangely re-enacted at Holly House; Richard the Architect, who must have wished he had never met me; and of course the builders, who get their very own thanks elsewhere in this book - Lets all do it again sometime soon (only joking).

Bricks and Torture

This is a book about purchasing and transforming a house of appalling mediocrity and bad taste into one of acceptability and stylistic calm. 'So what?' you say. Well, apart from admonishing you for being quite so pointed and rude, I will then go on to reveal, rather foolishly, that we decided to live amongst the carnage that was the rebirth of a building.

It is a diary of a personal story, but contains most conceivable human scenes and sensations, with a plethora of emotional ups and downs, laughter and tears, pathos, angst, triumph, teetering disaster, frustration, relief, bad language and awful dress sense. I have enjoyed writing it, even if emphatically, I did not enjoy the overall experience, but it has proved to be strangely cathartic.

The premise of the book, and the journey through, sounds deceptively simple, but since the experience was totally unlike anything I imagined, the book follows the same somewhat unstable path. It takes some diversions along the way, since in reality this was necessary to retain some sanity, but then a dead straight passage is rarely as interesting as a meandering change in scene and direction. In any event, the only thing likely to have been either dead or straight during the past 2 years is likely to be inhabiting the kitchen freezer cabinet, although there were a few perilous days in January 2003 when the similarities between the kitchen and the freezer cabinet were hard to detect.

I could tell you that the book is split into three sections, but that would be like pointing out the inadequacies of our rail system - blindingly obvious. Suffice to say Part 1 is the 'Where and Why' (a strange combination of desperation and inspiration), Part 2 is the 'How - Pt I' (parting the Red Sea might have been easier), while Part 3 is 'How (on earth) - Pt II' (sort of Texas Chain Saw Massacre meets Sound of Music within the arena of the Big Brother House).

I think to say any more would be so much expanded polystyrene - pointless (and very annoying) packaging.

Enjoy!

IN THE BEGINNING

12 October 2001. Well, to be precise, the full trauma of this project really smacked me in the face like an errant custard pie on 5 October 2001. Indeed, my senses were assaulted in other ways, particularly sight and smell. It must be a medical condition that on viewing houses whilst its owners are still in occupation, your vision and perception is apparently impaired, everything looks fine, reasonable and clean, the décor looks acceptable, the facilities look useable, yes this could be a reasonable home.

Okay, I already had in mind what only Estate Agents, shifty salesmen and gullible purchasers like me call potential. And I knew we would ultimately want to knock it around a bit to produce the dream residence. Yet I thought what did exist would be perfectly acceptable and comfortable, until such time as we could find the necessary ingredients to commence and complete the project. Something like money akin to a reasonable lottery win, the time equivalent of a serious jail term, and the inclination of a pervert in a convent.

There are probably few things in life that shock as instantly as the look of your house purchase once devoid of people and all their paraphernalia. Walls with the ghostly imprint of pictures and mirrors departed; kitchen cupboards and worktops bearing the wounds and scars of a thousand meals and the thousand knives that went with them; and the general detritus of time and life, built up in every corner, junction, crevice and gutter. These, I can accept and understand, and my sensibilities would have withstood the assault, but the naked truth of this inhabitance took my breath away.

You could have been forgiven for thinking the place had previously been occupied by a partially sighted Moroccan, witnessed by the pots full of a colour which I can only describe as dirty terracotta on just about any wooden frame or surface daring to be exposed. This was gloriously contrasted by acres of off-yellow on the walls (and the cupboards, and the plinths and the cornices and…..) – and this was just the kitchen! The yellow and terracotta theme continued across most surfaces that could be painted, and quite a few that should not even have been in shouting distance of a brush, throughout the house. This was occasionally broken by the odd artistic/vomit inducing (take your pick) swathe of mouldy green. Okay, maybe I can just about accept the taste in these matters is a personal thing – well, I probably could if you twisted my arm, locked me up for a week, and tied a rampaging bull to my testicles. But if we combine this with an ineptitude in application bordering on slapstick, then sorry, but I will just have to undergo the unpleasant surgery.

How was this manifested? How about painting around a built in wardrobe (which in itself did a remarkable impression of what passes for a house in the shanty towns of Rio) with a varied colour palette, without any semblance of precision, brush strokes meandering between wall and wardrobe. Of course, this meant that when the wardrobe was removed (not a difficult task in view of its relative impermanent construction) it left a strange and amusing paint effect on the wall. A riot and jumble which looked like a combination of Andy Warhol, Damien Hirst and my youngest daughter Cara's efforts during her don't-give-give-a-stuff painting period (about 18 months old).

Or, how about the carpet in the smallest bedroom (a disturbing deep blue colour that looked like someone had spilled a bucket full of black ink all over it), which had been fitted – no, sorry, glued and nailed – to the floor. And vaguely butting against the skirting (in some cases merely attempting to flirt with it), but in what appeared to be a jigsaw pattern created purely for the amusement of the fitter. One big lump covering two thirds of the floor, the rest in a complex hierarchy of smaller and smaller pieces which seemed to disappear into one corner. The peculiar thing was, once it had all been taken (ripped) up (for the purposes of some temporary decoration), it seemed impossible to reassemble. At which point some profanities which I had not uttered since the 6th form spouted from my mouth, the pieces went out of the window, and the bed was strategically reconfigured to cover the offending patch of bare floor.

And then there were the downstairs carpets. Imagine chocolate ripple ice cream. Now stir it up pretty severely. Now sprinkle on a liberal handful of dirty chopped string. Voila! You have the dining room carpet (except without the dirt). As for the lounge carpet, this was a hammer horror extra – during our rose tinted visit whilst the residents were in occupation it appeared to be a worn but reasonable cream carpet, albeit of apparent 1970's vintage. In the naked flesh it was grey and brown, but not of choice – this was dirt and stain of biblical proportions. And what was that smell? Our best guess was the presence of a dog, but judging by both the colour and pungency, my guess was the dog was still with us, but had merely expired and become blended with the rest of this matted condemned material.

And so it went on, but on the Thursday the property actually became mine, I seriously queried whether we should proceed to occupy the following week. My very words to myself (thankfully, all alone so the innocent were well protected), cannot be printed. Suffice to say the 'F' word featured. My heart sank deeper than the Titanic, as I wandered from room to room. I questioned my own sanity. I pondered suicide (which could probably have been done by rolling on the lounge carpet, thereby contracting a hitherto unheard of deadly virus). Perhaps total demolition was the solution. Whichever way I looked at it, we were lumbered, and here would begin a story of trial, tribulation and hopeful success, in the face of some odds which ranged from the merely irritating, through plain daft, to gobsmackingly outrageous. In the meantime, what else can a man do but go home, moan to his wife and shed a few tears.

So, how did we get here? Generally, through a series of very poor financial decisions, a desire to purchase the unavailable, and a gradual realisation that unless we did something, anything, we would be forever in housing limbo-land (aka renting someone else's house, with someone else's decoration, and someone else's carpet. Also, dealing with letting agents, whose combined intellect and appreciation of customer service challenges only that of a tortoise. And a sense of impermanency only epitomised by still packed boxes of personal belongings remaining in one place for such a long time, the carpet has become preserved underneath).

For many years, our dream, like millions of others, had been the purchase of a 'period' house with all the usual features and character you think you want, although in reality might just be a bigger pain in the arse (and the wallet) than you can possibly imagine – but more of our foray into the near miss purchase later. In truth, we had also been pushed by some of the increasing negative aspects of our current house. These included a garden whose proportions really were based on those of a postage stamp, a near neighbour whose propensity to use an angle grinder on sundry sad and sorry vehicles at 9.00pm in the evening had started to become very wearing, and an increasing tendency for the local youth to use the mini-roundabout just outside the house for both less than quiet conversation, and a starting point for drag races. These latter events seemed always to be between a lurid variety of badly modified and hand painted Vauxhall Novas, and a motley collection of Ford Escorts, usually finished in a fetching combination of white, rust and badly fitting (and completely pointless) spoilers.

Fortunately, we managed to keep these features in the background when the agents came to view the house, in order to provide a valuation. (Or, best guess/lowest price the fools will take/figure plucked out of The Sun, depending on how cynical you are about your friendly Estate Agent). Unfortunately for one of these Agents, I have some knowledge and experience of property and property sales. So when he thought he was looking ever so professional and clever by measuring the window openings, I was thinking he was either plain barking, or had temporary amnesia, and thought he was in Next trying to buy curtains. Either way the words 'arsehole' and 'complete' came firmly to mind. This quick character assessment was brought sharply into focus when he sucked his teeth and told us we would be lucky to get some £30,000 less than both the other Agents. The words 'crook' and 'total' should then have been branded onto his forehead.

No matter, like taxes, farts and Cilla Black, Estate Agents are a necessary evil, so on the market went the house, complete with adverts, particulars (with the front photograph fetchingly taken from the road, with the lamppost smack in the middle of the elevation) and the standard precarious sale board. Now bear in mind the twice weekly lads rave on the mini-roundabout, and you can imagine that on more than one occasion, the temptation to use this piece of temporary street furniture as either a makeshift bat or weapon of mass destruction was sometimes a little too great. Oh, the intellect and imagination of adolescent boys, and such rich, varied and colourful language. Still, it must have kept the local sign-writer in beer for a few weeks. And despite all this apparent distraction, prospective buyers were coming through in a steady stream – perhaps they liked the idea of a raucous party on their doorstep. Or perhaps we were just sickeningly prepared as model sellers, to include spotless kitchen, fresh coffee bubbling away, heaps of room fragrance and kids under strict orders that if they did not put on their topmost angel impersonation, a weeks solitary confinement in the garage would likely follow. The whole scene on discovery of an impending viewing was quite bizarre – the speed of movement and the blur of cleaning cloths and fluid must have made it look like a speeded up early slapstick film, only the laughter was replaced by swearing of barbaric ferocity. And then all was sweetness, light and beaming faces as the next mug came through the front door.

But it worked. True, the market in late 1998 was no slouch, but even so, to find a purchaser willing to pay the asking price within 5 weeks of going on the market, was pretty good going. (Admittedly, only after I had politely suggested to the Agent that one should never accept first offers, in this case at £2000 below the asking price – what was I paying them for exactly? Oh yes, to get the best price, and there was me thinking all they did was smile and chat inanely to people who wandered in and out of their shop). And such a nice couple too, which always makes it difficult to be hard nosed about any deal. But that was the easy part – now we had to find a house, and one we finally felt we could truly make our home. And to make it even more difficult, we weren't really in the mood to compromise, which is always a rather tricky position to adopt when your funds are limited, your search area is pretty specific, and your requirements match hundreds of others looking for the same thing. Call me naïve, but I truly believed Agents would welcome me with open arms, invite me to sit down in their most comfortable chair, make me a splendid cup of tea, provide me with a comprehensive list of properties matching what we wanted exactly, and ask me to choose. Hey presto, job done! Er, no, not exactly. Well, in fact not at all.

Welcome? More like a knowing sneer ('you'll be the 39th person I've seen today wanting that sort of thing'). Invitation? Rejection has never been something I bear well, and not a comfy chair in sight. Cup of tea? Metaphorical slap in the face more like. List of suitable properties? Ha! 'How about this enchanting 3 bed semi in a splendid rural location?'- shall I tell you what this was? A tarted up ex-council house, with appalling white UPVC replacement windows throughout, a front garden where they had simply strimmered the grass to death, alongside the A507, in the middle of nowhere. Sorry, also forgot the fetching view of the 40 metre electricity pylon on the other side of the road. Other than that, it was perfect.

By February of 1999, it was all getting a little tight and tricky. We had seen a number of houses that were too small, too expensive, time warps from the 1970's, even 1960's or just plain warped, some made you laugh, and countless made me cry, overlooked, overpriced, and over my dead body! But above all, I did not want to lose what seemed to be a good sale, at a good price in a reasonable market, so not for the first time, we made the decision to rent and that was my biggest, most expensive domestic financial mistake in the history of my domestic financial mistakes. What I innocently thought would be at most a 6 month temporary arrangement, turned into a two and a half year pit into which money was tipped, to disappear forever from view. Yes, we found a perfectly acceptable, pleasant house in one of the most attractive villages in the area, and we were comfortable and reasonably happy, with disruption generally kept to a minimum, but it was not ours. There was no mark or personal imprint we could make, no opportunity for the children to express their imagination in their rooms to create their own space, no stamp of personality or place that we could impart – it could never be home. It was more like a storage facility, a temporary refugee camp for those passing through to a place they had not yet found.

And to add to our frustration, we had quickly grown to very much like the village. A quintessential attractive 'sought after' English settlement, complete with a picture post card linear high street flanked with timber and plaster cottages, excellent pub plumb opposite a small green with a pump, magnificent church, whose spire towered over the village amidst swaying mature oak and horse chestnut trees. A small river right through the centre with not one but two quaint fords and a village shop and post office which sold most things you could think of, and many you could not. There were friendly residents and a collection of eccentric, disturbed geese, who regularly attacked anything that gave them as much as a furtive look. Some of the villagers even opened their doors on summer Sundays to offer teas and cakes, as, not surprisingly, those who knew this corner of Hertfordshire, came to soak up a world where most things seemed right, rather than everything being wrong.

So, okay, life was not exactly a miserable pit of despond and poverty, where we were living in squalor and had to undertake gross acts of depravity in order to keep mind and body together – or at least, I never saw such events advertised on the Village Notice Board. Perhaps they were hidden underneath the WI coffee mornings and lost Dalmation posters – or perhaps they involved both the local WI and a lost Dalmation, and I failed to understand the veiled meaning offered by these posters in close proximity, only understood by those wizened lifelong village residents who have their own impenetrable code of local communication and commitment to ancient rituals. Now if it involved sacrificing the odd local goose, I would have needed no invitation, but sadly had to make do with a swift reverse kick to the beak, so vicious and unpleasant were these beasts. Would you believe that shortly before we moved to the village, they had a local vote on whether to retain the geese, or deport them to some poultry equivalent of Siberia, probably to eek out a living as unwilling slaves to a group of militant chickens, or perhaps that was just my fondest fantasy. Anyway, there was an overwhelming vote to keep them ('an intrinsic part of village life' or some such lame excuse), so I rapidly came to the conclusion there was a very strong vein of masochism in the village. Who knows what goes on beyond the offer of Earl Grey and scones on a Sunday?

But it wasn't home. It would have been a wonderful place to have settled, but this was accessible and attractive Hertfordshire, and that spelt money – lots of it. You can see it in the proportion of Mercedes and (large) BMW's, in the mouth-wateringly picturesque and pristine cottages and the not insignificant number of rather grander residences. You can see it and hear it in the pubs (real ale, clipped accents, lots of discussion on cricket and rugby and even the odd cravat – I swear, its true!), and you can smell it. There is a fresh, warm, fermented smell in a well heeled English village, a heady aroma of leather, cigars, cut grass, wood fires, sweaty fly-halves, freshly washed cravats and perhaps the odd sacrificial and roasting goose. And that meant property prices well out of our range, particularly given our craving for the sort of house where the supply curve finally meets the demand curve, usually at a point close to the edge of the graph, where the price band has reached blood red, or otherwise has the notation 'if you have to ask, you can't afford it'. It is a terrible type of agony, badly wanting something you know you cannot possibly have. The sort of thing that used to haunt me at school when, invariably my lust for Sally Mercer was simply a sad delusion. While others literally got to grips with the sort of curves and crevices that 17 year old girls simply should not have had (or at least, not when I was 17), I could only pine and sigh, and curse the good looking bastards who used to flaunt her like she was a new sports car (albeit she had a better rear end, and a slightly more sedate but seductive turn of speed). In fact, wanting some of these oh-so-pretty cottages was much worse. Because I finally did get my hands on the lovely Miss Mercer, although I never quite worked out whether it was because she ticked off everyone else, and perhaps I was, as they say, the last turkey in the shop. But heh, while spoil it for myself! Sadly, none of these properties or their owners were likely to notice me staring vacantly, yet fondly, from the roadside, take pity on my plight and say 'there, there, its your turn now. You have the keys and make yourself at home', although funnily enough, I seem to recall Jez Wilson saying something not dissimilar to me just before my first date with Sultry Sally.

So, we settled into our refugee camp, and settled about tackling the local Estate Agents again. Oh, joy! I know Estate Agents are so lampooned and vilified, it is hardly novel to berate them, but god, do they deserve it. I dreaded the calls to the Agents to try and ensure they knew who we were, what we wanted, and that we were able to move at very short notice. And worst of all was the call on a Saturday morning, when almost without fail, you would have to speak to the 'Saturday Staff'. These are a peculiar breed, indeed I think there must be a laboratory somewhere, staffed by deviant professors that produces these characters as a trial of our ability to withstand the inane, stupid and sub-intellectual. It may be a man or woman, nothing sexist about stupidity, but in either case they would have the same traits. Answer the phone with the enthusiasm of a depressed sloth; a peculiar mid-range monotone delivery, the sort of voice you associate with the boring know-it-all uncle who usually wears a jumper, and a deathly variety of pale greens, beiges and greys; and often you will find when they pick up the phone they will be in mid discussion with one of their equally sub-intellectual colleagues, so what you might get on phoning will be "....did he really? Ooh, I would have slapped him one, the filthy bastard! Hello, Scratchit and Bile, Tracey speaking (yawn), how can I help you?". Well, Tracey, I doubt very much you can do anything to help me, and whatever you do, never, ever be tempted to take up a job with the Samaritans, as the suicide level in your local area is likely to show a marked increase.

It is the retention and application of information (or rather the lack of it) that constantly used to surprise and frustrate. Yes, I am the same nice Mr Neale with funds available, no house to sell, who rang 2 weeks ago to ensure I was on your list of those people who wanted a 19 bedroom mansion in 10 acres of mature parkland, and a complimentary staff of 20 flunkies within the £50 – £100 price range. But despite you appearing to have just this sort of house advertised in the local rag, you seem never to have heard of me. You don't have anything approaching my details in your records and in any event, the house has now been sold at half the asking price to a tribe of Mongolian cannibals, with no funds, a sales chain as long as Harold Shipman's charge sheet, and a disturbing propensity towards environmental destruction. Drat, pipped at the post again!

But we persevered, as only you can with Estate Agents, even though being nice and outwardly friendly to people that inwardly I feel failed to make the queue when they were distributing basic personality and acumen, does not sit comfortably with me. We tolerated being sent details of 1970's houses which had as much personality as the agents, and who then tried to persuade us that these really were characterful homes of charm and style. We endured the countless calls to try and ensure they knew who we were, what we wanted, and the circumstances of our ability to purchase. Despite the fact it became clear that even if I personally charged down the door of their office and branded the receptionist on the forehead with my details and telephone number and spray painted my requirements across their shop-front, just one week later a call would be greeted by "What did you say your name was again? No, we don't seem to have you on our list." We even stomached the crass incompetence of missed appointments, the unfathomable inability to return telephone calls, and the all pervading sneer of someone who finds perverse joy out of someone else's increasing despair at consistently failing to find anything that came within the same hemisphere of what we were seeking.

This went on for the best part of three years, including a period during which our faith had dropped to such sub-zero levels we simply didn't bother – which made the return to the market much more painful. There were a few near misses, including the chocolate box eighteenth century cottage with so many interior beams it looked like an ancient timber yard, and a wonderfully romantic long garden that swept up to a line of mature sycamores and chestnut trees. Granted, the downstairs bathroom next to the kitchen created potential for unfortunate accidents of bare flesh meeting hot objects and the less than sympathetic white plastic conservatory which made the rear elevation look like a hastily constructed railway station waiting room, did not add to the ambience. And despite the overall size, being one size up from a shoe box, and several scales down from what we were currently living in, we did attempt to buy. Indeed, at the time of our bid, a previous long running purchase had fallen through, and the owners had already committed to a move to Sussex, and seemed in need of a metaphorical purchaser on a white horse. Unfortunately, while we played the usual game of showing most, but not all our cards, along came the black knight with a straight flush, a heap of chips and the ability to sweep the table clean in a matter of minutes. Before we even had the chance to up our initial offer, the deal had been done, the door closed, and my heart had been ripped out. I felt as if I had been mugged and robbed, but truth be told, if you try and play clever in a game where you have neither the skill, experience or Swiss bank account, there is then a pretty fair chance you will come off the pitch way before the end of the match, probably on a stretcher.

But the nearest of misses came with the agreement to buy the rather euphemistically named 'Hillside', so named even though it was not located on the side of a hill. Next to a large village church, yes; perched on top of a bank beside the road, yes; owned by a belligerent German farmer, yes; one of the most peculiar listed buildings I have ever seen, yes; but crafted lovingly onto the mid slopes of sweeping downland, with evocative distant views over fields and trees it certainly wasn't. From the outside, the response it provoked was a deep quizzical furrowing of the brow and the simple question "What?". Sat sandwiched on a small chunk of land between a side road and the Church, Hillside was a strange double-fronted confection of whitewashed walls on the ground floor, red tile hanging to the first floor, a grotesquely grafted-on single storey garage that looked as if it had been stuck to the house with blue-tack, a shallow pitch roof all round which gave it the appearance of someone having sat on it unaware of its comparative weakness, and an array of white UPVC replacement windows of varying shapes and styles. The front garden was pleasantly mature with a gorgeous flowering cherry tree, smack in the middle, while the rear garden looked as if it had played host to absolutely nothing for about 5 years. Even without the adjoining graveyard, and the abandoned clothes dryer in the rear garden that was simply of industrial proportions, the signs were not good. And when you knew the house was owned by the local resident at the Manor House and until recently had been occupied by elderly tenants, the omens were not of the bright and sparkly variety. But internally, it began to intrigue and captivate in equal proportion.

The hallway ran to the back of the house, at the end of which was the wooden turning staircase to the first floor. I am a sucker for this vista on entering a house, it gives a wonderful feeling of depth and character, trying to seductively lead you up the stairs before you have even had the chance to take your coat off and drink your coffee. This feeling of being pulled through the house was accentuated by the long exposed beams that ran the length of the hallway, but at the same time, doorways led from either side of the hall, drawing your attention away, and inviting you take a different route – it created a little sense of adventure and mystery. And all this was further heightened by the clear age of the building written in its beams and changes in floor levels, although in some cases you had to see through the lamentable 'improvements', including a kitchen which had been installed by someone in a 1960's time warp and a clear obsession with the colour brown, a dire little tiled fireplace that all men of my age will recognise from their Granny's living rooms, and the entire stock of woodchip paper of B&Q in Harlow. As for the white UPVC windows, I have a pathological hatred of these things – they are an abomination at the best of times, but within a house of this age and (somewhat latent) character, it was sacrilegious. Windows should be wood, period. Metal belongs on industrial buildings and cars, not butted up rudely against plaster and brick.

Upstairs was a revelation – wonderfully bright open landing, wall to wall oak floorboards throughout, and three well proportioned double bedrooms. But the really interesting part were the exposed beams at floor and skirting level, while the walls and ceilings were generally devoid of anything. In fact, later investigation revealed the house was originally single storey, and what we were looking at were roof timbers. An upper floor had been added some 50 years ago, to a reasonable standard, if odd style, which explained the overall quirky nature of the house. In many ways, it added to its fascination, but was ultimately to cost lost time, patience, money and a fair percentage of my sanity.

I suppose the running damp on one of the lounge walls should have given me a bit of a clue, while the rather grey green furry deposit in the chamber of horror which was meant to be a downstairs shower, should have given me a firm nudge, and the curious discolouration in the hall should have shouted so loudly that I jumped back in shock – not to mention the rickety nature of some of the eaves, the peculiar smell in the second reception room, and the leaning retaining wall just about keeping the garage from parting company with the rest of the house. In reality, I already knew many of these problems existed and had accounted for them in my bid to take on the ridiculous liability that was Hillside, but still it came as a bit of a shock when the structural survey revealed its current state would have made it an ideal residence for any ghosts and ghouls that might want to pop in from the next door garden of interment, but less suitable for your average Hertfordshire family, where warmth, dryness and structural stability tend to feature high on the list of necessities. Okay, I exaggerate a little, but believe me, not by the greatest of margins. Damp was rife on the ground floor, but the cause was unclear, while subsequent prodding and digging around the foundations discovered there weren't any. Rather bizarrely, the garage was better anchored, but even then, if we did not correct the current torrent of water that ran around it and down the road when it rained, the garage could soon become the good ship 'Hillside Annexe', and float off into a new life of its own. Some other less costly, but still essential repairs were necessary, but perhaps most irritating were the sensitively installed UPVC windows. This was a listed building, and doing this sort of thing without the requisite consent is the equivalent of mooning outside No 10. It gets you into trouble with the authorities pretty swiftly.

Making these points to the owner is always a difficult job. Doing purely through an Estate Agent makes it tortuous. When the owner is a local landlord with no sense of reason or compromise, then pray that your hair is well secured to the rest of your head, or else baldness will swiftly result. He was not the slightest bit interested, and although the provisional price agreed did assume that the house would need more than a lick of paint and a self satisfied smile, I had not quite planned for the litany of corrective measures that would be necessary. However, desperation and desire are curious bedfellows, and together they conspired to persuade me I should press on, even though I knew this could be a prize-winning money pit. Strangely, a Building Society (not generally known for their services to poor house buyers) eventually came to the rescue, this being in the shape of their insistence that we obtain a full damp and timber survey before they confirmed any transfer of cash from their swelling coffers into my paltry metaphorical dented old tea tin. Said survey was eventually completed, although only after two visits, as the first hinted at the need for more extensive investigations – I had visions of a highly trained forensic team in the dead of night, all flashlights, hushed voices and white overalls, painstakingly digging around the flesh of the house in order to find the cause of its pernicious disease. Unfortunately the problem came from below rather than above – rampant rising damp caused by a concrete floor laid with little or no moisture barrier, the solution to which would demand the brutalisation of most of the ground floor and significant repair to some of the timbers and a rather major haemorrhage of funds from the old tea tin. Time for an ultimatum to the sellers, and even then I still could not quite get myself to accept the act of throwing good money after bad is generally not a principle to be admired and applauded. There would unlikely be a surprise party thrown to celebrate my liberation of this tired old house from the clutches of the evil Landlord, even if I was successful – which, thank god, I wasn't.

Belligerence and obstinacy must have been our local Shylocks middle names, and I pulled myself back from the brink of the abyss, having stared down it for sometime, been unable to see the bottom, and heard the clear voice of sense, which suddenly leapt out, grabbed me by the lapels, and told me not to be such an arse. We walked away a little saddened, but ultimately pretty relieved, not to mention a few quid short. To my great and twisted delight, about a month later I received a call from the agents who enquired rather embarrassedly whether I might still be interested, as the owner might, erm, be prepared to, er, well, shall we say, erm, discuss matters. My immediate response was to want to do an impression of one of the standard evil characters in the James Bond films – sneer slowly, and in an overexcited drawl say "well now Mr Bond, you want to discuss matters with me after all, do you? I fear the time for bargaining has passed and you have an appointment with Igor and his diamond tipped chainsaw. Goodbye Mr Bond." However, that would have confused the Agent (not difficult), if only for the fact neither they or their clients name was Bond. So, instead I laughed (and, yes, it was mildly manic) as I savoured the moment, and although what I really, really, wanted to say was "F*** OFF!", I simply said, sorry, too little, too late, I am in the process of buying something else. Ha! (only without the Ha!).

And of course that something else brings us back to where we started. Holly House would have ranked a 500-1 outsider when we first started looking for a house, it so does not fit with what we said we wanted, but after the failure of Hillside, responsibility began to way heavily. Here we were more than 2 years after moving out of what had become a home, despite its drawbacks, and we were all starting to feel like nomads, with a growing sense of impermanency, brought into sharp focus by my youngest daughter.

"Daddy?"

"Yes, Cara"

"Daddy, when we get our own house, can I paint my bedroom the colour I want?"

"Of course you can"

"And will that be quite soon?" There was no malice in her voice or accusing look, which made it all the more painful.

I looked around her bedroom and realised that even at 7 years old she was growing up, and doing so with no sense of home or stability, and a constant sense of 'make-do'. I had moved them all from somewhere they had settled, to an unsettling environment, and no timescale or commitment to make it right. I was failing the whole family, and although they weren't exactly plotting my demise, I needed to give them some solid comfort and an end to the uncertainty.

Rather perversely, Holly House is in the same village as Hillside, but no worse for that. It scored on 2 big counts – quiet, friendly village location (complete with no-nonsense pub), and a big plot. It fell down dramatically on the third point – it was a shit house! Smack in the middle of the village conservation area, and carved from what was once the garden of the adjoining handsome Georgian House, you would have expected it to have been designed and built with considerable sensitivity and style, yet it had the all sensitivity and style of a verruca. Built in 1985, it could have been supplanted from any one of a thousand border-edge dreary housing estates that litter towns and cities across Britain, all mixed proportion, style and emphasis, and a squatness which always makes me wonder whether there is an invisible ceiling they are afraid of hitting. Externally, it was built of rather indeterminate brown bricks, although at least they had some variety in tone and texture, topped with a roof that at least had a good pitch which helped to lift the building a little, but only a little. The windows were of the Woolworths variety – cheap and functional. Personally (and I accept my view may not be shared by others, although god knows why), windows and window openings are one of the best architectural and textural features of a property. They break up what can otherwise be a monotonous elevation, and their style can either emphasise, complement or (in this case) argue pathetically with the rest of the house. These were wooden, stained, flush asymmetric casement windows of subtly different sizes across the front and back of the house. The jarring impression they create when you can clearly see that one half of the window is a different size and proportion to the other, makes it look as if Mr Blobby has taken up a job as a carpenter. And houses have texture and perspective – flush windows on plain fronts make it look like one of those cartoon houses that pop-up from the pages of toddlers first play books – no depth, no interest.

And, at the risk of sounding like some architectural pseudo, the house had no rhythm. No, I was not expecting it to have a soulful voice and be clicking its tiles in time to James Brown. Think of a typical Georgian House, it has clear vertical emphasis, accentuated by its big tall windows, generally of the same height and position, lined up in the same plane, and all in harmony with its doors, roofline, even its chimneys. All the proportions are right, the vertical bits of the house don't demand a pistol fight at dawn with the horizontal bits. It is handsome, rather than pretty, you admire, rather than swoon. If it were a singer, it would probably be Bryan Ferry rather than Robbie Williams, whereas Holly House is more like your local pub singer down the Red Lion on a Friday night – dire and dull, all at the same time. Inside, it was as the architect said 'built to a budget', the budget being just slightly more than you might have proffered for 2 pints of lager and a packet of crisps at said Red Lion, but probably less than a barrel of best and a case of pork scratchings. It was compact and bijou, but without the bijou, although I had to hand it to the builders, how they managed to squeeze 4 bedrooms into such a limited frame was a masterpiece of logistics. The entrance hall was in fact an entrance patch, barely able to fit a cat let alone contemplate swinging one – it was so small the front door opened outwards, because it could not be done any other way. From it you could either go straight up the stairs, immediately left to the lounge or immediately right to the dining room, one step either way taking you fully into those rooms. This meant access around the ground floor was by one route only, and from dining room took you (in fairly short order) through hall and lounge to the kitchen. Meal times then were a comedy, and for those sitting in the lounge it must have looked like a farce in a restaurant with a constant stream of people rushing backwards and forwards across their field of view, bumping into each other and getting increasingly manic in their movements.

Upstairs was an equal hotchpotch. The landing was very marginally larger than the hall, while the bathroom was a small, thin affair where standing at the basin you felt you should pull yourself in to make room, as if squeezing by in a tight queue of people. The bedrooms were small, save the largest which was a reasonable size double, but then possessed two of the biggest quirks in the house – a door which was so configured that it caught on the upstairs chimney breast and so only opened about two thirds, and a shower built into a cupboard which not only looked as if Bob the Builder really had fixed it, but was also totally devoid of any lighting. Of course this latter aspect was a fundamental problem, since on closing the shower/cupboard door, you could not even see the hand in front of your face, let alone the soap and the rest of your body. Needless to say, it sat unused, a fitting empty monument we felt to the strangeness that was Holly House.

Turn your back on the house however, and its foibles disappeared. Whatever the shortcomings of the owners in terms of style, taste and DIY, they certainly did know about creating and maintaining a garden. To the rear and right across the back of the house, was a not unpleasant rockery, where over the first 12 months of our occupation, something new and surprising was cropping up almost every month. A small path through here led up to a modest lawn with mature borders resplendent with lupins, lilies and roses, while a hidden seating area had been created to the far right. From there was an arch from which tumbled a clematis that in the summer burst with huge flowers of shimmering lilac. To the left of the rear garden were a couple of semi-mature chestnut trees, but perhaps best of all was an arching laburnum that dripped vivid yellow flowers and created an almost surreal frame for the whole scene. Indeed, behind the garden were fields of wheat and views across the gently undulating landscape, and from the upstairs window, this view, framed by the laburnum, was almost too picture-postcard. The front garden was a much larger affair, but as the plot and house were largely side on to the road, it did not have that 'buffer zone' feel that you have with many front gardens, like an intermediate piece of ground that is part yours, but part public, open for all to see, comment on, deposit their litter and possibly defacate in. And since it was all very mature with tall hedging in part along the boundaries, not to mention the good manners of the people of the village, this was never going to be the case. A good size central lawn was the focal, but least interesting part. Fruit trees were abundant, producing plums, damsons, pears and particularly more cooking apples than you could shake a pie at, while more mature trees, particularly towards the far end of the garden created our own little woodland glade, the ground interspersed with ferns, ivies and hostas. And then there were the buddleias, carnations, and more roses peeping over and around the fence. The rest of the garden had been thoughtfully planted almost giving the appearance of a well tended oasis on the edge of a mature copse. Despite not being what you could ever describe as grand, it still had little walks and vistas, nooks and crannies that created real interest and a sense of restfulness.

The space around the house, or at least front and back was good, although the width of the plot did not leave much to play with. Nevertheless, there was clearly sufficient to spark my brain into concocting plans of extensions and improvements, even as we viewed the house for the very first time. The episode with Hillside and its aftermath had rather sharpened my senses, and although the house was clearly not what we wanted, the plot and location certainly was. Of course, it is particularly easy for your senses to sit comfortably in the green zone on a bright, warm sunny perfect summer day in July, seeing only what you want to see, and thinking only positive thoughts, yet be as blind as the proverbial to all those little, and not a few rather large and obvious problems that might put a metaphorical banana skin under your plans, which is where we came in.

THE BIT BEFORE THE START

Let me start with a confession – I am not a fully paid up member of the Architects Fan Club. Indeed, if one existed one suspects its Chairman would probably be in the throes of persuading doctors of his mental stability. It is not necessarily their dress sense, which is at best quirky, possibly unkempt and at worst faintly bizarre. There is usually a generous amount of brown within their clothes, teamed with something outrageously bright, a scarlet red, a cobalt blue or lime green. On meeting them I often find it very difficult to resist suggesting they might want to tuck in the half of their shirt that is flapping in the breeze like a sorry looking sail, and perhaps even pulling their tie knot a few inches to the right or left, so it is at least within respectable distance of the middle of the collar and looks vaguely related to it. Even more difficult to resist is the urge to pull out a comb and propose that some sort of semblance of order is restored. But having said all this, they can be disarmingly charming and amusing people, often with a great passion for what they do, although, just like my maths teacher in the 5th form, sometimes with a complete lack of ability to transfer such passion – granted, passionate about maths would appear to be an oxymoron, but hey, someone's got to love it.

With all this in mind and no real idea about whom I should choose to make my plan reality, I hit on the idea of a beauty parade, though without the need to dress up in skimpy swim-suits and tell me how they wanted to devote all their time to saving monkeys in the Congo. I selected four likely looking local Architects, wrote to all with a background to the house, an explanation of what I was looking to achieve, and a request for proposals, prices and timescales. One never even bothered to reply, a decision that says much about their business, but may ultimately have proved in their favour. The other three all wanted to visit, two on the same day, which appealed to my sense of deviousness as I booked them in back to back, like a cocky seller of a prize sports-car, hoping they would both meet each other and feel intimidated to bid against each other. In the event, that didn't happen, probably because I got very bored with the first one. Dressed in a long (yes, brown) coat and multicoloured scarf, he looked like he was halfway to a Doctor Who convention, and the discussion was equally left field. There were suggestions of re-fronting the house, and creating a rather weird glass atrium type structure as a stairwell, and a constant inability to discuss the matters and issues that I (as a mere simple prospective client) wanted to discuss. When he then went right down the end of the front garden, started waving his arms about and 'framing' the view of the house, I had reached the conclusion he probably was a time-lord. Number two was a completely different proposition, and most definitely from the same galaxy as me. A smartly dressed lady who was faintly intimidating and I felt had sussed me out in fairly short order. It became clear her practice were rather more noted and inclined towards 'modernism' than I might have been prepared to stomach, and illustrated by some literature she brought along to include an extension to a house that looked like an upmarket aviary – fine if you are an exotic bird, less so if you are an average human being. I was rather left with the impression she thought me a less than desirable client and that was indicated by a fee quote which confirmed my inadequacy.

Dear old Richard however, seemed to fit the bill rather better. He had all the attributes of what I was expecting (see first paragraph), including a degree of charm and the look of a man who had done and seen it all several times over. Whereas it might have been unfair to say his face looked like a bed that had been slept in, the duvet cover was certainly not straight out of the packet. He seemed genuinely to have had experience of similar projects, and I judged him as someone who had reasonable practical knowledge of how these things work in reality, although of course the mud on his boots could have come from his back garden. However, he had a kindly and confidently pragmatic air about him and seemed genuinely interested in what I wanted and why I wanted to do it. I was also amused by his dirty and slightly battered Fiat Punto and began to form the view that here was a man and a practice that was never going to have a huge and prestigious client list, and was certainly unlikely to win awards for cutting edge design, but was at least workmanlike in its ethos, easy to work with, trustworthy in its principles, and probably a damn sight cheaper than most of its rivals. My prediction on the latter point was confirmed a few days later, and so began a relationship that had all the trials and tribulations of a 20 year marriage, condensed into little more than 18 months.

At the same time as identifying an Architect, I also took a deep breath and commenced discussions with the planning department of my local council. This is an activity for which you must take the deepest breath possible and prepare to be transported to the twilight zone. Some may have felt I was fortunate in that I have some knowledge and experience in dealing with planning officers and their departments, but I have learnt over many years, playing the professional in these circumstances can be a big disadvantage. And being professional in a purely personal capacity I could see had the potential to create more conflict and confusion than Saddam Hussain. So it was, I played the ignorant-and-simple-member-of-the-public routine and met a planning officer, talking in such feeble and pathetic tones that even I started to cringe at myself. It is actually quite difficult to talk to someone about something you know quite a lot about, but pretend you are totally ignorant, and I had to resist the temptation to quote legislation and government guidance. My clandestine approach worked reasonably well. The planning officer was helpful in his suggestions and seemingly supportive of my basic ideas. But my cover was nearly blown when, without prompting I asked for the correct forms and certificates in order to make a formal application. After a two second blank stare, I laughed weakly, held up the little 'Guide to Making a Planning Application' and blurted "Did a little bit of reading while I was waiting for you! Thanks for your help, bye!" and rushed out of the building with indecent haste. His uncertain look was worrying, and when I next met him he was a little guarded, but I think my impersonation of Mr Ignorant was reasonably successful.

Metaphorically waving an in-principle agreement from the planning officer, I triumphantly met my architect to discuss just exactly how we were going to create the proverbial silk purse from a decidedly down at heal pigs ear and one with a bit more space and logic than a Barbie House. The restrictions of the width of the plot and the sensibilities of the neighbours pretty much made our decision as to where we would extend, but how and what it would provide internally met with some debate. Moreover, was how we were going to treat and improve the house externally, adamant as I was that the finished article would be as far removed from the current tribute to dullness and lack of imagination, as it was possible to get. Having said that, it needed to be simple and well balanced, and as clichéd as it seemed, I began heading in the direction of creating something with a Victorian flavour. Houses are predominantly two (or more) storey structures with generally some clear vertical emphasis. Yes, I know this omits bungalows, but since I would like nothing better than to ensure the entire world permanently omitted bungalows, you can see my point. Dwellings should have structure, height, depth, proportion, interest and a deportment that does not look as if someone has beaten it to death with a mallet. You can't really see the urban landscapes of Bath or Dublin making such an impression on us if the streets were lined with buildings that barely came above your knee. I admit, plagiarism is not necessarily something to be applauded, but in the position Holly House was in, it had to reflect some of the virtues of the houses in the vicinity, but without being twee or creating a sickening pastiche. Above all, it had to be simple and reasonably classic, and that rather limits the options.

Closest neighbour was a splendid Georgian House, with plain front, big sash windows and tall roofline. On the other side (if we conveniently ignore the bungalow) was a later and smaller Georgian cottage, originally two, now one, handsome red brick, more sash windows, and good pitch roof. Further afield were some much older cottages, many thatched and timber frame, all climbing roses, pastel walls and picket fences, but unless you want to look a real fool and commit architectural hari-kari, you cannot turn a 1980's brown brick house into an 18th century chocolate box cover. You wouldn't, for instance, try and make David Beckham look like Bobby Charlton, not unless the comb over suddenly made a miraculous return to the fashion scene as a must-have – can't even see Beckham going for that. So verticality, simple character, and a bit of texture were needed, particularly to reflect exactly some of those elements already in existence in the vicinity.

The verticality we planned to introduce with new projecting gables both front and back, together with a cunning/expensive (delete neither) plan to replace every single window and door. New simple box sash windows would go in throughout the whole house and I considered the joy I would experience on seeing the current horrors extracted, discarded and destroyed in a ritual sacrifice and celebration to the all-powerful god of good taste, and a two fingered salute to the deity of dross. The simplicity was to be maintained by ensuring windows and doors in line, with harmony across both vertical and horizontal planes, but with the greater height of the windows constantly emphasising the vertical plane as being the dominant form, especially within the gables. Okay, anorak off -looking at the front, from the left, window top, window bottom, door, window top, window bottom, the end. However, it did not necessarily start like this.

The first sketches produced by Richard either exposed his skills in the practical department but also his lack of flair in the design department, or he genuinely thought what I really wanted was a house in suburbia. As he went through them, I sat impassive, lips becoming tighter. As he saw this his speech became slower, and his eye contact more frequent as the realisation was dawning that he was not about to be hailed as the great saviour of village design. Finally, he stopped, looked straight at me and said

"You're not too impressed are you?"

"Mmmm…No."

"What did you envisage?"

"Not living on a Bovis Estate."

It could have come out of the pages of a developers standard house design guide, even of early 1990's vintage, but it had become clear fairly soon in the relationship that I would be leading the design ideas, while Richard made them and in some cases had to change them into practical reality. While I could mourn the fact we were not going to produce something desperately innovative, I wasn't sure that most of Anstey knew the meaning of the word. And I really didn't want to create something which looked as if the village had been visited by an alien intelligence, or Richard Rogers (that is of course always assuming Richard Rogers is not, in fact, of alien intelligence, although this was exactly my thought when I first saw the Pompidou Centre in Paris).

We pressed on and finally produced the first set of plans that seemed to do the trick. The gables front and back and the new windows and doors all round gave a reasonably handsome, if modest, appearance. The effect of the gable extensions was to create much more room internally, which in turn allowed us to re-plan the interior generally. Whereas previously on the ground floor we had our comedy circus of kitchen into lounge, through hall, into dining room (and vice versa), we now had a small but useable entrance hall, and one where there was the novel ability to circulate and access the whole ground floor. The current dining room was to become a study, part of the kitchen was to become a utility, while the majority of the rear extension was to form a good size kitchen and dining area. The lounge was to become even longer than it was at present (running completely front to back, or dual aspect if you want to speak agentese). Upstairs we were finally to have a landing worthy of the name, together with some natural light. The smallest bedroom was to become the new bathroom, and the rear extension was to be a new bedroom for Cara, who had already started to plan a colour palette which would have been at home in Willie Wonkas sweet factory. Sian's bedroom would be largely unchanged, while the adult bedroom would be extended into the front extension, and we contrived to be able to squeeze in an en-suite shower room, only this time with the ability to see what you were doing. The plan also included a conservatory on the flank wall of the lounge, in order to provide another ground floor reception, and add a little width to what was a somewhat narrow room. Okay it wasn't going to be Buckingham Palace, but neither was it likely to be Fawlty Towers.

My deliberate plan all along was to totally remodel the house, so when finished, it would not only look less than embarrassing, but have the appearance of having been built originally exactly as the finished article, and for there to be no obvious signs of bits having been stuck on, like a longstanding and ever expanding lego construction. I also proposed a plain front to reflect the next door property, particularly on the projecting gable extension where we originally planned two windows top and bottom, perfectly in line and centred. I proudly showed these plans to my new friend, the planning officer at a meeting on site, on a perfect cold, crisp December morning. Planning Officers are generally people who have a slightly misguided sense of public duty, but quickly have to develop a propensity for masochism. Their dress sense could often win first prize in an Architect look-a-like competition, but their demeanour and personality is many and varied, from the uncompromising dictator to the gregarious pragmatist. Mine was a touch uncertain but affable, dressed in a sober but smart dark blue suit. Perhaps he was new to the job, untainted by many verbal assaults by members of the public and slick housing developers. To my great satisfaction, he seemed to continue his general support, although griped about two things which would cause difficulties for some weeks to come.

One was the fact that we were planning a level of extension that took it some way beyond their unwritten rule of 30% of the current space. I pointed out that 30% of not very much equated to not very much and if we were going to make some impact on creating workable living space, this would be inevitable. It also seemed to escape him this did not mean we were creating a 20 bedroom hacienda from a two-up-two-down terrace – it was a 4 bed house now, it would be a 4 bed house when finished.

"Yes, that's true," he said rather wistfully, as if I had just unlocked some dark secret and told him where to find the elixir of life.

More troubling was his distinct lack of enthusiasm for the treatment of the front gable, which he felt was a little plain and flat. I could see where this was going, we were entering the land of the lowest common denominator and speeding rapidly towards Average-town seeking room at the Hotel Run of the Mill, in the delightful suburb of Standardised Housing. Oh, god, he wanted a Bovis House too.

We parted, and later that day I penned a letter on the basis of striking first in the, probably forlorn, hope it would reinforce my view and influence his. Without actually saying 'You're wrong, I'm right', I did try and point out the error of his ways, although avoiding any personal reference to my perception of his inability to spot an interesting design if it came up to him, slapped him around, and shouted in his face. To my surprise, a response came back within a matter of days, but in dealing with a letter from a planning officer, you have to have a degree of ability in analysis and dissection of English, without which its true meaning is less than clear. This approach of course comes from years of having to protect your back and covering every angle possible in order to demonstrate what some may interpret as explicit democratic even handedness, but others may view as sitting so firmly on a fence that splinters in your arse are an occupational hazard. Personally, I wouldn't be a planning officer for all the tea in China AND all the money in the world, even if you threw in a lifetimes supply of Wadworths 6X and promised me I would never have to watch another episode of Family Fortunes again. Ultimately, he had accepted the size issue was a non-issue, but persisted that the front of the house, and in particular the front gable, needed a different treatment. So, I did what we would all do when faced with advice from those in authority – I ignored it.

I continued to pursue a route of presenting the proposal on very much a personal basis rather than letting the professionals do so, although ultimately I was to be forced to rethink that particular strategy (aka swallowing ones pride). I prepared a veritable novel of a supporting statement to accompany my formal application, full of subjective hyperbole and somewhat biased viewpoints and conclusions, but I thought it stood up rather well. In truth, it was probably a little too personal and insular, like a poem about a favourite toy or teddy bear from your childhood, looks fine and reasonable to you, but totally cringe-making to others. But, hey, I was just a simple member of the public, how could I know any better? However, one solid theme I flogged heavily was that here was a pretty dire house in the middle of a village conservation area and here I was proposing something that would render a dramatic improvement. You would have expected it to be fairly compelling to all, particularly the good old British Institution, the Parish Council. I even gave them advance warning by sending them draft plans before the application was submitted and inviting further discussion. They then had a copy of my full application and plans at the same time as they were sent to the Council, when normally it would be some two or three weeks after the event they would receive them. I thought this was all rather inclusive and accommodating, all in the spirit of communication and discussion.

So it came as a bit of a shock when a few weeks later, I discovered the Parish had formally objected to my application. I had received no communication, no phone calls, visits or letters. Perhaps it was a misunderstanding, so I telephoned the Clerk to the Parish Council.

"Yes, I was going to telephone you," he said rather embarrassedly. "I'm afraid the council rejected your application, there were some things they weren't happy about it seems."

'What?' I thought. Had they been holding the plans up the wrong way? Had they misread the scale? Did they think I was proposing what was there rather than what was going to be there? Or were they just plain daft, vindictive or both? Thankfully I had not uttered these thoughts out loud, otherwise my already tenuous relationship with the Parish would have crashed and burned.

"Are you able to tell me what the problems were?" I said through almost gritted teeth

"I think you had best speak to the Chairman, Peter Sapsed."

So I did.

"Well, the council were concerned about the size of the extension, and the affect on neighbours," said Peter Sapsed rather apologetically

"But you know I have spoken to both my neighbours and they have no concerns?"

"Have you?"

"Yes."

"Well, there were concerns about the encroachment out the front and the conservatory at the side."

"Tell you what, why don't you come round to have a look at the house as it stands? See some of the problems we are trying to solve and I can also explain the plans to you, because I think they might have been misread and I know that is easy to do."

We agreed to meet on Saturday morning.

Normally in these situations, my patience is limited, I confess my opinion of the Parish Council and I suppose by inference Peter Sapsed, was not high. To me, this was an open and shut case of crap house being replaced by good house in sensitive village location. What else was there? It should also be confessed that I am no lover of local politics and councils, in my experience, they rarely have the altruistic motives they should in this position, but as you are now acutely aware, I am a cynical bastard. Peter Sapsed was actually a delightful man, the main local farmer, of a gentle nature, but still of some presence. He looked significantly younger than I bet he actually was and had been Parish Council Chairman for many years. With gently greying hair and moustache and a wonderful rural burr, he looked and sounded like everyone's favourite uncle. I showed him around the house and he clearly recognised the space and circulation problems, but remained concerned about the extent of the works. We opened out the plans, the extent of the misconception became clear and I worked through ticking off the concerns one by one.

No, the extension to the front would not need us to completely reposition the drive, it was not that big or extensive

No, the rear extension would have no effect on the neighbours to the east, given the garage already fell between us and they had no windows which faced in that direction. They had also given their full support.

And no, the conservatory would not be particularly noticeable from the road as it did not come much above the tree, hedge and fence cover.

"Well, I can't see any problems," he said. "I am happy to speak to the other councillors, but of course I can't say whether they will be prepared to change their minds, but certainly I can't see any problems."

In the circumstances, there was not much more I could do, Chairman of the Parish Council onside, that should sort it. Err, no.

In the meantime, I was pressing the Planning Officer to see some progress on the application. Thankfully, he had not been particularly swayed by the Parish Councils objection, he too thought they were being less than logical. Their concerns seemed to be on issues of size and encroachment, while he was still harping on about the design, especially at the front. Clearly, I was starting to reach a stage where simply turning my back with my nose in the air, stamping my foot and saying, 'sorry, you are talking bollocks' was beginning to have its limitations. And now it appeared the Conservation Officer was pitching into the argument. Oh, shit! Conservation Officers are to be feared in the same way you would fear a demagogic History Teacher, footsteps pounding up the corridor, drunk with power and authority, and utterly obsessed with the view that his view is right. Indeed, it is so right, it is not a view, it is fact, indeed, it should be law, in fact why isn't it law? They are correct, if somewhat deranged, you are a worthless individual. Period.

I had however, met this particular conservation officer before, when discussing the prospects of extending Hillside and to my great surprise, he had been most helpful. In fact, he had even drawn a little sketch which seemed to comply with the sort of thing I had in mind, and discussed matters with the (same) planning officer on my behalf. What was I to make of this, was it a cunning trick? No. Hillside was a Listed Building and was in some state of disrepair. I had what they wanted – the inclination to rescue the house, the conviction to do it properly and the prospect of this was rather better than dereliction and disregard by the local landowner. Holly House was a different matter and I was beginning to pick up vibes of discomfort from people who knew of its existence, and perhaps were now exposed to the shame it was ever built. That I could understand, what I could not understand were the apparent persistent objections to do anything, as if making the house remain in its present state would serve as some sort of perverse lesson. I think this is called 'cutting off your nose to spite your face', or more correctly, blind obstinacy. At least the planning authority were happy to see the changes in principle, but the detail of the design, especially at the front was now causing some angst. Time for a meeting to try and thrash something out. This was duly arranged for late afternoon on a rather warm weekday in April.

What is it with council meeting rooms? They seem to be designed to be cramped and uncomfortable, always internal without a window in sight, with a temperature range that seems to mimic inhospitable regions of the world. Today, we appeared to be in the Kalahari Desert, except there is almost certainly a bit more room there. Within a matter of moments we had all removed jackets, loosened ties, while some were going a nice shade of pink, giving the impression we had been in there all day, negotiating some major international deal. Sadly, we had barely begun, the subject was the front of my house and to my irritation, the back as well. I thought I would set the general scene, trying to promote a friendly tone, and working up to why we thought our plan and elevation was splendid, and they should accept their opposition was worthless – except, in not quite so few or direct words. There was however a persistent view from both the planning officer and the conservation officer that not only was the front too 'plain', but the pitch of what amounted to two new gables, front and rear, should fall below the pitch of the current roof, so they were 'subservient'. What? Do they expect the things to tug their forelocks in deference? Should we design them so they look perpetually ashamed, with drooping windows and eaves as a symbol of their place in the hierarchy? They persisted that gable extensions from main houses always were 'subservient', in order to 'step the structure down'. They then produced some sketches, which in part started to resemble some of Richard's earlier schemes, but essentially looked to lower the roof lines of both extensions and tart up the elevation of the front.

I could stomach the changes to the rear, although the lowering of the roofline and the pitch meant the dining area extension could not have a roof that was an extended plane of the main roof, which I thought might look quite good. However, the pronouncements on the front were starting to make me really rather cross and worse still, I was starting to show my irritation, which is something you really should not do in these meetings. I maintained and reinforced (and almost shouted) my objections and the contrivances being put forward made me wince. The last straw happened when they were proposing what they considered to be in keeping with local vernacular, and came up with a jettied front. Oh, Lord, help us! Jettied houses are almost always timber frame houses (often black and white) in town locations, they were built that way to create as much room at first floor level, while their ground floor footprint occupied something rather less, a sort of lateral thinking land-grabbing tactic. They are found in many old towns in East Anglia, always in central locations where land was at a premium, frequently in High Street locations and along old coaching routes. Anstey is not a coaching route, nor does it have a recognisable High Street and unless history has failed to record that the village used to be a long since forgotten major commercial centre, it cannot be described as a town where land was at a premium. I looked at the conservation officer, I looked at the planning officer, I looked at Richard and I dropped my head. Fearing I would pull a samurai sword from my bag and commit Hari Kari as a protest at the stupidity of all of this, Richard took control. I lost interest, but would have waved a white flag if I had had one. The rest of the meeting is a bit of a blur.

I regained the will to live once I was outside and my body encountered fresh air, at which point Richard and I were able to talk intelligibly about the consequences of the meeting and what we should do next. My overwhelming preference was to hire a Sherman Tank and wipe the East Herts planning department off the face of the earth, but I accepted it would not have been a very civilised or productive thing to do, although immensely gratifying. I had visions of how I could make part of the Council building jettied, easily done I thought with my tank removing a large section of the ground floor. However, I was persuaded to talk more sensibly and Richard agreed to go away and come up with some alternative revised drawings for the front and rear, get these to me for feedback, and then seek approval with our friends in their very un-vernacular office. In essence, this was going to mean some sort of bay front and if this was the worst I would have to suffer to get approval, then I suppose I was going to have to accept, even if I would keep thinking 'Bovis' half the time.

A few days later, I received a couple of alternative sketch designs, one of which looked very worryingly to have a frontage like the very one we were trying to replace and consequently caused a furrowed brow. The other was a simple tweaking of the bay front idea, but at least making it of some substance and style, whilst dropping the pitch of both extensions, so that they dutifully kept their place as minions in the presence of the main roof. Richard seemed to think this would do the trick and I told him to press on and get agreement from the conservation officer in particular, in the absence of which I might be looking up 'Threatening & Menacing Services' in the Yellow Pages. A telephone call from Richard the next day confirmed this would not be necessary.

A set of revised drawings dutifully dropped through the letter box a short while later, and these seemed to be in order. Knowing the value of neighbourly support, one of the first things we did was pay another visit to the occupants in the next door Georgian House. They had already expressed significant support for the scheme, but I felt it only fair that I should let them have sight of the new plans, given the changes to the front elevation. To a mixture of both delight and alarm, they professed a preference to the original scheme, so perhaps I was not the only one who thought the conservation officer needed a different vocation. Still, thankfully they accepted it was all still vastly better than what existed at present and gave their blessing. This however, was not reflected in the attitude of the Parish Council. Despite my kindly Chairman's efforts in pressing my case, having given him a full explanation for the changes and the support now of both planning and conservation officer, as a group they appeared unmoved. As a group, there are possibly a number of places I would suggest for their movement, but I feel it best to draw a veil over this particular forum.

The requisite number of revised plans were sent to the local authority, but within only a few days I was pestering the planning officer to the extent, he might have considered a restraining order. Unfortunately, these things have to follow the formal processes put into place and that meant another round of consultation for at least another 21 days, possibly the longest 21 days I have endured. While we expected (and got) little from the Parish Council, it was difficult to understand who the other substantive consultants might be. It would make sod all difference to the normal statutory bodies like highways and water whether we had a bay, a gable, a jetty or a life size mock up of the Cutty Sark at the front of the house. But of course in all of this, I was forgetting my neighbours. I subsequently discovered they had asked to ensure that the window from the bathroom, the only newly created window, which would look directly onto their house and garden, would be of obscure glass. It had never occurred to me this would be anything else. I certainly had no desire to inflict upon them glimpses of my less than athletic frame as I either alighted from the bath, or more likely stumbled in still half asleep at 6.00am on a standard weekday. I duly agreed to confirm this matter in order to allay all concerns.

So, all 'I's' dotted and all 'T's' crossed then? Well possibly, but finding out progress was like extracting the proverbial life essential fluid from an inanimate lump of rock, but I should really not describe the planning officer in that way. It still had to go to 'consultation' with the Chief Planning Officer, particularly as the Parish Council had not withdrawn their objection. This is one of those situations over which you can have no direct control or influence, other than lobbying one of the attendees to support your view, hence the planning officer had risen to the top of my birthday card list. While I admit I had now become rather obsequious, and squirmed at my own actions to get what I wanted, I only had a vague assurance from my new friend that 'It shouldn't be a problem'. Then one Friday morning, having left yet another message on the voicemail of my (now) best mate at the council, I received a call back, even though I was at the time driving at some haste down the M11. In the tones and inflection that could only come from someone steeped in local authority workings, I was informed that everything was now clear and agreed and he would be putting the planning consent in the post within the next few days. I cannot possibly recommend or condone the act of screaming 'YES!' and punching the air whilst driving in this manner and those in the cars around mine may have felt the urge to get as far away from me as possible, but I excused myself in this instance. I did at least wait until I had come to a stop before I phoned Sharon.

By the time the planning consent landed, it was mid May and we were well behind my original schedule to see works start in the spring, ensuring everything was done by autumn, or at worst, early winter and we would have an entirely disruption free Christmas. Not only that, but all the work could then take place during what you would hope would be reasonable weather. As we now had to prepare detailed plans and specifications to allow the work to be priced, even well before we could look at work starting, my ideal timetable was looking about as firm as that for trains from Stevenage to London, which I had recently discovered lack any foundation at all, other than the certainty that every train would be late, which was very fitting in this comparison. Impatient as I was, I appreciated it would take a little while to get the full tender pack prepared and I had little to add to the package that came in my direction to approve. I then agreed with Richard who we would ask to price and could do little more than take his advice on the appropriateness of the recipients. For all I know, these could have been made up names, down at heel architects masquerading as reputable contractors, or Richard's extended family, but there are times when you have to trust your advisors in these matters. And since the only builders I knew were multi-million pound corporations whose interest in a little old job in a little old village in little old East Herts would be precisely nil, I realistically had little choice.

The return of the tenders was nicely timed to coincide with our return from a week away in glorious East Devon. It is fortuitous that it was a reasonably pleasant and restful break, as the shock I was to get on return, was one which needed some reserves of mental strength and fortitude. Unfortunately, I had neither of these and on opening one item of mail from Richard, promptly, and literally, fell off my chair. Without revealing the cost of the works in their entirety, it would be fair, indeed accurate, to state that one price returned was a six figure, rather than the five figure sum expected, while the other was as good as double what we were expecting. How quickly gloom can overcome optimism. I was incredulous. In fact, I had not been so shocked since I witnessed 'Eddie The Eagle' trying to become a serious Winter Olympian. While he crashed and burned in failure some little while after becoming the most ridiculous type of celebrity (ie, those celebrated for being totally crap), failure for this project was looking a little more imminent. We simply did not have the money to match the requirements of these particular builders, and were being faced with the very real prospect of a perfectly good planning consent that we could not implement. I felt like I had an Aston Martin sat in my garage, but didn't have the ability or funds to drive it, although it could not be said the plans for the house, no matter how good, quite match the drop-dead gorgeousness of the DB7, possibly the most achingly beautiful thing on the planet. But we digress.

While I was shocked, I was also very angry. I viewed Richard as someone who could lead me gently through this process, which meant giving me a clear steer on the cost we could expect for the project. With that in mind, either these builders were extracting the urine, or Richard's judgement was miles off track. Either way, it prompted an e-mail from me with steam issuing from the keyboard and a demand for an early meeting. This duly took place a few days later and I confess my mood was such that the reception I gave Richard may have been gathered from a light sprinkling of frost which had enveloped my demeanour. I am not a man for confrontation, but I made plain my concern and anger that we seemed to have veered so far off course, we were now drifting into another continent, and it was one where I could not afford the standard of living. I am not entirely sure about the explanation as to why this was the case, although it would seem elements of the spec had been priced particularly high, and for the tenderers there seemed to be some concern about the cost of working around us while we remained in residence, but essentially I think it could be best put down to a good old fashioned cock-up and significant miscalculation. None of the calming words from Richard had much of an effect. I had little faith in being able to negotiate down some of the elements. The better and potentially more productive tactic was going to be in finding some more reasonable builders who did not have the propensity to make me pay for them all to have a 3 month Caribbean cruise.

By now, we were well into the summer and it seemed to take an inordinate amount of time to establish contact with alternative builders who would be prepared to take on the job, and might have the inclination to do so within a sensible timeframe at a reasonable cost. At the same time we had to ensure that any outfit who were going to come and effectively live with us for four or five months did not have any habits or proclivities that might make them unsociable, untrustworthy, unreliable or criminal, or did not fit the all too often well deserved stereotype portrayed by riding into the scene on horses, shooting up the place and then pissing off again. Two very local firms came to the fore, one of which was extremely local and for a time, was getting my vote on the basis that generally any firm would be very ill advised to, as we say, shit in their own backyard. The process (eventually) boiled down to these two and tender prices were sought. While I continued to hang on to the prospect of work starting in August ensuring all would be done by Christmas, it was becoming more likely I would get a phone call from Kylie Minogue asking for a date. After some cajoling, a price was returned from our fairly local builders, while the very local mob seemed to require a cattle prod. Some questions began to arise as to their commitment, especially as Richard relayed one phone call during which our man in charge professed he was a bit tired after what was a warm day and couldn't really be bothered to get anything to us. In return for this, we couldn't be bothered to give him any work, which might have been a difficult decision if our remaining firm had given us a stupid price, but thankfully, we were now firmly back into five figure territory. It was still significantly more than the budget figure provided by Richard, but the relief felt that it was at least now financially within our reach and *so* much cheaper than the previous piss-takers, was of colossal proportions.

So, the contract was duly awarded to our fairly local friends, but we now went through the painful process of trying to establish exactly what was going to happen and when, with us continuing to try and cling onto the fast disappearing hope of a disruption free Christmas, even though it was galloping away into the sunset, while we were unseated and thrown off into the bushes. In fact, I think the thing more likely took a complete tumble at Beachers' Brook, died in the whole unpleasant process and now was a veritable deceased objective. We were tantalised with possible start dates in August, which then slipped into early September, which then drifted out to late September, but in truth we still had no clear idea when we attended what would be our first meeting with the builders in mid August. Steve was not the stereotypical builder of your imagination, as he was of modest build, about my age, possibly a little more youthful, did not have the girth proportions to suggest excessive beer consumption, reasonably smartly dressed, no swearing, he wasn't Irish and there was no sign of the jeans being worn slightly low at the rear in order to provide the almost expected glimpse of the posterior. In short, he instilled me with a good sense of confidence, and we agreed the key to success and even tempers was to work closely and pragmatically together, offering regular cups of tea wherever practical.

It was a warm summers afternoon and the meeting lasted for well over an hour while we talked about a variety of fairly detailed, but important issues, ending with a firm handshake and a plea to extract from him a firm start date as soon as possible. While I would not call him evasive, he would probably have been pretty good at hide and seek, but I understood that starting on one job depends on completing on another. Still, he was of better character than I had expected, the weather was glorious, I got myself home early and we were off on a weeks holiday in a few days time. Perhaps this would not be so bad after all….? Then again, my lottery numbers might come up…..

WE'RE OFF!

30 September 2002

Nearly 12 months after we hauled ourselves into Holly House, work was scheduled to start on its miraculous transformation – or was it? Pinning down builders to specifics is a bit like trying to swat a fly, only more difficult. You think you are there, the conversation peppered with lots of clear nods, 'yeps' and other miscellaneous affirmative gestures, and then right at the end there is the little get out, like the small print on an insurance clause. 'Of course, this does all depend on us finishing off Mrs Bloggins' conservatory, and assuming George does not have a repeat of his allergic reaction to brick dust, or there is an 'R' in the month, while shares can of course go down as well as up, minimum terms and conditions apply.'

In theory, they were going to begin on 23 September. Well, yes, erm, possibly, but er, maybe a day or two after that. As the day loomed, this became well, er, no. Probably move in some equipment and materials during that week. No start then? No, but probably the week after. Was this the week after, er, yes, or the week after, er, no. There I was trying to murder the bluebottle again, and all it was doing was buzzing past my face as I swore and swiped just that fraction too late.

So today, I had expected to arrive home to find the house in much the same state as when I left in the morning – ugly and expectant. But what is this I see? At first sight, it looks as if someone has dumped a lost railway carriage in the drive. Either that or Anstey is to become a new transport terminus and Holly House will be reborn as the Hertfordshire hub of a new environmentally friendly thrust to encourage trips to the countryside by train. Closer inspection reveals the name of the builder on the side, so I surmise at least something has been delivered to site. I park the car with some trepidation, wondering if the rear of the house has suddenly been demolished in double quick time, making up ground on the lost week. All I find is some curiously placed small orange bollards and pieces of wood nailed in at various points – one in the garage wall, one on the house wall, several along the small wall that borders the fish pond, and something that looks like a leprechauns hurdle in the middle of our weed ridden patio. A deranged carpenter? Some particularly peculiar pervert that gets a kick out of running into peoples gardens while they are not looking, and furiously nailing pieces of wood into strange positions? No, it was the builders' time honoured and necessary ritual of setting-out – or making sure you definitely build where you are supposed to. Thus ensuring you do not end up with a kitchen that is 20' x 3', and can only be accessed up a three foot step and through the downstairs toilet.

Well, it was a start. Granted, we weren't seeing any digging, breaking, cementing, brick-laying, swearing, spitting, football stories, long tea-breaks or any of the other activities you associate with builders on site, but it was at least a beginning. Not quite sure, however, where it might end. I pondered the prospect of months of dust, dirt, grime, lack of heating, disruption to daily life, forced moves from room to room and volcanic family arguments and just hoped it would all be worthwhile. Not for the first time, I drew a deep breath and crossed my fingers.

1 October 2002
Either work has started in earnest, or I am being investigated as a serial killer with no imagination, as they clearly think that like countless others before, I can think of nowhere better to hide the bodies than under the patio. Now, unless they really think I would put people in long thin trenches, then the former seems the most likely answer. In fact, the true scale of today's events became clear as I swung my car into the drive and only just prevented the unfortunate and unintentional melding of Jaguar with dirty great skip, or rather skips. One of these was completely full, so it was with some curiosity that I ventured around the back of the house half expecting to see something akin to a scene from the battlefields of World War I.

The patio had gone and the ground had opened up in a pretty serious way, but in fairness to the builders, the mess was at a minimum, which was no mean feat given the depth of some of the trenches. Bollards, plastic fencing and temporary warning tape was erected all around, but in a fit of rebellion I breached the security cordon – no helicopter suddenly hovered into view with a piercing searchlight, accompanied by hordes of armed police and ferocious dogs to accost me, read me my rights, and push me forcibly into the back of a waiting police car, so I pressed on. If you have seen one trench, you have seen them all, but it is always a little distressing when this type of devastation is happening on your own property. In preparation, paving slabs had been pulled up, a small wall obliterated, but most forlorn of all was the sight of a semi mature laurel bush which had been emasculated at the base of it's trunk, the remains lolling about by the side of the trench, like a head that had freshly rolled from the base of a guillotine.

The deepest trench was covered by large sturdy planks, but its extent could be clearly viewed at one end. It was much deeper than I had anticipated, and the pool of still dirty water at the bottom rather added to its abyss like qualities. In the twilight you could have the beginnings of a classic monster horror, as some flesh tearing beast leapt from the trench, and pulled me deep into the underworld, accompanied by the usual piercing screams echoing about the garden. What actually happened was at the other end of the spectrum as my daughter excitedly bounced out of the back door, looked down the hole with me and said

"Cool!"

Yesterday I understood things had finally started, but now here it was, large and loud. It was a bit like queuing for Tower of Terror at Disneyland, considerable excitement, and more than a hint of fear, but this time without the pile of obese Americans crowding the pavements, the almost permanent smell of hotdogs, and the wonderfully creepy bell boy who guides you into the lift for one of the most extraordinary theme park rides I have ever encountered. Unfortunately, this was unlikely to be quite so much fun.

3 October 2002
I could have persuaded myself earlier in the week that although it was clear work had begun, at least the place did not look like a building site. However, on the usual arrival home tonight, the scene had been transformed into a building trades wonderland, complete with a pile of sand and gravel of sufficient proportions to become the new highest point in Anstey. Not one but two, not single but double, cement mixers (just how quickly can you use this much concrete?) enough planks to build a sturdy ship and trenches filled to the brim with concrete, like a huge grey setting jelly.

Okay, so the foundations were done, so what on earth were they going to do with the rest of the sand and gravel and cement, got to keep those very impressive cement mixers working? Would this be a little like any amateur DIY'ers dilemma when filling holes? You know the sort of thing – must fill those 2 small holes in the landing wall before painting, get the obligatory packet of polyfilla, make up twenty times more filler than you need, complete the two small jobs, stand back, and realise you still have enough left to reface the entire wall, with plenty to concrete over a new patio. You go looking for holes – you can usually find two or three that probably (just about) warrant a smidgen of filler, but then you start to get a bit desperate. What's that little hole there? If I poke around a bit…. oh, dear lots of plaster come away, well that will need filling. And then you go wandering with a menacing look in your eye, armed with filler and extremely dangerous.

"Any holes you know of that need filling darling?" you ask the wife

But she has seen this before. In a panic she tries to distract your gaze from anything with the merest flaw or indentation, otherwise you will be at it before you can say 'plasterboard', and before you know it, you will be trying to fill holes in the fridge door and sundry coffee mugs. There are few things more disconcerting than a man with a pot full of filler and a plan to fill.

I consoled myself with the thought that, unlike your average DIY man, the builders knew what they were doing. Just had to hope all the doors and windows were not concreted by close of play tomorrow.

6 October 2002

Like probably most reasonable households, Sunday tends to be a day of relative peace and relaxation and sometimes a bit of a laugh, the latter frequently prompted by the mad person that is my eight year old daughter, Cara – she is truly Princess Mad of Mad-world. As my wife knows only too well, she was a difficult birth and for the first eighteen months of her life was more trying and wearing than we care, or dare, to remember. Indeed, our memory of that time seem to be of consistent and persistent crying, screaming, kicking, later laced with tantrums and defiance and that was just us, as parents. She has always been a character, sometimes good, not infrequently bad, but always (with the notable exception of the first 18 months) entertaining. True, all children have a clarity of thought and imagination which makes you ashamed of the cynical, weary and doubting adult you have become, but Cara seems to do it with a sparkle that makes you laugh and smile at yourself as well as her. While walking with my mother some weeks ago she apparently said, in the deep and animated way that only children can.

"Ooooh, I love the smell of holiday!"

"Do you? What does holiday smell of then?"

"Well, it smells of the sun, and grass and fresh bread! It makes me feel all happy inside."

And so it should us all.

Sunday was a bright and uplifting day, the sort of early Autumn weather you always hope you will get, but seldom do. Some of the leaves on the trees had just finished the thought process of turning colour and were now proceeding to do just that, some getting ahead of the game, having floated gently to the ground, littering parts of the lawn. Most of the plants in the garden were also thinking it was about time they said their goodbyes, save the resplendent pink rose at the bottom of the garden who clearly thought she ought to show off her wares for a few more weeks yet. There was still the predominance of summer, all greens with a smattering of bright colours, but now with a colourwash tinge of browns, yellows, reds and oranges, a noticeable keenness and chill in the air that carried the scent of earth and wood fires – change was clearly on its way up the path, but the last dregs of summer were going to hang about for as long as they could.

I went out to inspect exactly what had been going on the previous week and Cara was firm about wanting to join me.

"Okay, but its not too warm out, you need to put a fleece or something on – and not something decent if you are going in the garden!"

While I peered wistfully into the big hole around the back of the house, now levelled ready for the first course of brickwork, Cara appeared by my side in what was merely the latest in a long line of comedy moments when Cara decides she will dress in something rather unorthodox: a pair of old brown trousers, discarded some little while ago because they clearly were too small, witnessed by the gap between foot and bottom of said trouser leg; purple fleece, fine in itself, but in close proximity to the trousers, probably an arrestable offence in Hertfordshire. And an enormous deep red furry hat, just made the whole thing hilarious. She looked like a very bad kids impersonation of Jay Kay in early Jamiroquai days.

"What *do* you look like?"

"I don't know," she giggled and then bounced off into the garden complete with my 7m metal rule, which clearly she thought was an indispensable extra for this outfit and would no doubt be put to good use somewhere.

In fact it was, as we suspected, a typical prop in another episode of Cara the Nutter, as she proceeded to inspect all the building works in a mock knowing manner, measuring everything she could, including the foundations, cement mixer, heap of gravel and the half filled, battered multi-coloured skip. Once this sort of thing starts, there is no stopping Cara, she has to continue this exercise. So she then proceeded to investigate the entire length of the rule, and whether it could measure the front garden and before long, the whole thing had turned to joyous farce and mayhem. It is impossible not to laugh, even if the dull inner-adult suggests you really should not be doing such a thing. True, there are times when these escapades go on a little too long, or go just that bit too far, which usually ends in an escalating call of "Cara," at least three times, the last of which has to be shouted with some menace and eyes wide. But even then, she can catch you with a skip, a stifled giggle and a nonchalant "Okay," and the anger has melted.

My inspection revealed little, other than an expectation of some even more serious ground work going to get underway soon, and a realisation that looking at works at this stage cannot possibly give you a correct impression of what the finished article will look like. No doubt things will become clear soon.

7 October 2002

Arriving home late and in the dark, simply accentuated the senses tonight, but by the dim lights of the house, and a faint wispy moon, I came across the proverbial bomb site. All bollards, mounds of earth and gravel, scruffy ply-boards over holes, bags of sand and cement, buckets and pieces of wood. I half expected to come across bodies, paramedics and smoking shells. In reality, I probably was doing an injustice to the builders, but given the chill in the air and the lack of daylight, it did have a creepy, surreal and somewhat chaotic appearance.

Inside the house, my eyes were instantly drawn to a piece of wood propped up outside the kitchen window, which clearly was a gallows – tall, thick and large wood sections, with a sturdy right angle, braced across from mid top to mid side. Good God, had one of the builders gang dug a hole in the wrong place, had he measured in inches rather than millimetres, the punishment for which was to be strung up outside the clients premises? Was this a particular village ritual I had failed to appreciate? From my position, I stood and stared at this for some little while and could not make out what it was, but having ventured outside to inspect further, discovered it to be one half of an external door frame.

This could mean only one of two things; either they were planning to carry out said gruesome ritual, creating not one, but two, makeshift gallows, or they were very shortly to extract the existing metal patio doors and replace (in part) by the new French windows. The latter meant that the inside would be breached very soon. This was when it would get serious, this was when it would become clear exactly what was happening, this was when the fur would fly, the shit would hit the fan, reality would bite and all the metaphors in the world would be of little use – but it was too late now.

8 October 2002

You have to feel a bit sorry for drains. I mean, you wouldn't want to be one, would you? They carry all the really horrible stuff that you don't want (and the odd thing that you do, but by the time you realise that, its too late), are stuffed away underground where no-one can see them, and are constantly prodded and poked when they have a little blockage problem. When you see them revealed, you understand it would be rather difficult to live without them, unless you want to return to the early nineteenth century practice of covering a passer by in a bucketful of your personal bodily detritus – not recommended for them or your local environment.

So on return home tonight, I was fascinated by the burrowing and digging which had taken place, yet more trenches hewn out of the ground around three sides of the house. And the new drainage runs that had been laid, exposed to the elements, revealed like the strange skeleton of some ancient subterranean beast ('Neolithic Drain Dinosaur found in Herts Village'). In order to avoid the otherwise inevitable incident likely to result when child (or wayward adult) meets building works, especially when there are holes and trenches involved, there was now a mass of bollards, temporary fencing, metal poles and barrier tape, which now created an interesting route of the non-scenic variety to the back door, taking in sites and features of the garden and driveway that had not hitherto been visited. It was just like an archaeological dig in your own garden, only less messy and more interesting, with the added benefit of not having a manic Tony Robinson bouncing around the place asking silly questions, nor having to tolerate eminent University Professors dressed in either very loud sweaters, or impossibly large bow ties.

This all looked very impressive and efficient, until I noticed the out-fall from the kitchen was now looking rather lonely and forlorn, in view of its complete lack of attachment to anything. Up to this morning, the two external pipes from the kitchen taking waste from the sink, dishwasher and washing machine fed into a small open hopper which then took all the water and its unpleasant baggage down into the drains and away to the septic tank (ah, yes the septic tank – I'll tell you about that another time maybe). Unfortunately, the new drainage ran in a different direction and there was not even the hint of a temporary connection to take said effluent. Rather it just poured pointlessly into what was left of the old drain and spewed out over the soil in all directions. Now, It is a bit of a problem to have no drainage from your kitchen. Bear in mind, my children get through clean plates and cutlery like there was a supply crisis. They then pile up the dirty stuff in the sink until such time as the overall height reaches a point where its stability is such that walking within 3 feet of it could bring it crashing down. In addition, their ability to produce dirty clothes far outstrips the ability of the washing machine (or the wife) to keep pace. Ergo, a problem, as some form of washing has to be done.

Thankfully it was dark, but for all I know tomorrow morning, the whole of the rear garden could be a veritable lake of unmentionable liquid, but let's not go there.

11 October 2002
A day off from work and of course I was going to do with this day what all right minded people do when they are released from the general drudgery of their desks – order our new kitchen. Well, it beats (marginally) clothes shopping. Better still, this was to be done in the salubrious surroundings of an industrial estate in Harlow. The scene of this transaction takes little imagination on the readers part, if you simply picture your average conglomeration of fairly battered 1970's sheds clustered around a bleak and weed strewn courtyard, every unit fronted with the traders self-made name boards and advertisements in all shades, shapes and colours, cars parked like they have been dropped at random from the sky and the inevitable burger van of Bedford Truck Vintage. Admittedly, this compared rather unfavourably with an alternative supplier in a rather swish showroom formed from a converted coach house in Bishops Stortford, but whereas he was all suave, irritatingly knowledgeable, and frankly too much like a Paul Whitehouse character, our man from Harlow was basic, stoic and somewhat chaotic, but had the particular advantage of being a personal recommendation. Being the snob I am, I wanted to turn and run back to the bourgeois setting of shiny worktops and clinical steel at Mr Suave, but I had been persuaded to discuss matters with Mr Stoic.

Like so much in life, what appeared superficially to be a bit shallow and untrustworthy turned out to have more substance. His sales patter was modest and he was happy to let his even more modest showroom and pricing do the talking. This was in fact our second visit, having dismissed Mr Suave as being, well, too suave and yes, expensive. We had also dismissed the company whose name shall be a secret, but has more than a passing association with an instrument that attracts metal objects, and is usually drawn (even though you never, ever see them like this) as a horseshoe with two red ends. The obese greasy haired woman (I think) who greeted (or should that be grunted) us did not create the best impression, but the chances were then blown by the revelation that despite having a showroom open to the public, it was impossible for you to sit down then and there to discuss with someone what you wanted, we would have to make an appointment. I thought this was a bit like Tesco's telling me if I wanted a tin of beans I would have to order them first – rather defeats the object really, don't you think? So, Mr Stoic won the day, his wares looked just as good as everyone else, he had a glowing reference from a friend and he was cheapest – can't ask for much more.

The day also allowed me to meet the merry band of men that were gradually both destroying and building our house all at the same time. Having heard reports they generally appear before 8.00am, they promptly did so, in a convoy of two battered white vans, but otherwise pleasingly individual in their appearance. Steve and Andrew were the bosses, brothers jointly lending their name to the business. Steve was not the effusive, bluff typical builder you might expect, but was rather reserved and always seemed to wear a look of modest concern as if he was never quite sure what you were going to say to him, but would nevertheless prepare himself for a verbal onslaught. Andrew was more communicative, again in his forties, with an altogether more contented and confident air and a little more hair – perhaps there was a connection here. Both were of modest stature, neither of which you would pick out in a line up and swear they were builders: no bulging muscles and beer guts, no tattoos and choice language. I found this all very reassuring and a little uplifting – it's always gratifying to find something that demolishes a stereotype.

The rest of the outfit were however somewhat quirky. One had hair the length and style which would have won him first prize in a Limahl look-a-like competition, or for those of you of a less mature vintage and who need a simpler description, long white/grey mullet with a degree of disruption on top. The final member (on this day at least) was a rather elderly looking man with a permanent baseball cap, so tightly fitted that I had no idea whether he had any hair or not. Unlike Limahl, he was fairly voluble and felt compelled to make conversation every time he saw us, pleasantly so, but when he began to spout what sounded like welsh, he marked himself out as the comedian in the group. So there we had it – serious boss, confident brother, moody early 1980's faded pop star and Max Boyce impersonator. Would you entrust your house to these people?

In fact, the order with which they were proceeding and the fact they expressed annoyance when the brick delivery was two days late gave me some confidence. Indeed, that they washed up their tea mugs and left them neatly draining beside the sink in the kitchen, like some tidy well trained group of schoolboys doing some good deeds for the elderly of the community, was quite touching. And when Steve suggested perhaps some of details in the Architects plans were not necessarily workable, you knew they were paying attention. In the meantime, their final task for the day was moving all the bricks (finally) delivered from the drive around to the back of the house, ready for the Monday and creating space on the drive for us to continue to park. The well-ordered and industrious nature of this exercise was like watching Snow White and the seven dwarfs at work, only without Snow White or any dwarfs and there weren't seven of them, but you get my drift.

12 October 2002
Rain, wind and a change in both the weather and the season, so sudden, it was almost shocking. Only a week ago, summer was clearly hanging on and doing so pretty gamely, but she had now been comprehensively heaved out of the scene and a far more brutal regime had taken hold. Although it was no doubt accentuated by the greyness of the skies, there was now more than a tinge of brown and orange across the trees. What had been a light covering of leaves on the ground had now turned to a rather generous spread, as if an entire army had tipped bucket loads of them across the ground. The prodding chill in the air had turned to a stab of cold and you wondered if Autumn had abdicated and Winter had leapt in to fill the void.

This change had also had a pretty dramatic effect on the works around the house and the scene started to look more and more dreary and muddy as the day wore on. Little rivulets began to trickle down the piles of sand and gravel that were placed at the front of the house. Our very own outdoor swimming pool was rapidly forming in the concrete base that should at some point be the new floor of the kitchen. Tarpaulins over the skip and piles of bricks dripped incessantly and the breeze blocks began to resemble giant sugar cubes in coffee as they sucked up the water, turning an ever deeper dark, sodden grey.

The space now left on the front drive was limited, but just about sufficient to park the cars, providing you had no problem with the front bumper of the first car getting intimate with an empty oil drum, while the second car looked as if it was getting frisky with the first. That also meant getting to either required some all-terrain experience, necessitating navigation around a skip, a concrete mixer, two oil drums and pile of indeterminate material which seemed to be an agglomeration of sand, mud, gravel and any other small granular material that happened to be lying about the garden at the time. In negotiating this particular obstacle, foot had to come into heavy contact with said muddy mound, and the science of these things predictably dictated that several inches in sole and heel thickness was added, but these newly developed platform shoes were neither fashionable nor practical. They just made normal walking rather precarious and driving the car requiring substantial adjustment of the seat to accommodate the new found leg length, as shoes now the weight of a hod of bricks, squelched sickeningly against throttle, brake and carpet. Going in the other direction from car to house was just as bad, but the greater length in journey from mound to back door was a stagger of steady deterioration, as your shoes were now muddy magnets for anything that was not fixed down. And by the time you reached the back door, you were six inches taller than when you started and travelling at half the speed.

It was not pleasant to contemplate the progress of work if this type of weather now set in and clearly the mild and clement conditions we had enjoyed through September and early October were likely to be a distant memory very soon. Still, I consoled myself that thus far the awesome foursome had remained cheery and committed and somehow I could see our Max Boyce impersonator revelling in such conditions, although Limahl's hair might take a bit of a battering.

14 October 2002
I am cross. OK, it will not be the first time, and I am not exactly apoplectic with rage, but I hate it when things are not done as I had asked, or as were indicated to me. Unfortunately for those around me, my anger and reaction is generally inversely proportional to the size of the problem. It is probably because I view small problems as irritations, as matters that really should not be happening, matters over which we should all have reasonable control, therefore should not be the subject of cock-ups, errors, omissions or acts of stupidity and such things just get right up my nose. Bigger problems I find easier to deal with – perhaps it is because I can think more effectively about wider, more strategic issues that inevitably surround big problems, maybe it is because I subconsciously relish the challenge, or it may simply be I am a stupid masochist.

An early arrival home had meant I could view what had been going on in the last fading daylight and my eye was drawn to the fact that external brickwork was now going up at some pace. Unfortunately, on peering further around the corner, it seemed as though someone had got a taste for that pace, slammed it down a gear, floored the throttle, wound down the window, and blasted off into the distance hoping to eventually disappear off the horizon. Alternatively, we could have a brickie on speed, perhaps Limahl had sampled a long forgotten stash of 80's hash, aided by Max Boyce sniffing a few too many leeks. It could of course simply have been that someone was not paying attention, and merrily piled brick upon brick forgetting the fact that they actually should have stopped this particular course of bricks back at the first mornings' tea break. In the overall scheme of things, it was not a big problem, not one that required a carefully thought out wide ranging strategy and plan to resolve the issues, so it irritated the hell out of me and caused me to shout "SHIT!" even though no one could hear me.

The rear extension consists of a gable extending out about 11 feet to accommodate a kitchen on the ground floor and a new bedroom above. The original plan was to extend the roof line of one side of the gable down to ground floor ceiling height and to construct this all in glass, creating a very light dining area adjacent to the kitchen, almost doubling the ground floor area of the gable extension – all very Homes & Gardens. However, no hint of a hyper Irish garden designer to suggest it should all be built in papier-mache to make it organic, or worse still, dear old Laurence LB to propose a retro-chic Indian gallic inspired 1970's mock aluminium painted pink with heraldic motifs picked out in gold leaf. We did however, have to compromise as the curse of overbearing regulations struck again and it was impossible to have that amount of glass across walls and roofs. The compromise was therefore, to tile the roof and build a low brick wall around the base, off which would come the full height glazing along all walls, right up to the apex of the dining room extension, where it met the main wall of the gable extension.

The problem was, this low plinth wall had been built as a high plinth wall, and the way in which it had been built would give the appearance of some dire half wall with windows mounted above, like so many tasteless cheap extensions and conservatories people frequently threw up next to their houses in the 60's and 70's, and then proceeded to fill them with either all the junk that wouldn't fit into their garage, or rapidly turn it into a greenhouse, since its modest construction and thermal abilities (not to mention poor aesthetics) dictated it really could not be used for normal habitation. Hence the anger and shouting.

Quite irrationally, and out of all proportion to reality, I tried to phone the architect. Given it was now seven o'clock, it was not very likely that even the cleaner would be in residence, let alone any member of the practice. And even if they were, what would it have achieved? He was hardly going to come round with his own hammer and chisel to take the wall down a few courses. But like all irrational behaviour, this didn't matter, I simply had to complain. So of course the modern substitute for good old fashioned talking and listening is the e-mail, and one of some vitriol, misplaced criticism and plain unreasonableness went shooting out of my PC, probably giving the system at the Architects a bit of a rude shock on landing. It was all very unnecessary, but it made me feel a little better.

Tuesday 15 October 2002
My mobile rings, and I know from the number displayed it is Richard.
"Richard!" I answer with rather curtly, ready to launch into a verbal sequel to my evil e-mail of the night before.
"Hello Alan. Yeah, this wall, we'll reduce that to 600, is that OK?"
"Er, yeah."
I am left with little else to say, all anger and concern dissipated like a dark stormy day suddenly replaced with blue skies and sunshine. It is of course the only professional way to deal with a mistake – admit it, provide corrective action and move on, and in doing so take all the proverbial wind out of the complaining sails of your ungrateful, emotional and rude client. I accepted my punishment with merely a whimper and realised what an irrational arse I had been.

The human form is a sophisticated mechanism which ought to be able to think, plan and respond reasonably and logically, but sadly too often we fail to think, rarely plan and react accordingly in time honoured knee-jerk fashion. Personally, (and I appreciate this is a very subjective thing) I blame the raft of over publicised Premiership footballers who are usually overpaid sub-intellectual thugs, but there I am failing to think, plan and respond reasonably to those who think kicking three shades of shit out of someone who fails to worship them an act of acceptable social behaviour. Being the public figures that they are, I can legitimately take my cue from them.

I am suitably contrite, but not overtly so. After all, I am the client.

Thursday 17 October 2002

Nothing. Well, not very much. Well, very little to get excited about, unless you count a few more courses of grey breeze blocks. Now, my life may not be a riveting social whirl, nor is the day job one that others lust after, in awe of its apparent intrigue and interest. (You know the sort of thing, chocolate taster for a Belgian Confectioner or Test driver for Ferrari), but even I cannot muster any great enthusiasm for one building block being put onto another.

It could be the weather, it could be that temporarily they have lost interest, or it could be a plain old-fashioned cock-up. Not surprisingly, it seems the latter is the case. Like a scene from an Ealing comedy, they had turned up on site bright and early, replete with window frames ready to fit, only to find the said window frames did nothing of the sort. Wrong dimensions. Lots of head scratching and swearing no doubt, but thankfully I was not there to witness this, which is just as well as I think it unlikely I would have seen the funny side. So within half an hour of arriving, they decided that until they had the right frames in the right size to fit, there was not much else they could do except disappear for the day.

Let us hope we do not have too many more of these incidents, although (and yes, it could again simply be that I am reverting to type as a cynical bastard) something tells me this is pretty improbable.

Friday 18 October 2002

It being Friday, Sharon was in residence, but no sign of a builder. The wind simply whistled through the brickwork and propped up door-frame, like a scene from a bad Western, although to the best of my knowledge, Clint Eastwood was not particularly handy with a trowel and mortar. Lets face it, such implements would not have been much use against a shotgun and rifle, no matter how large and outrageous his poncho and how much tobacco he chewed and spat.

Let us hope that Monday brings better things.

Sunday 20 October 2002

At this point I could take you here on a very serious diversion, and am pondering the merits of doing so. Well, there is very little to tell you on the house front (other than discovering that someone has stolen 200mm from the Kitchen/Diner). Actual work on site will very rarely be exactly as on plan, and dimensions indicated and measured will always be magically transformed through some peculiar builders time-portal to arrive at something different on the ground. But since we already had a dining area, about at the width limit to avoid having to eat with your elbows, this was not good news. I felt myself getting cross again, but this having all happened on a Saturday morning, there was not realistically much I could do -I was beginning to master the empty shrug.

But then Sunday was not spent at home, it was spent somewhere which could not be further removed from a building site in deepest East Herts. It was spent in Guildford, within The Spectrum, one of those modern temples to what society perceives as leisure, although as fun as ice skating, swimming, bowling or playing a variety of sports might be, there is nothing particularly leisurely about it. Why I was there might take a bit of explanation but will be a familiar scenario to millions of parents whose lives out of work time (and occasionally within) revolve around the activities of their offspring. In addition, if you are, like me, a father of purely girls and are therefore surrounded by women, you will be nodding sagely in the knowledge that life is nothing if not interesting, depending on the activities your children pursue or (in some cases) are thrust towards. In my case, one of them is swimming, and from a parent's point of view, not a major consumer of either time or energy, but the other activity certainly is – dancing. This is not half an hours' ballet on a Wednesday afternoon, this is commitment un-thought of when I was my children's age. Three afternoons after school on weekdays, and private lessons on a Saturday, culminating in competitions spread across the four wet and windy corners of the region almost every other Sunday. And what is a Father for, if he can't support his daughters in terms of transportation, endless soft drinks and crisps and shouting ridiculous encouragement from the sidelines, not to mention deft use of safety pins to secure competition numbers. From Colchester to Chippenham, Sudbury to Stopsley, and even a god forsaken drill hall in Luton that looked like a set out of Dads Army in an area where tumbleweed would not have been out of place rolling down the High Street, and a body guard would have been a wise investment.

The whole dancing scene would warrant a novel, and is so full of drama, intrigue politics and pathos, that the potential to create a mouth watering docusoap is almost overwhelming. Even the dance school to which my daughters belong has a cast of characters and parents equal to anything Channel 4's scriptwriters could even dream of creating. Most competitions are events that almost defy description. Imagine a typical sports hall of modest proportions and too few chairs, into which is crammed hundreds of people, mostly girls ranging from 6 to 18 in age. Add the most motley and varied collection of parents imaginable, a plethora of costumes, some plain, some weird and many frankly outrageous, in the brightest most luminescent colours only man could produce, a truckload of sequins and glitter, a banquet table heaving with shiny plastic trophies, very loud music with the most persistent of disco beats and an atmosphere brimming and bubbling with tension, anticipation and hormones. Then throw all this lot into competition. If you could bottle the grossly unstable emotional by-product of these events, nuclear fission would be obsolete within days.

But this was no ordinary competition. This was National Finals. Now, I said I could take you on a diversion, but I could go off circumnavigating the globe on this one. Suffice it to say, the school had its fair share of representatives, all of whom had fought hard to win or come within the top three in qualifying competitions throughout our region, and yes, it included both of mine. Forty-four schools, more than a thousand kids and hyper parents, and for us, one dance school teacher so nervous and twitchy that she looked set to explode. Mind you, at 21 years of age, who could blame her? All I probably worried about then was whether I could hold down my tenth pint of Fullers, even though I knew the answer before I started (No).

Now, I will cut this short. A hatful of medals and trophies came in the school's direction, including a top six placing for the mad Miss Neale, which for a modest thinking parent like me was fantastic. Even a semi-final qualification for my eldest in the mornings competition was pretty damned good I thought. The Neale family are not renowned for their winning – we do quite a bit of there-or-thereabouts and even a modicum of never-mind-there-will-be-a-next-time, but podium top spots have not become second home. So there I am, sitting up on the side, proud as any proud parent that my eldest and her partner have got through to the final six of rock 'n roll. (Yes, it's still taught and danced with a passion that would have Elvis jumping out of his grave and forsaking a hamburger to watch), and I have even borne the extra tension of a dance-off between our two and another couple. Must be for fifth and sixth I ashamedly thought. I am calm and not unduly considering the final placing, looking on and listening out of interest, ready to congratulate them wherever they came.

"…and the winners are………………..Sian Neale and ……". Sorry, Laura (partner of Sian and mighty fine dancer in her own right), but shock hit my sensory system before they mentioned your name, and for four or five seconds, I simply held my hand to my mouth in disbelief. When I realised they had won, I ran down the steps like only a mad parent can do and the rest would simply be embarrassing in print.

Poor Sian – she is a fairly reticent girl, intelligent, bright and engaging, but like her father she lacks a bit of self-confidence and belief and is a touch too self-conscious. For us such individuals, driving yourself to achieve and doing something, which in its basic form is showing off, needs a lot of effort and energy, unlike Cara who just does it as a matter of course. When such effort bears the ultimate fruit, the shock can be almost overwhelming. She had a smile to make the Cheshire Cat look like a manic-depressive, and was shaking with a combination of pride, relief and astonishment. You will rarely see the emotion of the human form writ so large as this. Me, I just hugged her until she almost passed out. Life is thankfully made of such sweet and surprising moments.

So, who gives a stuff about the house today?

Monday 21 October 2002
Back down to earth this morning, which, courtesy of some appalling weather, was very wet and muddy, so progress to turn a building site into a remodelled house has not been rapid. I have now discovered, the missing 200mm from the dining area is the fault of the Architects and I am beginning to keep a running tally of problems. It is rumoured that the mismatch of windows to wall was an Architect's error, so the case for the prosecution is starting to build (unlike the house).

Talking of windows, they have arrived. What a joy to see well made, chunky wooden frames, apparently made to order just for me by the local chippie. And what an even greater joy it will be to see the old battered skip piled with the flimsy brown stained casements to be ripped from the house very soon. Perhaps I could set light to them in a new Hertfordshire ritual, but then I have no desire to attract the attention of the good people of Anstey, the local media or the Police.

Rather more ominous is notice that the builders are about to execute a construction oriented pincer movement, so we are back to battle-ground analogies again. While work goes on at the back, the cunning devils will move in on our blind side and execute some digging at the front in the form of yet more trenches – seems to me that I could make some handy money on the side by hiring out the entire plot as a grisly backdrop for a gritty drama based around the First World War. This means extension works at the front, which means disruption all around us and in particular a pointed requirement to move all personal items, valuables, furniture, small children, pets and dusty collections of magazines not looked at for 12 months, completely away from the front window and bay. It would be coming down soon and we would be finally exposed to the elements, although I was promised that Steve and the boys would put up a 'protective screen'. This could have been anything from a sturdy, wind and waterproof metal and wood shield with ready access, to a few metres of cling film stretched over the gaping chasm, like some half empty bowl of baked beans stuffed to the back of the fridge. And knowing the trouble I have with cling film, it would unlikely be a good fit.

With the vision of us sitting blissfully in the lounge, viewed through a large untidy hole in the front of the house, all brick, plaster and dust, we set about moving everything away from the front to anywhere else in the house it would fit. And if it didn't, it would be made to fit. In a dining room already replete with boxes, plants and pictures, as well as doubling as a laundry, it was difficult to create more space. But it is amazing just how high you can stack boxes, as long as you ignore the precariousness (usually done by running out of the room and shutting the door as quickly as you can). Perhaps more frightening is the rubbish and debris discovered under and behind furniture that has remained immobile for many months. These must be approached with considerable caution, lest a new super-breed of bug or beast has evolved in this undisturbed pocket of dirt. Stand back, and hover at a significant distance is my tip.

Tuesday 22 October 2002
It has indeed begun, more safety tape, temporary fencing and barriers than you can shake an Inspector Morse novel at. Trouble was, on racing into the drive, thinking I was now well versed in what stood where, and could park quickly and deftly with a quick twist of the steering wheel. I discovered almost too late, the trenches for the front extension now encroached right into the drive and hence a calamitous dumping of car into muddy hole was only just avoided.

Still no big hole yet where the grubby bay currently sat. Although the excuse for a front porch had been rudely torn down, only the long strip of lead flashing was left flapping, still nailed to the wall where the top of the porch once met the wall in a less than harmonious embrace. It troubled me not in the slightest that I was gaining perverse pleasure from seeing significant sections of the house pulled down, mutilated and trashed. Perhaps I should have invited the original Architect (perhaps even the planning officer of the time) to witness the initial brutalisation ceremony, but that would have gone into the bounds of cruelty.

Thursday 24 October 2002
Progress of a serious kind today, heralded by the arrival of a dirty great steel joist, all primed and pristine in red, rather menacingly propped on sleepers just alongside the front drive. It signalled for the first time that there was more to all this than a bit of cut and shove, more than some severe cosmetics and expansion of living space. Here was the first bit which necessitated someone to pour over the plans and certify that the thing was not going to be the missing property link in the infamous Three Little Pigs story, and fall down at the first hint of a passing fox. Ah yes, there were going to be a variety of structural elements throughout, like new bionic additions, only costing rather less than six million dollars.

This particular appendage was to lay across the dining area, spanning the width of the rear extension providing support for the new bedroom above. It seemed to worry Cara more than reassure her that this was needed to make sure that having gone to bed in her new bedroom, she wouldn't then suddenly land in a pile of washing up in the sink. Children's thoughts are simple and uncomplicated and of course what you don't know can't hurt you. Clearly it had not occurred to her, without something to prop up her room, let alone all the teddies, dolls, books, clothes and general pink paraphernalia, a major gravitational incident would be unavoidable. She was however, cheered by the gratifying sight of her bedroom window frame leant against the wall in the garage, the size of which in its open and raw state was certainly surprising.

"Wow, it's massive," she said, with only a hint of exaggeration. And when I told her it would open up and down rather than to one side, it was like her birthday. "Fantastic! I can open it and lean out and have lots of lovely air!" Why can't adults extract such simple pleasure from life?

Steel structural beams are fine, but I do have a problem with the junction of steel with brick and cement, somehow they just don't seem compatible. I mean, you don't put tomato ketchup on your cake, do you? Okay, it is pretty rare to propose a major construction of Victoria sponge and butter icing, but there is something unsatisfactory about an object so harsh, unyielding and singular next to the malleable, tactile and textured combination of clay brick and oozy, squidgy mortar. I do keep thinking that there cannot possibly be a decent bond between the two, and a messy divorce of this forced marriage can only be just around the corner, but then this is clearly why I am not a structural engineer. It could also explain why I am not a prolific maker of cakes, but I think it is probably much more to do with me being a simple old-fashioned bloke.

Sunday 27 October 2002

Let me tell you, a building site during a gale can be a rather unsettling place to be, especially when the builders clearly have not expected the sort of winds that tear branches from trees, and knock old grannies off their feet. What were once innocuous pieces of building material or builders general flotsam can become unpredictable missiles and serious hazards.

Work has progressed at a good pace during the latter part of the week, with the walls for the front extension, now coming out of the ground. But now they are building front and back, there are a lot of materials on site, including piles of bricks wherever you look, mounds of gravel and sand, pieces of timber, drainpipes, joists, boards of all shapes and sizes, bollards, and an excess of orange plastic temporary fencing, which is nothing if not bright. Given that the idea is to leave the place on Fridays in a modicum of order, and in a state whereby a call to the emergency services will not be necessary, these things are generally piled and stashed into a corner or against a fence, while the looser items (excluding Limahls hair) are covered by a variety of green tarpaulins and pinned down by odd bricks and small wooden sleepers of rather greater weight than their size belies. But the global elements are no respecters of tidy building sites, and during Saturday night and right through Sunday, the wind did its best to obliterate anything standing above ground level.

On Sunday morning, despite the blindingly obvious stupidity of the idea, I thought I should try and clear some of the leaves from both the front and back lawn. Bear in mind, I am a man and having planned this event more than a week in advance, nothing so modest as a full blown gale and tree limbs whistling past me was going to divert me from my chosen purpose. Even when I stared out into the half built extension at the back to see some of the piles of huge wooden joists rocking backwards and forwards and flurries of cotton-wool-like insulation flying around like some grotesque snow storm, my mind could not be changed. Not even the eerie noise the wind makes when it rattles and whistles through obstacles and openings could deter me, although the fact that I was instantly knocked sideways when I stepped out of the back door did raise the odd question in my mind. I proceeded to rake up leaves from the rear lawn and then stuff them into what seemed to be a bottomless black sack, but of course this was more than a little like running up an escalator. I cannot think that anyone else in the whole of Hertfordshire would even be contemplating such a task, let alone trying to carry it out, but once you are in a hole you may as well keep digging. It was not the clear stupidity and futility of the job which finally made me stand up and think that maybe this was not such a good idea, but a 'thud' I traced quickly to the pile of leaves at my feet. There beside this ever moving mass was a branch, about a foot long. But it was not wizened and brown, nor did it have the remnants of leaves all yellow, red and shrivelled dotted along its length. It was bright green, the fronds and needles of a conifer firmly attached, together with a bulging collection of shiny brown cones, right down to the end that until a few seconds before, had been very much part of one of the very substantial pines situated just the other side of the road. This end was stripped and jagged, and had clearly been brutally ripped from the tree, like a limb torn off an animal. I picked it up, turned round slowly to face the direction of its flight, and realised for the first time, perhaps conditions were not ideal to be working in the garden, as the trees were being flung around as though they were inside a tumble drier.

Having abandoned the rear garden as a bad idea, this did not stop me heading to the front, where on the way I was assaulted by an alien extra from a 'C' rate horror flick. Well, actually it was a voluminous green plastic sheet which covered one of the brick piles by the side of the house, but it had shrugged aside its sleeper and brick shackles and looked set to take off over the tree tops. Meanwhile, I was beginning to look like a refugee from a wind tunnel. Despite this, I made a foray into the front garden where I was joined by Sian and Cara. The latter of whom performed her usual ploy of pretending to help with the job in hand, but within 5 minutes had decided playing on the swing amidst this howling gale was far more entertaining. Sian made a more workmanlike effort, but even she soon decided that such wind and cold was not the ideal situation for a Sunday morning, and I was not far behind her.

By the end of the day, the gardens and the surrounding countryside looked like some giant hand had rather forcibly ruffled its hair at some length, but despite the builders neat piles and stashes being rudely disturbed and vandalised, everything remained remarkably intact and unbroken.

Tuesday 29 October 2002

Progress seems to have slowed a little, but we do now have floor joists, half the upper walls on the rear extension and an upper floor window frame, perched rather precariously on breeze blocks and held in place by a slender looking plank, propped against the frame in order to prevent its rapid descent to the ground. It is now starting to look noticeably like a building, but the amount of debris and water that seems to be accumulating and slopping about the floor, makes me feel a little uneasy. Indeed in the murky darkness of a wet and cold October evening, lit very fleetingly by the lights of the house, you could be forgiven for thinking, progress is actually in the other direction and the house is gradually being dismantled rather than constructed.

In the meantime, I pour over some documents received from the Architect, indicating a better representation of the glazed dining area and a copy of a faintly bizarre letter from the planning authority. Like most planning consents, conditions are attached, generally stating that you must commence work within 5 years, but also seeking further details of actual materials to be used. Seemingly this ensures they are happy that you do not intend to use a new organic bright green brick you recently discovered during a trip up the Amazon that usefully glows in the dark. Or perhaps you have taken a shine to some groovy tiles that have been made out of recycled bin bags, giving a warm multicoloured sheen to the roof. Despite the fact our drawings stated, we would match materials to existing, the authorities do like to have continued power and control.

The problem was that Steve had provided Richard with incorrect information. And despite my approval to the bricks we had correctly chosen (Butterley Old English Russett – yes, I know it sounds like a new Mr Kipling cake, but it was probably slightly tastier), for some strange reason, he had stated they would be Hanson Old English Brindle (whatever a Brindle might be). Richard had duly written to the planners on this basis, but in fact, there is no such brick as a Hanson Old English Brindle. You would then expect the planners to do their homework and write back rather haughtily to state that as far as they knew, no such brick exists and please supply further information. In fact, they wrote back and approved it. I need say no more.

Wednesday 30 October 2002

"Daddy, Cara's windows been blocked up!" shouted Sian, almost before the back door was half open and my shoe had made contact with the kitchen floor. Some people get a pleasant greeting on coming home at night, I more frequently get hit with shock tactics and a diary of the problems of the day (usually involving disputes with and between the children). In truth, it was a bit of a surprise to be told this fact, as we might have expected some warning. The fact that Cara still uses and occupies her room to the full made this action a trifle problematic.

Having first discovered that no-one in the house wanted to talk to me in anything approaching a civil tone (must have been a particularly bad day for all), I went upstairs to inspect. Sure enough, where once there had been a window, now there were breeze-blocks bound together with mortar and the plaster around had been chipped and blown away. Indeed, rather than looking as if a hole had been filled, it looked like one had been made, as if an explosive had gone off just by the wall, blasting away the plaster and paint and exposing the raw structure of the house underneath. It looked particularly obtuse and brutal against the bright pink paint all over the rest of Cara's walls and the general fluff-and-glitter ambience of the room that is her domain. It was not what you would want to make as a main feature of an eight year old girl's bedroom, not unless she had found her way into a 'Goth' phase before the teenage years set in, or perhaps was starting to take alternative interior design seriously at a very early age.

Later that night, on putting her to bed, it was clear she was feeling uneasy about this new development.

"When I wake up in the morning, I won't be able to open my curtains and look out!"

"We could put your curtains back up, and you could pretend," said Sharon encouragingly (civility had returned to a degree).

This did not seem to have much impact and you could see her point – not a lot of fun in throwing open your rather pretty heart and flower curtains only to be faced by a grey breeze block wall, six inches from your face. It all seemed a bit prison like. I think some temporary relocation could be on the cards.

Thursday 31 October 2002

It might have been rather fitting as it was Halloween, but I could not help but cringe at the dark and sombre view into Cara's bedroom this morning. Admittedly, since it was 6.45, then we were hardly likely to be bathed in brilliant sunshine, but it was so dark, I had to fumble my way in and then reach out hopefully to even find her face so I could give her the usual goodbye kiss. Indeed, I must have given Winnie the Pooh a bit of a fright, as he was the first to be accosted before I discovered human flesh on the other side of the bed. I then half tripped over what was probably Tigger, (the hundred acre wood is alive and well and living in my daughter's bedroom) on my way back out. It was not an uplifting experience.

It also seems I did the builders a little disservice (not the first, certainly will not be the last), as they had fully intended to talk to me yesterday morning. But as I am inclined not to hang around filthy building sites in my best suit, I had done a runner immediately after leaving the house. There was therefore an apology made to Sharon this morning and this is more disturbing evidence that we are blessed with builders who really do give a damn.

Friday 1 November 2002
I had been warned earlier in the day we could finally witness the outside work breaking in and this time it was likely the internal repair would almost certainly be of a temporary nature. So on return home tonight, the rear lounge wall was covered with two huge pieces of thick plywood, like a hasty repair job to a high street shop window following some particularly unpleasant vandalism by drunken louts on a Saturday night. While the lounge cannot be said to be in a state of pristine repair and decoration, it still jarred to see these great ugly sheets of wood next to the sofa, carpet and umbrella plant. Still it was a joyous occasion to think that the ugly brown metal patio doors had now been rudely confined to the skip.

For the rest of the evening, these odd additions to the interior décor continued to catch my eye, and as we had recently had the award for the Turner Prize at the Tate, the thought did cross my mind that I could be looking at one of Britain's great unrecognised works of modern art. ('The conflict of the raw wood with the bland interior, expresses the brutality of society at its most contemporary'). The other disturbing facts were that the wind fairly whistled through the gap and you could hear everything happening just the other side of this temporary shield to the outside world. Given the fact that sundry wildlife tended to wander aimlessly around the garden, goodness knows what we might hear tonight. More particularly, we have been plagued for some months by the noisiest pheasant in Hertfordshire. It takes to crowing at all hours of the night and day, but makes a sound I can only describe as someone trying to croak loudly and badly with a very, very sore throat. If I had a gun, it would have been dead several times over by now. If it performs this act outside the plywood portal tonight, I will do the killing with my bare hands.

Saturday 2 November 2002
This was always going to be the test of the room without a window. Up until this morning, the lack of a window in Cara's bedroom had made little difference, as the weekday mornings had been pretty dark and the time of year dictated the evenings drew in nice and early. So even by the time the girls returned home from school, night-time was upon us. This morning was bright

and sunny, but in Cara's bedroom it was dark and positively foreboding. You could also feel the stillness in the air, which hung rather heavily and oppressively. Cara sat on the edge of her bed less than impressed at this state of affairs, with the almost comic grumpy look that only children can put on their faces. Sharon and I pondered the situation, but I had to admit, I really did not want to perpetuate the circumstances – not only do I have no wish to impose anything unpleasant onto my daughter, but I could see the local Social Services asking some serious questions if word got out.

"Cara, would you like us to move you into the spare room?"

She sat with a quizzical look on her face, contorting her mouth backwards and forwards, head propped on hand, just like you might draw someone in a cartoon situation.

"Mmmmm....Yes!"

I must confess, I was rather hoping she would say no. As you will have gathered, there is not a lot of space to manoeuvre within. I had only now begun to wonder how on earth we could swap two small jam-packed rooms, particularly in the clear knowledge of the fact that the landing had all the storage capacity of a box of matches. Meantime, as per the normal Saturday routine, all the women of the house were scheduled to disappear for hours and do interesting things like dancing and swimming, while good old dad has the task of doing-those-things-that-did-not-get-done-in-the-week, and today this includes the logistics of transforming spare junk/play room into bedroom and vice versa.

You will all recall those infuriating puzzles still available in Woolworths crackers, where you have to transport the bottom right corner of the puzzle to top left, even though your ability to move said piece is limited by the fact that all other pieces are in place bar one. It's one of those games where ideally you have to think several moves ahead, a real challenge to the brain, a bit of cerebral limbering. Alternatively, it will get you so cross within 5 minutes, leaving you trying to physically tear the puzzle apart in sheer anger and frustration, smoke billowing from your ears and it will finally be discarded at ferocious velocity across the room, or out of the window. Such an exercise would have been good practice for this particular task, as moving one pile of stuff simply blocked my way to move another and within about ten minutes, all I had achieved was lots of piles of stuff in lots of different places, all restricting my movement even more than it was before. On top of this, I had to dismantle Cara's bed – I can only describe all of this as like trying to get dressed whilst being stuck in a tube.

Inevitably, expletives poured from my mouth, and finally violence ensued, as I kicked the bed hard. Practicality is not my strong point, but this little outburst had at least cleared my mind a little and it appeared that I should indeed adopt the tactics of the Woolworths puzzle. So finally, I got things done by packing the bathroom with as much stuff as possible, thereby releasing space in one room, to allow the introduction of alternative stuff and then replacing the stuff from that room with stuff from the bathroom, if you get my drift. It would probably make an excellent party game, but it would have to be played at something like two in the morning and only after so much drink had been consumed that most competitors could only play on their knees.

Like all dramas, once it was done, you simply would not know of the angst and difficulty behind it, so the fairly mute thanks and acknowledgement I received once the family had returned I felt did not truly reflect the heroic efforts of this fraught human. But, I am a father and a man and in these circumstances, one must accept ones position in life.

Monday 4 November 2002
I have not ever wished to experience the life of a troglodyte, but I think we may be forced to sample existing in the dark, or at least, seeing little of daylight. It had not occurred to me that while one end of the lounge was barricaded against the outside, that the other end would suffer the same fate, but that is what has happened. When you see a huge tarpaulin over the front of your house, where once there was a substantial (if very ugly) bay window and porch, you know something pretty serious has taken place. Indeed, with the cold and dark, it had a sense of menace and malice about it, like a protective screen surrounding a particularly gruesome and unpleasant murder scene.

Of course this made the inside of the house start to resemble something out of a war zone, parts of the building having been blasted apart and subsequently boarded up. It was pretty bizarre, wife and children sat disconsolately on the sofa, furniture huddled into the middle and both ends of the room sporting great big slabs of boarding, covering the majority of the walls, screwed and nailed securely into place. What made it infinitely worse, the boards overlapped where they were secured, hence chill drafts whistled through from outside. More critically, having removed the front bay, away with it went the main radiator for the whole room. It really did begin to look like the blitz, now complete with sorry looking occupants, wrapped up against the cold. All we needed were some candles, and the whole family sharing a tin of beans with one spoon.

But it got worse. The window had now also gone from the bathroom and although a new frame had been installed, that was also boarded. Perhaps we were to be part of some strange experiment, probably instigated by the slightly insane looking Professor Robert Winston, who seems to be on the telly most nights informing me how fascinating humans are and proving this by conducting ever weirder tests. Personally, you don't have to persuade me that people are strange, I accepted this fact many years ago. Meantime, the impression of living in an area of conflict and devastation was emphasised by the dust, dirt and rubbish around the bathroom, and particularly in the bath, a fact having escaped my attention until I was in it, and on trying to wash myself with the soap, merely removed several layers of skin as the bar had become a veritable sandpaper block, infused as it was with grit and fine builders debris. Still, it certainly made sure I came out of the bath clean, even if once the water had gone, the bath looked like the inside of a concrete mixer.

So, lets recap – four windows gone and blocked up, main heating disappeared from the lounge and a constant film of grime and dust. But, as I hear myself saying every time someone asks me, it will be nice when its finished – won't it?

Tuesday 5 November 2002

You know that scene in 2001 a Space Odyssey, where all the stone-age men gather quizzically around the black monolith (and I still do not know what the hell that was all about) – well, I had a little 'déjà vu' tonight on returning home. We have a motion sensitive light set to come on at night, and although it does sometimes seem so sensitive that a sparrow fart does the trick, it is useful in bathing the front of the house in light when I turn into the drive. Tonight, it revealed a fine upstanding piece of white sculpture standing proud some distance from the front door, and almost luminescent against the dark brown mud, bricks and rubbish around the front of the house. Okay, there weren't a bunch of grunting Neanderthals scratching their heads and circling it in wonder, but it caused me to double take. This was the front door frame, a part of the design we had never really discussed, its appearance on the drawings of little consequence compared to the other items of greater import. But now I could see it in the flesh, naked and proud, I appreciated it was going to be a very obvious feature. This was particularly the case, as it contained two very substantial side-lights in order to ensure we got maximum light into the hall, and in this state, the main frame looked like it had two rather large and long ears. I decided to reserve judgment, but bowed in reverence before disappearing to the back door.

A pitch black November night is not conducive to inspection of the works at the rear and with the windows gone from all but one of the first floor rooms that face rearward, there was no way to cast any light on proceedings. I had discovered the only way to spot what had been going on was to open the window in the spare room (now Cara's bedroom), climb on the windowsill and lean out. Please do not try this at home, especially if it is windy and rainy – which it was. Any passing observer may well have thought I had reached the end of my tether and was preparing to throw myself onto the mercy of the bricks and paving slabs immediately below. In fact, what I could (just about) see, peering through the murk and wet, was that the roof timbers had gone on, and despite the extension still being swathed in scaffolding, planks and netting, there was now the semblance of something whole and recognisable.

I thought I should celebrate this fact with a drink, but on returning to the kitchen in bare feet, was reminded there were still many trials and tribulations ahead of us before we actually had a home. This came in the form of the omnipresent layer of dry, crunchy dirt, which seemed to sit on the floor of the kitchen at the end of every day. Just a few steps accumulated enough sand, cement and other grains on the soles of your feet to make your own bowl of mortar and from there it got transported through the rest of the house. I had tried vacuuming, but it merely seemed to spread it around (a Dyson has never worked so hard, but I am afraid failed pretty miserably in these conditions), as did sweeping with a brush. Only one thing for it – spray the floor, get down on your hands and knees and mop the floor with a lifetime supply of kitchen roll. This is not an act I would recommend in a suit. Indeed, I can't say it is an act I would recommend, but it does the trick. However, it also reveals the true state of your kitchen floor, which in this case was several steps up from revolting. You don't want to know – you really don't want to know.

Wednesday 6 November 2002

Richard had called earlier, following an e-mail from me just headed 'Problems' – it pays to be direct in these matters. It covered my whinge about our enforced lack of daylight, the fact that icicles would soon be forming in the lounge and the growing lake now accumulating around the rear extension, as it seemed the soil had all the drainage properties of a plastic sheet. He pointed out the weather was not ideal (it was hissing down, in the cold miserable way you can only find in England), but there was hope that normal daylight service might be resumed shortly. In the meantime, in the view of the very unaccommodating nature of the weather, Steve and the gang would like to start work inside in earnest (well, in the house actually – forget it!). In particular, could we move everything in the dining room right to the outside wall so they could start to construct the hallway, and do similarly with the bedroom with the blocked window, so they could replace the partition wall.

Mmmm, lets see now. The dining room is already filled with boxes and bits from the lounge so gaining access required some combined knowledge of navigation and contortionism, creating more space was going to tax our skills. The windowless room was similarly filled with Cara's stuff (believe me, the amount of her stuff would leave Emelda Marcos in awe) and most of the gubbins from the play-room, so there was another puzzle to solve. Well, bless them, for the first part did not need much work as the weather had clearly been so atrocious in the afternoon, they decided to plough on and put up the frame for the partition in the dining room, and shoved everything they could out of the way. Shame they forgot to plug the fridge freezer back in, but thankfully there were no human organs contained therein to have suffered damage for being semi thawed. I did however rejoice at the fact that they had violently attacked the carpet (you know, dirty chocolate swirl?), having sliced it right the way through and removed a substantial section in order to fix the frame to the floor. It was only a pity that I had not had the pleasure of performing this act myself. Less satisfaction could be gained from the fact whilst mutilating the carpet, they had also sliced the telephone cable in two. So perhaps this is all a devious plan to gradually incarcerate us in our home and cut off our lines of communication. But then they would not have left all the doors unlocked if this were the case. Good job most burglars have probably never heard of Anstey, let alone be able to find it.

Having reconnected the fridge freezer, we then rearranged the dining room. We were miraculously able to shove more stuff in (some of the furniture had simply been decanted to the lounge) and threw half an acre of plastic sheet over it all. This was in the expectation of all hell probably being let loose tomorrow and we would rather it did not all fall onto our boxes of books, pictures, chairs and other stuff of admittedly questionable value. Windowless room was not so much of a problem. Well, nothing a bit of grunting and swearing could not solve, together with some stacking and squeezing that made up for in brutality what it lacked in imagination. It wasn't pretty, but then nothing in the house currently was and it was getting even less so.

Continued progress seemed to go hand in hand with a diminution in the ability of the house to keep warm. The work in the dining room had necessitated the removal of another radiator, while preparation for breaking through into the existing kitchen meant that one had to go also. So, the total number of radiators now left on the ground floor was…..one…….of modest proportions……squeezed into the far corner of the lounge…..with November temperatures dropping into deep Winter…..perfect! Could I be certain this wasn't an English version of the Trueman Show?

Thursday 7 November 2002
Shite weather, shite day, not a lot seemed to have been done, save a bit of concreting to the front and a big tarpaulin over the roof at the back. These were not conditions in which I would want to work, so who could blame them for making little progress.

My big moment today was a purely personal one. I had returned from Thursday night swimming club in my other work capacity as omnipresent taxi driver to my daughters. It was 9.30 in the evening, Cara was in bed, Sian was wrapped up in her nightgown on the Sofa, Sharon was huddled in an armchair, and both were clutching a hot mug of tea. The small convector heater I had thankfully discovered in the loft was whirring away rather asthmatically at one end of the room and was keeping the temperature on the borderline of acceptable. At the other end of the room, the rest of the furniture was crowded together like the inside of a removal lorry, while the bookshelf was covered with a grubby plastic sheet, a uniform film of dust sat over its surface. The large bare wooden boards across the walls at either end of the room were of course the main and obvious features, and our only protection against the outside elements. The finishing touch was the continued presence of the original decoration, all painted blown vinyl, dour colours that clashed and the stone clad fireplace, and somehow, this all seemed to fit with the appalling conditions.

I looked around standing rather speechlessly and just said "Sorry!"

"What for?" Sharon looked a bit surprised, as if I were going to reveal some terrible hidden deed.

"For taking all of you on a continued downward spiral of houses that could hardly be called home for the last 4 years."

"Oh, that's not a problem, it will be lovely when its finished!" Sharon said as a matter of fact and returned to her tea.

Personally, at that moment in time, I felt guilt and anguish, but clearly no one else was willing to back me in this campaign of self deprecation. Thank god for the family.

Saturday 9 November 2002

I always knew this morning would be a real tester for the darkened cave that was the lounge. Ordinarily, with a big bay window facing south and large patio doors at the other end, even on a dark, dreary winters day (and this morning was so damp, cold, and overcast, it was almost a parody of what people think of as the archetypal British winter day) it would be flooded with light. This morning it was awash with dark. It was a little strange to sit at 9.00am with a cup of tea, reading a magazine, with all the room lights on full blast. It was difficult at times to persuade yourself it was not time to go to bed, rather than begin something meaningful for the day.

Opening the door to the hall in order to get at least a glow of daylight was not really an option as it meant the temperature dropped to almost Arctic levels within about 5 minutes. In the meantime, the rain was incessant, with the roof to the rear only covered in felt and no means of proper drainage in place, we tolerated the constant background splashing of rainwater onto concrete. For most of the day it was like a tap had been left on outside. Perhaps this was what Chinese water torture was like, because it was certainly sending us a trifle mad.

This was not a place to spend a good deal of time, and suddenly the thought of the weekly trip to Tescos seemed positively uplifting. Now, I am a man of the modern variety and have no particular difficulty with shopping, as long as everything goes to plan, the shop has what I want and there are not too many people around – which is hardly the environment you can expect at a big supermarket at 10.00am on a Saturday morning. So much so in fact I have now come to loathe this particular chore. I am not an adventurous or particularly difficult shopper, you could very easily predict what I was going to buy each week, and 95% of the time, you would be right. You know the sort of things, bread, milk, beans, loo rolls, bananas, pocket nuclear fission reactor (well, this particular Tesco seems to sell everything else, so why not?). So why is it that for a store which opens 24 hours a day and apparently has the selling space equivalent to the deck of the Ark Royal, there are a lack of basic items and a surfeit of the useless ones? You want to buy the latest 20 slice carbon fibre toaster? No problem. Want a tin of Tesco beans? Er, sorry, sold out. Today, it was packs of 4 Tesco loo rolls, and at the site was a Saturday sales person. I looked at her, she ignored me. I kept looking, and wanted to say 'given the size of store you are, the money and people at your disposal, how the hell can you be out of 4 pack loo rolls?'. But all she was interested in was getting in the way and I suspected would not have understood my question. I could not stand the thought of her almost certain response of 'What?'

And there is a lot of crowding at Tesco on a Saturday, but we are not talking other shoppers here. How many shop staff does it take to fill an empty hole in a shelf? By my calculations, it is at least 4, often 5, and not unusually 6. However, this does not actually achieve the filling of said empty shelf. It does achieve a major blocking of the aisle, whilst at the same time educating all the shoppers around them as to the success of their individual social events of the previous Friday night. All this is usually expertly emphasised by the use of one of those caged pallets the size of a small juggernaut and I marvel at their dexterity in moving it around so as to cause maximum inconvenience. There are the makings of a day time action quiz show here, but all I want to do is buy what they do not have, pay money I would rather keep and get the hell out.

Ahh, weekends, a period of rest and relaxation.

Monday 11 November 2002
More trench warfare has begun and the front drive has been all but obliterated while they do their best to create new drainage runs for the rainwater. This is all heading towards the soak-away, which we are pretty certain is in the front garden, in very close proximity to a hawthorn bush. We know this, because every time it rains for any length of time, the bush becomes an island in its very own lake, while the area around it becomes a marshy bog. Where else could you get such changing landscapes and ecosystems? There aren't any gnomes in Anstey to the best of my knowledge, but if there were, I am sure it would have become a major fishing venue by now (what else do gnomes do, except look very stupid?).

The other major action seems to have been the placement of the front bay window frame in approximate position on top of what has so far been done on the front extension brickwork, and bugger, is it big! We may be going pale with the lack of light at the moment, but when this baby is in place, we will be able to place our sun-loungers inside the house several deep and soak up the rays for hours. It did currently look a trifle odd and at first I frightened myself that it had actually been fixed in place, as it sat very low. Despite its size and depth, I thought the bottom sill should come some way above my ankle, otherwise we will be tempted to do passable impressions of goldfish.

We now also had piles of tiles all over the place, ready to go on the roof and coupled with the mounds of sand and aggregate, the heaps of wood, multifarious door frames, bricks, and just about every other form of builders raw material, we could look at a quick change of use as a builders merchants. That might make a quick buck, but had the serious drawback of leaving no materials to finish the house. And anyway, I would have to develop an almost impenetrable language (mainly monosyllabic shouts and calls) and display a builders bum, so all in all, the appeal was pretty marginal.

Tuesday 12 November 2002
The weather has been nothing short of atrocious today, indeed November generally seems to have followed a rather consistent, depressing pattern. That in turn means work back at Holly House has been rather hampered, at least externally, although roof tiles have gone on one side of the rear extension. This has sorely exposed the problems when new meets old, or at least when new meets something that is at least getting on a bit and has the darkened colour of some seventeen years exposure to everything the British weather can throw at it. So while the new roof tiles are a rather brighter red than I had imagined, they looked positively Toy-town against the deep, almost brown red of the tiles on the main roof, coated with all the patina of years of wind, rain, snow, sun and abuse by errant leaves, twigs and more than a modicum of bird crap.

The weather had therefore forced Steve and the gang inside, a fact heralded by an almost overflowing skip full of rubbish and demolished breeze-blocks. I had rather hoped this would mean we had French doors now installed at the back of the house, but what it actually meant was, we now had a dirty great hole in the kitchen where they had broken through to form the hallway. A rather rusty metal prop sat in the middle of this perfect door sized hole in order to prevent a total ceiling collapse, and a wire snaked its way down the prop, ending in the light switch taped to its middle. It all looked pretty Heath Robinson, but while those contraptions worked, this one didn't and we were now robbed of some of our artificial light.

In conjunction with this exercise, they had also ripped down one wall of the stairs, as it would open out into the newly formed hallway, although this left the obsolete down-pipe from the shower-of-no-bloody-use exposed, remaining intact in its pointless position. A temporary wooden prop sat next to this, jammed in to keep up the floor, but looking less than sturdy, with sundry pieces of wood rammed in at top and bottom in order to ensure connection from floor to ceiling. Its less than perpendicular angle was a slight worry. While all of this was a complete mess, it did have the effect of opening out the area and making me wonder why on earth the original builders had not planned the ground floor in this way, thus creating a reasonable hall, access to all rooms from it and avoiding the need for traffic flow through the lounge to rival the M25. Granted, the dining room would have been smaller, but it would still have been perfectly useable for that purpose – and it would have saved me an awful lot of time and money.

The other fall out from all this was precisely that, dust everywhere, on everything, on every floor. Wherever you walked, it took no time at all to collect a tidy coating of brick and block dust on your feet. Whatever you touched had a nice gritty film (as in a physical covering, rather than a video of Saving Private Ryan or some other finely acted drama – don't usually have those lying all over the place). Although we attempted to wipe this away (including the on-the-knees scenario previously described), it proved difficult to get rid of, as it almost seemed to hang in the air and drift down to recoat the surface immediately you had finished wiping it. Indeed, I could swear my tea had a slightly crunchier texture to it than was the norm, while I was not entirely sure what was later remaining at the bottom of my coffee cup, was all sugar. Still, probably good fibre for the body.

Wednesday 13 November 2002
Shit. Literally. Well, almost. I am not what you call an optimist – crap days will generally get crappier – but I had rather hoped, the general dirt and mess yesterday might be about as bad as it would get. Wrong! When I arrived home tonight, I managed to bump into (it was dark) the electrician. I had not expected this degree of technology at this stage of the process. Bearing in mind nothing was yet wind and water tight, the walls were still looking like the inside of a remote far eastern prison cell, it had not occurred to me that we would be into wiring, plug sockets and light switches. The man was an affable, slightly built chap, with a whispy greying beard, not too happy that he had been standing in water most of the day to do what he does. (Personally, I always thought that the combination of water and electricity generally meant you were likely to be burnt to a crisp, but he didn't look very frazzled). He also told me a rather funny tale about his van, centred around the fact that because it had recently been broken into, the only means of access was through the tailgate of the boot – I couldn't quite link the two, but I took his word for it. Apparently, earlier in the day, he had had to charge off to get some more cable, but when he returned to his car, found someone had parked so close to the back of his van, he couldn't open the boot and therefore couldn't go anywhere. Just to add to the comedy, his parking ticket was about to run out and he urgently needed a gent's toilet. Of course, he also had to phone Steve to explain why he had apparently disappeared for so long. Norman Wisdom or Rowan Atkinson surely could not have dreamt up and acted a better scenario. The image of him crossing his legs, while on his mobile, hopping around trying in vain to open the boot of the van, while manically looking for the driver of the offending vehicle parked behind, made me chuckle. If I had seen him, I probably would have been looking for the whereabouts of the camera crew.

But back to the shit. The presence of an electrician meant installation of lots of wiring, meant drilling, gouging and general destruction of the existing walls and partitions to create holes and spaces, meant enough dust and grime to fill several bags and sell it for a tidy profit. When I said it was everywhere yesterday, I lied – yesterday, it was *on* most surfaces, but now it was *in* all surfaces. In cupboards, in cups, on plates, in handles, in your ears, up your nose, and probably find its way out of your bottom eventually. And while yesterday might have been a dusting, this time it was a positively quilted bedspread of a covering, and the act of removing it took some time, and not a little application, not to mention several rolls of kitchen towel. The feeling of whatever you did you were living in a persistently dirt laden and grubby environment was all rather depressing and hardly lifted the already gloomy ambience of the incarcerated rooms that were now a large part of the house. I begun to wonder whether we should simply have moved out for 6 months while all this was going on rather than try to stick it out like the stubborn Brits we were.

At least the roof tiling was complete at the back, even though the bright redness of the new finish might well have attracted alien space craft, thinking it was an earthly sign of welcome, a beacon of greeting, bidding them to our planet to sample its delights and friendship. Trouble is, if they had landed, they would have looked at the squalor that was Holly House and hightailed it back to Zog Minor III, then rapidly spread the word that the peoples of Earth were a disgusting disorganised bunch of heathens, who lived in self-inflicted conditions of filth and unpleasantness, in half finished and chaotic abodes, but at least they had really funky roofs.

The rather impressive front window bay frame had also now been put in its correct place, with brick all around and underneath, but in this half-built guise looked like a slightly lost sales or ticket booth. I could imagine standing behind it, charging entrants a modest fee to park on the drive, or perhaps some rather twisted individuals might want to pay good money to inspect the mess and mayhem. 'Entrance round the back sir, watch out for the dodgy pile of bricks, but you can't miss the door, its the one coated in splashed mud.' Perhaps I could even create an Anstey Lottery outlet, raising money to help the wretched and needy of Holly House. On second thoughts, it would be difficult to tempt people in when they couldn't even gain safe entrance. Personally, I would take one look at this particular house of horrors and run the other way. In fact, it was very tempting to do that anyway.

Friday 15 November 2002

It is Children in Need day today. I was rudely reminded of this fact when turning on the radio, where I was confronted by Tina Turner, singing 'Simply the Best'. Apparently, this had been requested by some misguided soul, who also had agreed to pledge £20 to hear it – I would have paid £20 to ensure I did not hear it for at least the next 5 years. I am sorry, and if you are a TT fan, bless you, but go and get help immediately. This woman should have settled into her zimmer-frame long ago, I cannot get out of my mind the ridiculous strutting walk she does to EVERY song – she looks like a cross between Mick

Jagger and a badly choreographed puppet from Thunderbirds. Sian, my eldest, does a superb imitation of TT performing this act, and my goodness is it funny. Thankfully in this particular case, the radio in my car has the benefit of interruptions for traffic reports, and I have rarely been so glad to be reminded that the A120 in Essex was moving freely this morning, while the M11 was getting busy around Stansted Airport. By the time we returned to the radio station, Tina had clearly had enough for the day, and presumably was now tucked up in her favourite armchair with a cup of cocoa and would soon start her knitting. I proceeded on my way to work in reasonably bright conditions, so at least hoped the builders would be able to make some progress today, unless they were all captivated by Tina Turner, maybe Sian would be teaching them the TT strut. I would find out later.

Indeed they had made some progress, progress in making even more of a mess than I thought was possible. Actually, that is a bit unfair. The weather had hardly been accommodating for the week, so it should have been no surprise that heavy traffic of man and wheelbarrow over the sodden soil should have created a small mud-bath. This generally transported all of this unpleasant gunge all around the house, while a not insubstantial amount was gradually finding its way into the house, stowed away on the bottom of everyone's shoes. In fact, the front extension was now moving on at some reasonable speed and by Friday night, another steel beam was in place across the top of the wall just behind the bay window frame, again looking a touch out of place amidst all the bricks and mortar. Moreover, we now had an extensive stage erected around the front of the house, courtesy of a jumbled configuration of scaffolding poles and planks, all sat on less than sturdy looking small wooden sleepers. In particular, this created a rather amusing balcony at first floor level, with direct access from Sian's bedroom window, should you have had the inclination.

Perhaps here was an opportunity to create some extra cash. Yes, I could see it now. Out of the strife torn war-zone which was the Holly House construction site, the embattled inhabitants had heroically created an impromptu arena and stage, and in aid of the Neale Family Sanity Fund, proposed a mega gig, the like of which had never been seen by the UK, or at least the eastern side of Anstey. Unfortunately, David Bowie and Robbie Williams had found themselves double booked and had to send their apologies to the fans. Instead we had Cara Neale on her amazing recorder, Sian Neale on her slightly scratchy violin, all backed by an astonishing sound system expertly managed by Sharon Neale, or otherwise known as an S Club 7 CD on a modest little hi fi sat on the window ledge. The revered Alan Neale, trying to hold the garden torch still while slipping precariously around in the mudbath, provided lighting. Perhaps not. Funds raised were unlikely to be substantial, whilst the danger to life in performing on dodgy scaffolding were likely to seriously outweigh any benefits.

Saturday 16 November 2002

Seeing the scaffolding and the rest of the mid point construction in daylight, together with the unremitting mess all around rather made me catch my breath this morning. It also reminded me why I would much rather this had all been done in the summer. As has tended to be the norm on Saturdays, the morning was spent clearing up much of the mess from the preceding week, while the afternoon presented an opportunity for the good Mrs Neale and I to commit yet more expenditure – when you are feeling a bit down, make it even worse by putting yourself deeper in debt I say. In fact, I confess, I rather like shopping, as long as I do not have the kids in tow, as their attention span and interest is limited in these circumstances. There are only so many times I can tolerate the phrase 'I'm Bored!' or 'Can we go home now?', before I just give in and return from whence we came, having bought nothing, but acquired a mountain of frustration and a hatred of all other drivers, especially all those who quite unreasonably want to use the same car park as I do at precisely the same time. Can't they see I want to shop in peace, on my own? It is one of life's greatest pointless exercises.

But this afternoon, we were devoid of all offspring. Despite some growing backchat from Sian and the complete inability of Cara to do anything with her possessions other than leave them exactly where she had finished with them (kitchen floor, stairs, on top of the bin), I had not yet been tempted to nudge one of them into either the open cement mixer or the gaping trenches. Cara had conned, sorry gently persuaded, one of her friends and their mother to spend of the rest of the day at their house, while Sian had pondered the prospect of the shopping trip and decided an afternoon at the nearby grandparents and an armful of home work was far preferable. You see the sense of excitement and wonder I instil into my children? So free of these ties, we proceeded to our local bathroom supplier, having been prompted by both the builders and the Architect to get on and order sooner rather than later. I had not worked out whether this was because they would soon be in a position to install, or if they all simply and desperately wanted a decent bathroom and toilet to use. I could see their point.

I had not realised that bathroom suites could come in quite so many styles, colours, shapes, sizes and configurations. All we wanted was a reasonably modern straightforward white bath, basin and bog, but that was rather difficult to locate in this emporium of indulgence. It wasn't just the fact of taps being gold, although there were plenty of those, but you could have ones looking like Mickey Mouse, or with a very strange top that looked like a big blue pen in a pen holder – handy if you want to write at the same time as wash your face. There were combined baths and showers, including one that had recently been extracted from the bridge of the Star-ship Enterprise. It had an almost fully enclosed capsule at one end, above which was a huge metal spray-head and miles of shiny pipes and tubes running all around and top to bottom. It just lacked Captain Kirk in mid transportation and Scotty over the other side of the room shouting 'I canna hold it Captain!' And then there were the Jacuzzi baths big enough to hold a blue whale, with jet nozzles I suspect may recently have been more at home on the wings of a jumbo jet, complete with digital control pads that put my laptop to shame. The prices were equally astronomical, but then I suppose if you are going to have an intergalactic bathroom the size of Birmingham, you don't quibble about the cost, but even they must have gulped at a radiator costing some £1500. I mean, I could sink my own oil well and create my own heating system for that. Most outrageous of all however, was Tilevision. Yes, you've guessed it, television in the bathroom. I have always thought the bathroom was a place of tranquillity and peace beyond the stressful realities of everyday life. The last thing I would want would be pictures of pain and suffering in Africa, or Arsenal at home to West Ham (misery and affliction levels vaguely similar) whilst soaping my unmentionables and playing wistfully with my duck. If my kids ever got hold of this, they would never, ever come out of the bathroom again, the fire service would have to be called to extract Cara in particular.

Needless to say we plumped for something a little simpler, less complicated and without the need to sell my children for a princely sum, although that always remains an option.

Sunday 17 November 2002
November is turning into one of those seemingly never ending dull, dreary, wet depressing months, which seems to typify the British Winter in the eyes of visitors. It seemed to be forever cold, grey and damp and given our circumstances within the Chamber of Mess and Dark, a Sunday spent inside getting more and more depressed did not appeal, so I suggested an afternoon at the Cinema and dinner out afterwards. That seemed to cheer everyone up, although we all agreed we would not join the mass hordes all clamouring to be the latest Harry Potter fans. I like to take my time with these fads, I can't stand being seen as one of the first to see or do the latest craze. Much better to wait until the rush is over, although by that time you are a bit sick of people saying 'Have you seen the latest Harry Potter?'. No, but then I won't be queuing five times around the block, looking like a poverty stricken housewife in a bread queue in Azerbaijan. The problem was the only other film left suitable for all was Disney's just-about-finished-its-run cartoon, Lilo and Stitch.

Before we could settle into our seats however, we had to negotiate our way through the Cinema foyer. Now, I am old enough to remember how cinemas used to be, and although they may be rather euphemistically called flea pits, they were generally pretty clean and tidy and like policemen, the people who worked in them seemed very much older than they do today. Like all weekend retail outlets that do little more than take your money and tell you to piss off, these places are staffed with those of a more youthful persuasion and the manners of a fruit bat.

"Family ticket for Lilo and Stitch at 3.35 please."

"Firm tick?" the girl behind the counter grunted, or at least I think it was a girl. Whatever, I wasn't sure what this question was about. Was there some extra deal being offered today, or was I being offered some reward for saying please, so I got a firm tick on my pass rather than a weak one for being so pleasant?

"Sorry?" I leant forward and cocked my ear towards her

"Firmly ticket!" she grunted louder. Aha, she wanted confirmation that I indeed wanted a family ticket. Glad we got the translation out of the way quickly.

"Yes please."

She took my credit card, swiped it, produced the tickets, and got me to sign in an almost seamless blur. What she lacked in coherence and interpersonal skills, she certainly made up for in speed.

Across the other side of this grubby entrance hall, three male youths were chatting and jigging about behind the refreshment counter. It is of course a matter of opinion if you consider insipid coca cola from a hose and nozzle that looks like it would be better used on my car as refreshment, not to mention the piles of sweet and sticky polystyrene sold as popcorn. While these three clearly felt talking and mucking about was a greater priority in their job description than serving customers, one of them did at least ponder the question of general tidiness. He looked at his counter, scattered with popcorn, gave a furtive look across the foyer to see if anyone was looking, and swept it all off the counter onto the floor *in front of him*. Either, he didn't give a toss, or he was too thick to consider for his own embarrassment, that it might have been better to at least removed all the debris to the floor behind him. But then I came to the conclusion, that clearly nobody in this place gave a toss anyway, as the whole foyer floor was covered with popcorn, drinks straws, crisp packets, discarded children and dead dogs. Okay, there weren't any dead dogs, and the discarded children were momentary escapees, but I can't think that even if there were dead dogs lying about the place, anyone would have bothered to do much about it.

Indeed, on getting into the screen where we were to watch the film, any nagging doubts I had about general care and cleanliness in this place were sadly confirmed. I didn't need to look under the seats to check for rubbish and the odd expired mammal, most of it was around the place, but worst of all was the state of the floor under the seats. It was like stepping onto sellotape, but of course the only thing on the floor was a film of everyone else's spilt drink, a disgusting layer of sticky, dirty sugar laden and sugar free Coke, Fanta and god knows what else. Each time you moved your feet, the noise of shoe reluctantly removing itself from the floor, reverberated and you had to remove your thoughts from what exactly was going on at floor level. What a pleasant and edifying experience it was.

And the film? One of the most bizarre I have seen in recent years. I can only describe it as a cartoon cross between Men in Black, Bugs Bunny and Annie, set on what looked like a Caribbean island, but the kids enjoyed it and it took my mind off the state of my immediate environment.

Tuesday 19 November 2002

Another white framed monolith sits at the front of the house tonight, but this time rather precariously perched at first floor level. The wall construction on the front extension had proceeded to the extent that the single replacement window for our bedroom was now in place, albeit held there by two rather flimsy wood splints, nailed rather brutally to the new window frame at one end, and the existing window sills at the other. As we had two windows currently to our bedroom, we had opted for just about the deepest window we could put in place as its single replacement, and its width wasn't of modest proportions either. Coupled with the large bay window at ground level, they made quite a statement as you looked at them, a sort of carpentry equivalent of Arnold Schwazenegger, 'Don't mess with me, look at the size of my windows!'.

And this wasn't the only beefy construction to have taken place today. Finally, the steel support structure had gone into the dining area at the rear, although I struggled to understand why such a powerful means of support was going to be needed for what was a fairly modest piece of roof. It now looked like part of a weird temple entrance, with strong red metal beams spanning the width, two huge uprights at either end and two shorter sections back to the main two storey construction. Once again, the red metal looked incongruous against the brick, breeze block, mortar and general builders detritus, and rather added to the eerie feel, significantly enhanced by a swirling and cold mist that wafted around. Perhaps we were witnessing the beginnings of a builders' temple of worship, where strange and obscure ceremonies would take place in the dead of night, or more likely just after the 10.00am tea break. You know the sort of thing, rolled up trouser legs, impenetrable language, presentation of strange implements, rituals involving cutting and swearing – a normal day on a building site really.

Alternatively, this could be linked to the increasingly bright nature of the rear extension, and its suspected function as a beacon for extraterrestrial forms of life. The tiles were now going up on the sides of the walls, their newness and almost luminescence were increasingly surprising. I had asked Richard about this, and wondered whether we could do anything to age or darken them, particularly as if this were repeated at the front, the appearance would likely cause road traffic accidents. Although he briefly mentioned there might be a spray to do the job, one of the most popular and successful treatments is….wait for it….yoghurt. Right, OK, let's think about this. Problem number one – If I went and purchased what would probably amount to the whole of the nearest Tesco's entire supply of yoghurt, chances are I would at worst be arrested on suspicion of yoghurt fetishism (outlawed in Hertfordshire since 1967), or at best become an instant outcast for bizarre behaviour. Problem number two – my car boot surely does not have enough room for this size carton of yoghurt ('Excuse me, do you have any larger sizes of yoghurt cartons? What size do you need sir? Jaguar Boot size please!'). Problem number three – the thought and imagery being created of crawling around the roof, probably hanging dangerously from the chimney, spreading strawberry yoghurt across the roof tiles with wild abandon did not appeal. Problem four – the smell of decaying yoghurt, which would soon fill the air, would knock that from the nearby chicken farm into a cocked hat. Needless to say, this suggestion did not find favour, although I could not get out of my head the picture of me kneeling on the roof, dog-eared rope around my middle, pot of yoghurt in one hand, spooning implement in the other, dolloping dairy product left right and centre. I could not even think this would ensure the good people of Anstey would take me to their heart.

Wednesday 20 November 2002
A bit of general progress today, nothing dramatic – a bit more glowing tiling, a bit more brick and block work out the front, window now installed for what will be the en-suite shower room. And (at last) roof beams over the dining area, so the temple of doom was beginning to take shape and in fact, look rather less like a temple.

Having said that, mysterious white scrawlings had appeared on the walls of what would be the kitchen and indeed, even inside what currently was the kitchen. This I could only see by peering through the current kitchen window, so I did my best Arthur Conan Doyle impersonation, entering dark, dank chasm with torch, but alas not dressed in Khaki suit with shorts and pith helmet. Were these some unfathomable doodlings of a hidden East Herts tribe, that only came out when the weather was crap, and building works were taking place? Sadly, nothing so interesting. I had called back my kitchen supplier to take some actual measurements, especially as we had discovered that the whole rear extension was 200mm narrower than planned and 275mm deeper. Quite why this had occurred, I had not been able to figure out, suffice it to say, if I had got the Architects and the Builders together, they would have stood pointing at each other shouting 'It was him!'

When I had bumped into the electrician last week, he had assumed the current kitchen plan was as it was going to be, but I hastily had to point out that reality would be different. Too late however to prevent him marking out where he thought some of the appliances and associated plug points would go. Now Terry the Kitchen had arrived today, he had used his own piece of chalk like a school-kid scribbling out his enemies' drawings, and putting his own in place. So, there were big white lines and crossings out together with barely decipherable writing denoting 'Oven' (self-explanatory) '600 bse'. (If my kitchen speak is up to date, this means 600mm base unit), '600 d/w' (struggling here a bit, but possibly 600mm drawer unit). And what looked like 'scrxxx' (either my kitchen phrase book is not this advanced, or he had simply lost the plot by this stage).

Inside the kitchen, in a big circle was '520 MIN'. A ransom demand? A reminder for payment? A prompt that by 5.20, he really should have removed his Mini? No, in fact, it was a prompt to the builders to make sure they left him enough room to put in a planned dresser unit, although personally I liked the idea of him looking at his watch and saying 'Blimey, better go and move that blasted car.' We do have zealous traffic wardens in this part of Hertfordshire, but mercifully, they have not yet begun to roam the streets of Anstey.

Thursday 21 November 2002
It is probably a good job that I get up as early as I do – 6.00am. I confess, I do not leap out of bed, full of the joys of anticipation of the day ahead, and anyone who does at that time in the morning, in the middle of November, when it is as cold, dark and wet as it has been are in need of a thorough medical examination, concentrating on the brain and its function, or lack thereof. Having completed my ablutions and fumbled my way down stairs, I then stumbled into the lounge and found the light switch. Now I wear contact lenses, but I do not bother with their installation until just before I leave the house, so as well as being cold, grumpy and half awake, I am also visually challenged. However, my ears work perfectly well, and what I heard woke me up and made me say very deliberately 'Oh, shit!'

'Drip, Drip, Drip' was what I heard, and I quickly homed in on the far corner of the lounge, where I discovered an armchair soaked through, a sodden radio, and a ceiling issuing water in constant and consistent drops. 'Shit, Shit, Shit' I shouted, rather nicely in time with the dripping. Now men are not good in these situations, so I turned one way and then the next, moved the chair partly out and then stopped, turned again and turned back, it was like an involuntary and useless robot dance, which wasn't getting me anywhere. Eventually I thought I had better do something positive, so I finally moved the chair right out, took the sopping cushions off, and rootled around the kitchen to try and find some sort of water retaining receptacle. Why I first of all looked where we keep the glasses, I have not got a clue, but eventually plumped for a plastic dish in which we normally cook rice. Granted, this was not ideal, but it was a start and anyway I was being rather distracted by the constant dripping and my own chants of 'shit, shit, shit'.

Having partially stemmed the problem, I then ran upstairs putting on every light, but quickly realised that illumination was of little use if I could not actually see and make out very much. So, I then lurched into the bedroom, and coupled with the floodlighting upstairs, this woke up Sharon

"What *are* you doing?" she said rather annoyed.

"We've got a leak in the ceiling." I blurted

Now think about this. Pipes leak, buckets, even tyres leak, but since the principle job of a ceiling is not to hold anything, liquid or otherwise, it is difficult to see how it can leak. Granted, water was issuing from it, but unless our particular ceiling had hitherto unknown powers or an undiscovered molecular structure, I was clearly talking bollocks.

Sharon is Mrs Practical, and as usual took the situation in hand in fairly short order, encompassing a reorganisation of affairs, a rapid assessment of the problem, followed by the most appropriate corrective measures – she would have made a great Army General. Why had I used the rice bowl when there was a bucket in the downstairs loo? Why had I not got out a towel to mop up the excess water? Where was it coming from? Why am I generally so crap in these situations? Answer to the latter is very simple – I am a bloke. She quickly discovered, the problem related to the bathroom. And on pulling up the tatty green floor tiles and opening up (or rather ripping down) the panel at the head of the bath, it seemed that the source of this difficulty was the rather cruddy bath taps. They had been perniciously issuing water for some time, judging by the widespread thin puddle that was revealed. Perhaps this was the bathrooms last revenge before we tore the whole thing down, cackling in delicious evil as we finally rid ourselves of the disgusting mucus colour bathroom suite and the tasteful green wood panelling.

Either way, we had stabilised the condition, and would ask Steve to perform some delicate surgery to ensure the lounge remained reasonably dry, even though my preference would have been to treat the bathroom to a small nuclear device. I therefore shot off to work for the day. Except, I was soon shooting back again. I thank God, my children are ridiculously healthy individuals, they simply do not do ill, other than the odd sniffles and colds, and these simply do not keep them away from doing things. Indeed, Sian had a less than pleasant cold when she competed at Guildford. Not too much immobilises them, but today was the exception that proves the rule, and lets face it, when your guts are telling you all is not well, indicating it wants to evict its contents, you cannot press on in stoic fashion. So, Sharon got the call from school, I got the call from Sharon and we split our nursing duties morning and afternoon, returning home at lunchtime, child laying quietly on the sofa, her pallor bearing a remarkable resemblance to the bathroom suite, so perhaps it had got the last laugh.

I spent a surreal afternoon running between laptop precariously balanced on a filing box in Cara's room, and periodic inspections of Sian languishing in a less than sprightly manner on the sofa in the darkened lounge, surrounded by the sound of workmen from every angle, banging, sawing, drilling, carrying, mixing, whistling, shouting and singing. With my laptop wire trailed across the room right across the entrance, an outside observer with an interest in slapstick would have had hours of fun watching everything go flying, including me, several times, accompanied by barely stifled colourful language. Not the best of days this.

Saturday 23 November 2002
Bless them. Even if in most other things, I find dubious products and questionable service which I always suspect has behind it the sentiment of 'Do I really *have* to do this?' my builders emphatically do not fall into that category. The weather has hampered their progress, although they have still worked outside in some atrocious conditions, they want to catch up. They have therefore, requested if they can work this morning. So, let's just take a moment to understand this – they want to do the job, get it done on time and have asked me, the customer, if they can effectively work overtime, without extra pay, to ensure they can stick to their side of the bargain. Please take note, those companies who have failed to provide me with even a modicum of this outfit's commitment to customer service, most of them large household names. Libel laws probably prevent me from naming and shaming some of these, such as the organisation meant to look after my money, but the only attractive thing about it is the nice bright shade of green in its logo, and a rather fine black stallion that graces its shop fronts. It strikes me that a more appropriate pose for this horse, rather than rearing up in apparent readiness to gallop to the rescue, would be for it to be shoving its ample arse in the direction of the customer. Certainly, more truthful of the service in my experience.

So back they all were this morning, the entire gang under Steve's control, together with the roofer and the electrician, the latter of which seemed to be in less than jovial mood. Perhaps he had been taking lessons from a Woolworths shop assistant, but either way was definitely not happy in his work. However, while such surliness in Woolworths usually means you get handed the wrong thing and incorrect change, our man beavered away running wire all around the kitchen extension, and a semblance of order was beginning to take shape as boxes and feeds for sockets and switches materialised against nominated positions. At the same time, the floor had gone in above, and I was finally starting to get a more tangible view of what the finished product was going to look like. The completion of the roof tiling and a tarpaulin over the dining area meant that at long last water was no longer feeding the indoor pond, which had been in existence for weeks. The installation of the roof light completed the feeling that we were now getting to a stage where the extension would soon be a part of the house.

However, the front still remained an ugly confection of scaffolding and partially built walls, but had the benefit of considerable activity this morning. Despite the continuation of the deluge now threatening to bring Noah out of retirement, they persisted with their work, putting more courses of brick into place and even getting the small roof extension over the en-suite room in place and felted. This was a little troubling, as I peered nervously at the timbers sloping downwards, which were a continuation of the existing roof. That being the case, the point at which roof timbers coincided with head height would determine just how much room we had in attempting to carry out the normal tasks of washing and using the toilet. My pessimistic calculations (scientifically estimated by putting my hand on my head, then putting my hand against the wall in our bedroom and then trying to eye that with the roof some 2 metres away) suggested I would have to either develop a stoop to challenge the Hunchback of Notre Dame, or pick up a hard hat on the way in, possibly both.

Monday 25 November 2002
A day planned to be a short opportunist escape with a day away from work, but you know what happens to the best laid plans. First of all, Steve and Richard had felt a site meeting would be worthwhile. So, I mentioned I would be around on Monday, thinking half and hour would do it. Two hours later, it was finally drawing to a close, but it had at least been of significant value. Secondly, sickly child syndrome appeared again, and I sped ambulance like to Sian's school to find her pale, hot and decidedly unwell. Thirdly, a score of calls on the mobile ensured my mind remained firmly on the day job for a good deal of the time.

The site meeting had the benefit of making me feel like a client. For most of the time, I see little of the builders, merely witnessing the fruits and aftermath of their toil, but simply knowing I was paying, did not give me the satisfaction of seeing something substantive being done for my hard earned cash. I suppose this is akin to wanting to see your car being built, although not terribly practical. Yet it is always nice to see people *doing and making*, in a society increasingly dominated by *facilitating and servicing* – something tangible and practical in return for cash and an ability to appreciate what is being done and check it is being done well. When my bank cocks-up with a bankers draft (as it did), I have no idea where or why it went wrong, how many people were involved, whether it was one person's incompetence, or a conspiracy of crass stupidity (the latter is my best and favourite theory). With building works happening, I can see what is being done, good or bad, I can *appreciate* the work and the product and so far I have much appreciation. During the site meeting, talking about a myriad of largely fairly small matters of detail, we toured the site, including my first faltering steps up a ladder and onto the lofty stage of the scaffolding. It gave me my first face to face encounter with the wall tiling, and I confessed I rather marvelled at the fact, they appeared to have been hung perfectly and symmetrically, almost too perfectly and symmetrically. I suppose I have got used to imperfections equating to character in houses. You know the sort of thing, wonky door frames, lilting walls, uneven floors, worn skirting-boards, beetle ridden wood, chipped tiles, the sheen of age, but hardly the sign of good workmanship. I couldn't see me going to shake the hand of the roofer, for making sure half the tiles were hanging off, the battening was on the piss and water was coming through the roof.

We then went around the back of the extension, and clambered through the open window, into what was to be Cara's bedroom, and it was then, I was struck with satisfaction. Despite all the elements that had literally rained down on them, this room was not so far away from completion, with ceilings in place, floor boards down, basic electrics installed, and even the wall cut away where the entrance door was to go. This latter piece of work was immediately behind the toilet in our current bathroom, and while we knew this was scheduled to disappear very soon, I just hoped they would remember a little warning beforehand. Breaking through while said toilet was in use might bring a whole new meaning to the phrase 'shit a brick'. I admit, I was in wonder at the progress, and the fact that within a week we would probably have a useable room, indeed, the plan was for Sharon and I to use this room while our current one underwent major and dramatic surgery. Of course the hope was in doing so, the point of access and egress would be rather better than an aluminium ladder roped to the scaffolding, a blind scramble along the dirty planking, and an ungainly heave through an open window without glass. As it was, with all the current internal chaos, a trip through the house and up the stairs already carried a frisson of adrenaline, more than that would probably keep me awake.

The rest of our meeting did nothing more than confirm my increasing approval of the builders, but also rather neatly highlighted what must be a time honoured tense relationship between Architect and Builder. It is one that clearly states 'it may be drawn like this, but we can't build it like this', as minor corrections are made on site to try and put into practice what the Architect thinks can be done in theory. I have witnessed more than once, a rolling of the eyes from Steve, and an explanation of what *can* be done, rather than what *could* be done. This included pointing out, the roof over the bay at the front as drawn would require those who stood in the bay to tilt their head forward, or back, or indeed anywhere but up. As doing this would cause a collision between head and roof timbers as they cut through the ceiling plane above. Mmmm, problem. Well, no, simply solved by moving the roof slightly higher, although this also meant a slightly shorter window above to the bedroom, which also meant a change to the…….you get the idea. I liked this 'can do' attitude, rather than the 'Oooh, can't do that guv', ' Nothing to do with me', or 'drawings? What drawings?' manner I often encountered. They toiled away for the rest of the (dry) day, and by dusk were well on their way to a roof over the extension at the front.

Meantime, I was again juggling with discussions with builder, tending to sick child, tapping away on laptop, and holding conversations on my mobile phone. The last of these tasks is a bit tiresome, since the level of reception in

Anstey means the conversation is a bit like a turn by Norman Collier. I seem frequently reduced to wandering around the house like a man with a Geiger counter, desperately searching for a strength of signal that will register something on my phone. I have even taken to climbing onto the chest of drawers in our bedroom and, believe it or not, leaning out of the spare bedroom window, in order to maintain some sensible and intelligible conversation. I am not sure such a scene would be a good marketing shot for a mobile phone companies ad campaign, but probably good for a public information clip about health and safety around the home. 'Remember, no matter how poor your mobile phone signal, do not attempt to climb your roof and strap yourself to your chimney in order to converse with your friends at the local hostelry, careless talk costs lives.'

None of this however includes the other requirements of the day, notably taking Cara to school, collecting her from school, taking her to Brownies, collecting her from Brownies, and creating some evening nourishment for all for the evening. Not sure I could be a househusband, and by the looks of the playground at Cara's school, it is not a popular choice amongst the male population of this part of East Herts. This is always a peculiar and uncomfortable experience, particularly as I know few of the mothers in attendance as we all gather either to drop off or collect. As a man, apart from being outnumbered substantially, I feel a little outcast, as if I am being eyed up suspiciously. 'What is a man doing in the playground, shouldn't he be at work?' Perhaps their suspicion goes deeper 'Perhaps he is out of work – do we want unemployed people in our school grounds,' or worse still 'Maybe he hasn't got a child here, he's just lurking around for a likely kidnap victim!' Okay, this is the height of paranoia, but the longer I hang around, shifting from foot to foot, not talking to anyone and feeling more and more remote, the worse the situation seems to become. Perhaps I will set up a special club for occasional dads doing chores, and we can all gather round, swop experiences and provide group support. On the other hand, that would be the height of sadness, I think it better I tolerate my temporary, and possibly imagined isolation.

By the end of the day, I had given up on all these exertions, in favour of a cold beer, a comfortable seat, a darkened lounge and a decidedly immobile mobile phone.

Wednesday 27 November 2002
I have never slept on board a ship. Well, actually, that's not true. I did once attempt to induce a state of unconsciousness on board a rather rough and very uncomfortable ferry from Harwich to Holland. Problem was the constant movement, noise of the engines and incessant snoring of my fellow occupants guaranteed I stepped onto Dutch soil very bleary eyed. However, last night seemed to be akin to sleeping aboard a large sailing ship. It is true, we have had so much rain and the ground is so sodden that if I woke up in the morning

and found the house had drifted down the hill to the pub, it would not have entirely surprised me. Yet this was not the real cause of this illusion.

Work yesterday had centred on trying to complete all the new roofing as soon as possible and the presence of another sacred dry day had obviously focused attention. However, while they had clearly moved along as quickly as they could, neither the small roof over the bay or the main roof to the front extension were complete, and in consequence, a huge green tarpaulin (looking suspiciously like a relative of the flapping green alien that attacked me not so long ago) was draped across the main roof, with a smaller thick plastic sheet across the bay. In fact, these temporary means of protection gave me the feeling of work going the other way again, as if someone had just maliciously stripped the roof, rather than the roof being put in place. And last night in the cold mist, without a clear view of what was in place, all I could see was the soaring scaffolding and a lot of flailing sheeting. It was like an abandoned church tower roof, robbed of its lead covering, waiting forlornly for local people to raise the necessary funds to reinstate. Now, there was an idea! Perhaps I could make up one of those fund raising boards, complete with badly drawn giant thermometer and a collection tin, the 'Make Holly House less Ugly' fund. However, I think I would be in little danger of using very much red felt tip to colour in the progress of the fund up the thermometer tube, difficult to mark 23 pence on a scale up to £90,000.

The ship impression was as a result of these loose coverings fluttering and flapping in the wind and generally doing so within feet of our bedroom window. It was like lying in a (very dark) galley of a large (but mysteriously rock steady) sailing ship, sails being ripped and flung around and creating a hell of a racket throughout most of the night. I was tempted to open the curtains in the morning, put flat hand to forehead shielding my eyes from an imaginary piercing sun, peer into the distance and shout 'land ahoy!' Apart from being completely unable to do this in view of the fact it was pitch dark, and all I could see out of the bedroom window was a breeze block wall and a covered window frame, it would also have attracted unimagined abuse from Sharon, since such disturbance at 6.00 am was unlikely to be welcomed. Shame, I have always fancied being a ship's captain.

By the time I returned this evening, the noisiest of the covers over the main roof had gone, good progress again having been made while the rain, for a change, stayed away. Overall however, we were still looking like a scene out of Scooby Doo – dark, misty, half finished building site, rustling and creaking from every corner and a definite sharp chill in the air. All it needed was Scooby himself to come piling by, closely followed by that irritating nerd Shaggy and the obligatory man-dressed-as-ghost. They would be much better named Stupid and Thicky, although having said as much, it does seem strange that Scooby seems able to drive a van. Either way, if they come anywhere near me, I will have great pleasure in tripping them up.

Thursday 28 November 2002

4.30 am. It is cold, there still remains the sound of flapping outside and Cara is throwing up in the bathroom. The lack of sleep, and the whole depressing and less than ideal current environment not surprisingly has Sharon in tears. Suicide can, they tell me be painless, but ultimately unproductive in this situation. I mean, who is going to approve the design for the canopy over the front door? Exactly, so I won't do that just yet. And anyway, if I jump out of the bedroom window, I will simply land gently on some of the new floor beams and will look pretty stupid standing inside the new extension with not a stitch on. So I definitely won't do that then. Well, not yet anyway. Maybe the whole thing was not such a good idea, I do feel at times as if I am dragging the whole family deeper and deeper into crap.

Arriving home tonight presents no different face on the situation, although Cara thankfully has a colour which is at least tinged with flesh and blood, rather than looking as pale as a bucket of wallpaper paste. This roofing lark clearly takes some time and we still have some covers over the front, but the shape of the finished article is now very clear. I have to say, even in its unfinished state, it is a vast improvement on the monument to blandness that existed previously. I have today pleaded to get some light into the lounge before the weekend, otherwise we will develop stoops, lots of hair, start wearing animal skins and saying 'Ugghh', as we revert to our base ancestry. I am promised a result by tomorrow night. I live, almost exclusively at the moment, in considerable hope.

Friday 29 November 2002

I was asked this morning, as I occasionally am, how the work was going, the questioner usually doing so with a slightly knowing smirk, aware that the combination of substantial building works, the middle of winter and continued occupation, is great territory for serious amusement. I tend to reply that it is almost impossible to describe the circumstances within which we are trying to live, but perhaps I ought to try.

Externally, it is as you would expect a building site to be in late November, a god awful mess, with scaffolding front and back. The scene replete with stacks and piles of materials, ladders and planks dotted here and there, cement mixers, poles and not a few depositories of things meaning nothing to me at all, like the long white plastic beams that look like they have escaped from a giant air-fix kit. The standing water around the rear extension has now been in place for so long that I expect a German to come along shortly, put up his sun lounger and plonk a towel down to grab his place. Meantime, the garage is being used as a paint-shop store and general dry gathering place, while all our stuff has been shunted so far up the far end and in such a tight pile, it now gives the impression of the inside of a rubbish lorry. Access around the works at the front is easy, if a little circuitous, although all the gravel off the drive has gone somewhere (not sure where), while walking around the rear entails both hurdling and limbo skills, and the odd ability to swing from bars can prove useful. The external works are as they are, in mid point, but other than a little bit more tiling and roofing, glazing to the windows already installed, and a few more existing windows yet to be trashed, outside work is not far from complete.

Inside is either a confection if you are weird and unhinged, or a pigs ear of a bloody mess if you are just plain normal. Given the original state of the house interior when we purchased, you could be forgiven for thinking the current internal changes were an improvement. But as much as I hate the current décor and layout, I would not wish our current conditions on anyone, save possibly Osama Bin Laden. Or even the woman in W H Smith in Bishops Stortford who manages to serve me without looking at me or saying anything, yet chats inanely to her equally rude mate while doing this. The kitchen is a perpetual shit-hole, thanks to the constant stream of people going through and depositing dirt like they were re-enacting the tunnelling from the Great Escape. Indeed, the hole that was blasted through to the new hall created a not incongruous backdrop to such an imaginary scene, although I don't remember seeing too many yellow walls and cheap laminate flooring in Stalag 17, or whatever it was. The single large window in the kitchen, apart from now being a very dirty, dirty green on the inside, is coated with grime and water stains from all the work on the extension, just on the other side. As a consequence, it looks like the windscreen of old Ford Cortina that has been dumped in a breakers yard for the last 10 years. As we step through this opening, taking care not to brush the jagged edges of breeze block and crumbly plaster, whilst also avoiding the hole in the floor created by ripping out both wall and radiator, we arrive in what was the dining room, but is now the hall separated from what will be the study by a half finished stud wall. All clean wood and plasterboard on one side, un-boarded on the other, the skeleton of the wall revealed, riddled with reams and loops of wire and boxes for the switches and sockets to come. More depressingly, half the room is filled with a pile of chairs, books, ornaments and mementos, and our trusty old dining room table, covered with a now very grubby and dusty plastic sheet in vain protection. The hall looks like the aftermath of an earthquake, plaster having been torn and broken away around walls and ceilings in the zeal to rip out the old in preparation for bringing in the new. This is all nicely complemented by a temporary rough wooden prop acting like a stair newel, but wedged into place with a scrappy piece of wood against the ceiling. More comically, the impression of bare survival is confirmed by the light switch for the study taped un-permanently to this post with reams of black gaffer tape, the wire snaking overhead and through the stud wall.

A very short step away is the beating heart of depression in the shape of our twilight lounge, light banished by the brutal bare boards at either end, carpets rolled back at the junction with the boards and most of the furniture piled down the far end. This together with books, ironing board, CD player, magazines and other everyday survival items ushered and stacked around the area in a futile attempt to create space and maintain some sense of normality. Thank god for an airer, which forms our mobile mini laundry, touring all the rooms of the house in an epic journey to find the best place to dry the washing. Today it's back in the lounge, but we maintain some clear space in the middle of the room for the sofa, one armchair and the perennial television. Amongst all this disturbance and transitory living, the grotesque crazy-paved clad fireplace is barely noticeable, but I still look forward to the day with relish when I can tear this down, it will be then that I will truly feel, this house will have the imprint of me, rather than the strange dwellers of the past. We can go full circle from here, through the gaping portal that once took the door back into the kitchen, but is yet another monument to the builders delicious bluntness of destruction of the old, the inner blocks of the wall and its plaster coating exposed to the passing traffic. Just before we pass back into the kitchen, under the stairs and the hard working boiler placed less than neatly underneath, to the left is the downstairs cloakroom, now without window, stifling without ventilation, sporting a neatly filled and plastered hole where the window once sat. Of course this is all tastefully finished with the bright burgundy suite, and the dusky (dirty) pink painted radiator – I don't think these ever belonged to Barbara Cartland, but I cannot be absolutely sure.

Dust continues to coat everything. Indeed, I recently discovered the video remote, grey and caked, looking as if it had just been discovered in a grandmothers loft after years of neglect, but had merely sat beneath the television for less than a week. The rather well filled see-through dust cavity of the Dyson sitting at the bottom of the stairs is witness to the dirt embedded.

Going up the stairs, be careful not to err too far to the right, as the wall no longer exists, another exhibit of the progress being made. At first floor level, there is little destruction, but a fair bit of disruption. The bathroom sports another filled orifice, but this time with a new frame in place, albeit boarded until the window and glass can be inserted, and at the moment it is rather a rough piece of work, internally completely unfinished, plaster, wood and mortar spilling across the sill. The aftermath of the leaking bath taps is evident with the hole in the panel still gaping, and the ghastly green floor tiles still removed from the surrounding area, all gathered and unceremoniously stuffed under the bath. The problem with not being bothered to put the floor tiles back, is the glue remains on the floor. Standing at the sink first thing in the morning, you then have to unpleasantly unpeel your feet from the floor, as if you have discovered a wayward piece of chewing gum in the wrong place. Elsewhere in the bathroom, all the usual personal bits have been stuffed into several boxes, ready for the obliteration of the toilet and cupboard above in order to form the door into Cara's bedroom. This generally means an unseemly and bad tempered rummage in the morning to find the razor hidden within and beneath toothpaste, dental floss, hair removal wax, and hair spray, like a peculiar and slightly dangerous lucky dip.

Sian's bedroom is pretty much untouched, which is probably why she often has a mild smirk of self satisfaction, but her day will come when they replace her window, ha ha! In the meantime, she does have to suffer the storage of at least one stack of toy boxes that have now seen just about every room on the first floor. Next door, what was Cara's room, and will eventually be the bathroom, is totally dark, featuring another perfect transformation from old mouldy window to seamless reformed and replastered wall, splendid in grey pink, blending into the same plane, and soon to disappear as if nothing had ever been there. In the far corner is yet another pile of books, clothes and toys, crammed into as small a space as we could manage, covered as well as possible with another dusty plastic sheet.

Our bedroom is again, much as it was, only with rather less space. This would be a good party game, or perhaps a feature on The Generation Game – how many boxes of toys, puzzles, dolls, pens and pencils and other loads of children's paraphernalia can you cram into an already crammed bedroom? Well, you can pile loads under the bed, but just make sure you don't move too much while you are in the bed, otherwise the Mousetrap game immediately under your left buttock is likely to need some quick setting glue. The top of the wardrobe is also a favourite stash place, but squeezing things rather brutally between wardrobe and ceiling, followed by a swift punch, tends not to ensure its future integrity. We have also moved in storage cupboards to put next to existing storage cupboards, even though there really isn't any storage space left, unless you are happy to make sure that on entering the room, you only do so sideways – which we do. And finally, Cara's chest of drawers had to go somewhere and there was no way it was going to fit into her room, so we have stuffed it next to ours. Being strategically placed in front of the airing cupboard, it squashes the round dirty linen basket, now very oval, rather than its original perfect circle. And of course, in order to access the airing cupboard, it is necessary to heave the small chest of drawers out into the room, stand on top, and then hang inside the cupboard like an insane trapeze artist. All good fun, I'm sure you will agree. The windows from our room are almost as grimy as the kitchen and light almost as limited. The view is of pleasing grey and damp breeze blocks, roof timbers above and a view down into what will be the extended lounge below, filled with cement, bricks and general rubbish – it's a bit like peering into a disused lift shaft, only dirtier.

Cara's room is what you might call multipurpose. You might call it multipurpose, I call it a nightmare. It is the only room in the house within which the computer will work and standing on a good size computer desk, it takes up a good deal of the room. Cara's bed is opposite, complete with purple canopy which I agreed to put up in order to distract all eyes from the fact that she was really sleeping in the junk room. Her bed is piled with the usual toys and fluffy cushions, and it looks a bit absurd against the scruffy, pock-marked white walls and the repulsive brown floor tiles that cover (most) of the floor, not to mention the flaking, orangey red window frame, nicely stained with remnants of black mould. In truth, the presence of both Cara and her personal entourage brightened up the room considerably, even if it also limited the available space to the size of a hamster cage. Also located in this room is the keyboard, squeezed up against the near wall, but an item of much light relief for both Cara and Sian. With headphones on, dancing around, plonking apparently aimlessly on the keys and singing gently, she looks and sounds like an unhinged DJ, escaped from a nearby unhinged DJ's rest home.

So there you have it, an oasis of peace, space, serenity and harmony, if you want me to lie so much that a fire tender will be required to douse the flames from my pants, as the children's saying goes.

Saturday 30 November 2002
I had not paid much attention last night, but magnificent things had happened yesterday. Most astoundingly, light had reappeared in the lounge, courtesy of a neat pair of French windows, exactly as we had ordered. I almost felt as though I should stagger outside, in torn clothes with 2 months beard growth, shielding my eyes from the sun, moaning quietly 'I'm free, I'm free!' The people of Anstey would rush down from the back garden to help me with a firm but gentle hand, paramedics would rush to my aid. National news-reporters would jabber excitedly into their microphones, staring into the camera lens of a hundred television stations, and a tumultuous applause would swell from the surrounding crowd that thronged the scene – or have I been watching too many poor television dramas? Trouble was, I couldn't have staggered out of the French windows, owing to the fact, the bottom board remained firmly screwed to the wall, this because the doors were not secure, and the hole adjacent, where the door to the dining room would go, remained just that – a hole. Security (and draft proofing) was therefore rudimentary. No matter it was progress, and a welcome sight.

Outside, to my continued surprise, the scaffolding had completely gone from the front. The brickwork and roofing is finished and although some sheeting remains over the front bay, I can now pretty much see what the finished article is going to look like. Okay, the front gable and bay does still look like an impersonation of a Bovis house, but the terrible clash of supreme dullness and the fencing match between vertical and horizontal has gone. When all the windows are in and the old ones replaced, the house should start to get a real sense of style and proportion. It is not going to win any architectural prizes, and some of the elements do still look a little odd, by my goodness, even in this unfinished state it look so much better than before. Around the back, the roof over the dining room is complete, but as yet no windows or glass in place, so the ground floor remains like a modern draughty stable. I do know however, some plastering has taken place, so I clamber ungainly onto the scaffolding, peel away the black cover across the window of what will be Cara's room and see that they have indeed been hard at work. Still drying, in varying shades of dark and light grey pink, all walls and ceilings have been beautifully finished.

I call to Sharon and Cara, and I help them up onto the stage beside me.

"Do you want to see your new room?" I say rather patronisingly to Cara

"Yeah, Yeah, Yeah!" she shouts – thankfully, she does not recognise the shameful adult trait of talking patronisingly.

I pull back the sheet again, and show her

"Wow! Its huge!" she says in genuine wonderment. And she is right, it does seem much bigger than we imagined it would be.

I heave her through the window, she dances around in celebration, this performance given all the more credence by the existence of two workmen's floodlights on stands in the corner

"Ladies and Gentlemen, Cara Neale!" she announces herself, before flouncing around this bare, darkened room again.

A little bit of joy in a week that had become far too depressing for my liking. Roll on more of this please.

The calm before the storm part I

The calm before the storm part II – good riddance!

The Evil has landed – The builders transform the drive

Beware – foundation excavation in progress.
Note the novel use of empty beer crates. Of course it could be that an errant drunk has dumped them along with his stolen bollards

The uneasy feeling that part of the house's stability rested on these oversized pogo sticks never quite left me

The new Stalag 17 compound emerges

Industrial Architecture is alive and well, and living in Anstey…….

Not a lot of room for the car

I know what you're thinking – wouldn't it be fun to run up to one of those wooden struts that appear to be supporting the entire bay, kick it away, and leg it. Fortunately, none of you lived in the vicinity at the time.

The front door from hell

Splendid views from the front room, if you like plywood – all light is banished, as the window disappears

A veritable confection of brick, block, scaffold and roof trusses. The rear extension arises

The death of the original bay is shrouded to spare those of a weak disposition, while the new front door frame does a passable impression of Prince Charles (think ears!)

The local café opens up for the morning. One of the builders searching desperately for all the ingredients to make the first cup of the day.

The skeletal frame of a new stud wall rather unfortunately
(but accurately) looks moderately prison like

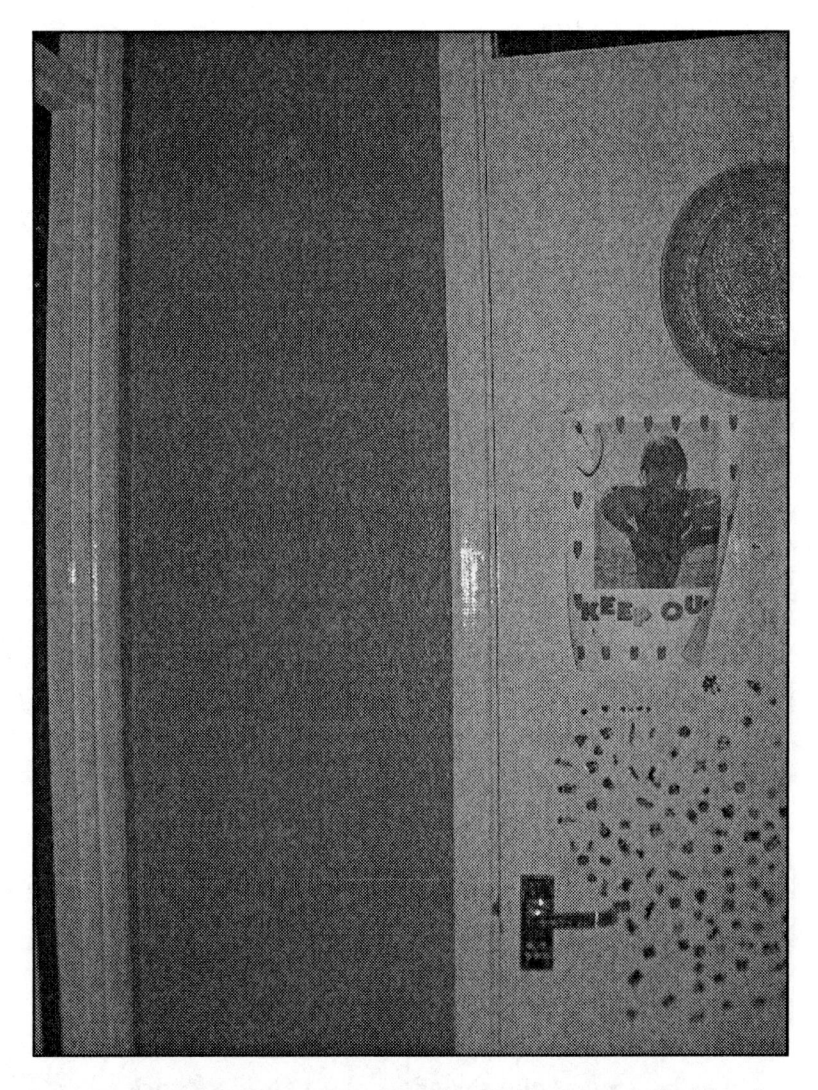

Cara does all that she can to disguise her current bedroom door.
For those of you in black and white nothing can hide the horror of rancid
red against mouldy banana yellow

The bathroom minus window plus new blockwork –
bit of an improvement if you ask me

The beefy new bay frightens passers-by

Not sure whether it's all going up, or fast coming down

Dancing Queen Number 1 – Cara celebrates her triumph at the Guildford Finals, with a bit of thumb sucking and a hug of her partner. Ooops, sorry, no, that's Winnie the Pooh.

Dancing Queen Number 2
**Sian (middle, right, *top step*) does her best Fame Academy impression,
while the judges stare in admiration and awe**

Be warned – this is what happens to your 8 year old should you be so foolish as to live in a building site

Our Laburnum tree looks rather gaunt and troubled against the frenzy of activity – rather like ourselves.

The new French windows and the rather crude method adopted
for keeping us in the house

Any resemblance between this and a fairground House of Horrors is purely intentional

The new bedroom tries to dry out. Interesting doorway that indeed is blocked up, but more worrying is the retention of the overflow pipe from the toilet on the other side.

We've broken through! The builders probably ran screaming when they saw the kitchen colour scheme

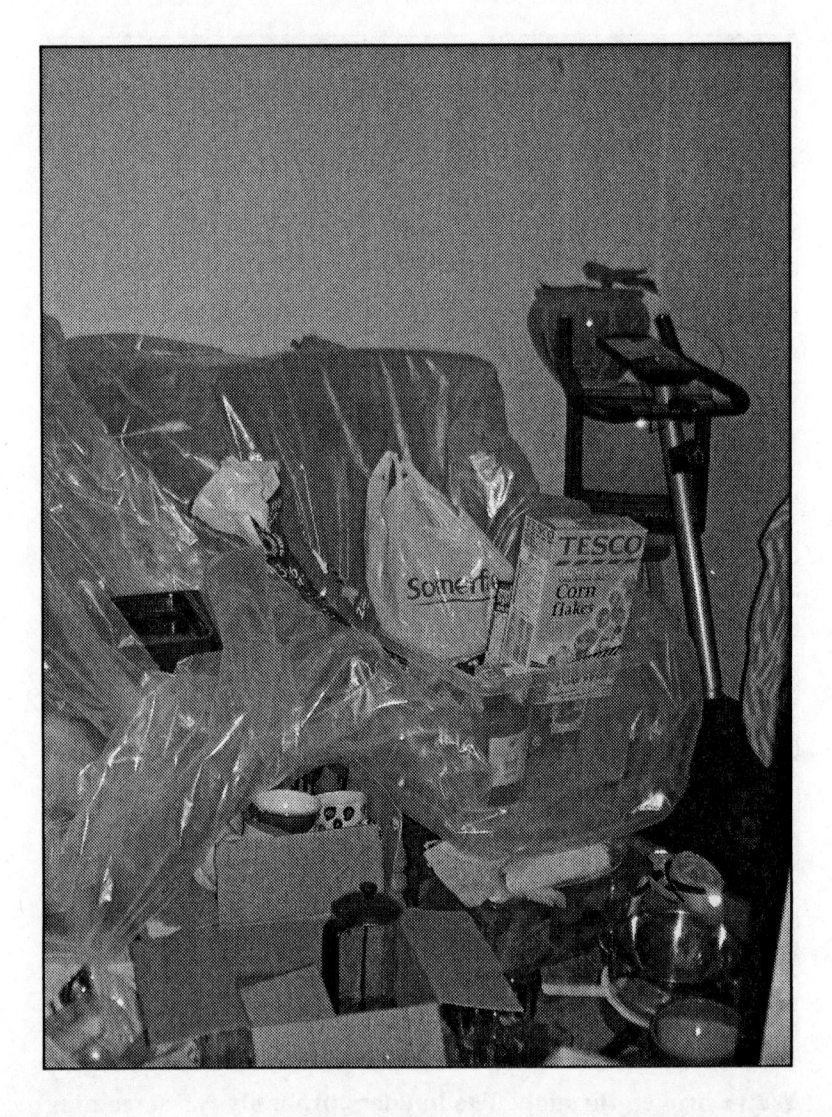

The dining room that was, aka study to be, but at this point served as the storage room from hell. I will try not to draw your attention to the barely concealed bottle of gin.

Changing rooms woz here – the kitchen in original guise, with rather fetching new orifice

How we lived – all human (and other unidentified) life is here

How we lived, part 2 – Note the temporary door way cover, cunningly created from a sheet circa 1973

Sharon ponders whether it might actually be better to live in the garden for the next 3 months

Sunday 1 December 2002
Vomiting. Wall-to-wall vomiting. You don't want to know, you *really* don't want to know. Not me, but Sharon during the night and Sian early this morning (of course Cara had played her part particularly well earlier in the week). And it's pissing down with rain *again*!

It is also my mother's birthday, so Cara and I escape for a short while in the afternoon, to deliver presents and drink a germ free cup of tea. On the way back home, the radio is on, and unfortunately, just to make my day complete, Mariah Carey is taking up the airwaves on this particular station. I groan, Cara and I briefly discuss the fact that she, allegedly, will not sing live. I say allegedly, but unless you are a blind devotee of this woman (and I really do mean blind), this fact is obvious and clear. I was at first incredulous, but then in hysterics when I happened to watch her on Children in Need a few weeks ago. I have seen some bad miming before, but this was miming as a comic art form, she can mime about as well as I can dance, very badly. But more frighteningly, she clearly thinks she is doing it well. The exaggerated manner of her lips (generally out of sync) and overall movements adds a delicious thread of unintentional humour – she almost looks as if she is taking the piss, but it is apparent she feels she is consummate. Oh dear.

"Why doesn't she sing live Daddy?"

"I don't know Cara, I really don't know."

"It's a shame, because she's really pretty." Out of the mouths of babes. She looks good, but what's the point in that if she can't do what she says she can.

Uncannily perceptive, my children.

Monday 2 December 2002
"Remember, if you need the toilet in the night, you'll have to go downstairs. I don't want you piddling on the floor."

A space has appeared in the bathroom, where once there was a toilet, whilst a mystery white door has materialised just behind where the loo used to be, blocking what will be the entrance to Cara's bedroom. Since the bathroom already looks pretty weird and chaotic, this does not look so out of place, screwed to the wall with a makeshift wooden bar across the top, and sporting a dirty dustsheet stuffed around the edges to keep out the draught. If you were particularly imaginative, or just plain peculiar, depending on your point of view, you might see this as a mysterious gateway to a strange and extraordinary world, an entrance to a land created by C S Lewis or Tolkien with unusual creatures and fantastic landscapes, leading to soaring adventures and stories of intrigue. On the other hand, you could just see it as a grubby improvised boarding of a hole in the wall, leading to an unfinished room, filled with dirt and debris, created by B&G Builders, paid for by me. Sorry, romantic is not on the menu tonight.

Neither is there anything romantic about the thick brick and block dust that is the inevitable by-product of demolition work and which particularly coats everything in the bathroom. Walking on the floor feels like treading on the interminable contents of the very bottom of a cornflakes packet, all crunchy, grainy, sticky and unpleasant. The only solution is to wipe everything down several times with a wet cloth and in the process, making the sink of water used to rinse the cloth look like the inside of the builders concrete mixer. Unfortunately, no matter how many times you wipe the floor, some still clings like it has a magnetic attraction. I confess at 7.30 pm on a Monday evening, it will just have to do.

This is all a portent of things to come of course. Within the next few weeks, possibly days, Sharon and I will be evicted from our current bedroom and incarcerated in Cara's new room while they work to incorporate the front extension into the house. The entrance into Cara's room will be where the mystery white door now stands and will give us uninterrupted views across to the bath as we enter, waving to any poor soul using the bath at the time of our passage. I have never before pondered the question of an open plan bathroom and we may be the first family to experience such a thing. It's a good job that we are all pretty brazen and unashamed in Holly House, naked flesh abounds and the act of washing has long been a favourite spectator sport, indeed Cara even sometimes fails to close the door when using the toilet.

"Well, I can talk to you then," she not unreasonably reasons.

Outside, work seems to have been fairly limited, the tiling on the wall of the rear extension is now pretty much complete. A lintel has been put in place to create the door into the dining room, but the gaping hole that remains stuffed with a strange thick foil covered polystyrene remains a gaping hole. The lower board on the inside at this end of the lounge maintains its stance as security and other than the disappearing loo, inside everything is much as it was 24 hours ago – in a state of dirty disarray. But at least everyone seems to be keeping their food down.

Tuesday 3 December 2002

There are times when returning home can have a frisson of excitement, not knowing what you are going to find on arrival. And since we are getting close to completion of external works, the surprise, and shock, at the internal upheaval, can be all the more great – take the vanishing bog of yesterday. Will the bathroom have disappeared completely, has the front wall gone from our bedroom, will I in fact wake up from a bad dream, emerging Bobby Ewing like from the shower, to find the house remains in its original, intact but ultimately depressing, form? Actually, that would be a tad difficult as we never had a shower, apart from the darkened cupboard masquerading as a shower, in which case, I would probably never be able to find my way out again. Come to think of it, that would have been a much better fate for Bobby Ewing.

The surprise tonight was the removal of some of the kitchen units, in preparation for the sink to be temporarily moved to the back of the room and where the utility would ultimately be placed. A big fat waste pipe had appeared in the corner, with virgin pale pink dusty plaster all around, the clothing of the old units removed to leave the wall as naked as the day it was skimmed. A hole had also appeared in the ceiling above, from which ran a couple of new grey plastic pipes. Mmmmm, so if the pipes go up through the ceiling, it must mean they are going somewhere upstairs, so lets go and have a look. Sure enough, Cara's old bedroom was positively bursting with pipes, flanges, taps, valves all clean and shiny, but rather brutally exploding through the floor, not unlike the emergence of the beast in 'Alien' from poor old John Hurts stomach, but without the blood and flesh splattering over everyone, and definitely without the screaming and hysteria from the cast. Oh, and I didn't jump out of my seat this time (which would have been difficult as I was not sitting down, but we are straying off the point here). Instead, the floorboards had been broken and smashed to make way, splinters and chipboard debris littering the room.

Later on during a quick external recce, I noticed the roofing over the bay had now been completed, including all the impressively intricate lead work and the final cementing around the tiles and ridges. This included some interesting large metal uprights with little swirly hoops on the end, but I have not got a clue what these are, or what they are for. You could hang your washing from them, though they are a bit high. You could hang your Christmas lights from them, but I would be hard pressed to believe – even in a world that takes ridiculous gadgetry to the extreme – someone would actually sell such an article. If I was in a mood of particular parental angst, I could use them as temporary storage hooks for naughty children, but they would look a bit untidy, hung outside the window. I subsequently discover they are ridge irons, in place to stop the ridge tiles sliding down and falling off. There does not seem much chance of that, and in any event, the size of them would probably prevent even a bloody elephant sliding off.

Thursday 5 December 2002
Lets work backwards. Somehow, such a concept seems to fit neatly with our domestic situation, seeing as we seem to be working down the evolutionary ladder from comfortable home, through rented anonymous abode, to unremitting shit-hole, all in the space of a few years.

When I *finally* arrived home tonight, another hole had appeared and the bathroom seems to be receiving the brunt of abuse at the moment. This is the doorway that will lead from the landing (currently the bathroom) to the new bathroom (currently the windowless ex-youngest daughter's bedroom). Around this new and definitely unfinished portal, lies yet more mess, and little boxes of plumbers fittings, conversely all neatly arranged and stacked just inside the doorway, as if someone were setting up a little plumbers merchants, or perhaps here was a tradesman with a strange obsessive compulsive disorder, who just *had* to have all his bits and pieces all neat, tidy and accessible, without which he just simply could not work. The latter was unlikely, not just because the thought of a neurotically tidy builder was just so improbable, it would rank alongside the prospect of the Pope being Hindu. But if such an animal did exist in this house, then why the hell had he not tidied up the bathroom, cleaned out the bog and left a bunch of carnations in a vase beside the basin? I rest my case.

However, by the time I noticed this element of the day's efforts at the house, it was half past midnight. It would have been more like quarter to midnight, had I not noticed something awry with the handling of my car while half way home. Actually, if I had not noticed the handling of my car as awry, there is a fair chance I would not have made it home at all (not to mention I would have had to be pretty stupid not to question why the car was wandering and tugging me towards oncoming traffic). Having stopped to investigate, I discover a flat, or rather deflated, tyre. Great, and here I am in the middle of nowhere, on a hill, with no real prospect and certainly not the inclination, to change the wheel. To add insult to injury, a police car trundles by, slows to peer at me, clearly decides I am a grown and mature man and appear not to be pissed, so why stop? Thank you for your assistance.

I decide to soldier on, very slowly and carefully, hazard lights ablaze, as home is only a few miles away. Trouble is, at 5 miles per hour, this journey seems more like a return trip to Newcastle. With my window open and a hell of a racket coming from the tyre, as it flaps and grinds away at considerable volume, I feel like a rather odd kerb crawling pervert in a limping Ice Cream Van. Thankfully, no one tries to stop me and buy one. Good job, as all they would have got would be a torrent of abuse and a slap. I was not in jovial mood.

And I was in a non-joyous frame of mind before I even got into the car, owing to the fact that I had sampled travel by rail into and out of London during the late afternoon and evening. Yes, I know that like Estate Agents, this is hardly a new subject for a pile of invective, but when there is *nothing* good about it at all, is it any wonder? It's all the usual stuff – lateness, dirt so ingrained I think the seats were actually made this colour with chewing gum and grime pre-ordered, overcrowding to the extent that life as a sardine seems positively palatial and roomy, with passengers from another planet. Oh, and the cost of the ticket is clearly in inverse proportion to the pleasantness of the journey. Apart from that, it is a wonderful way to travel.

Friday 6 December 2002
A day off to give the credit card a hiding it will not forget until Christmas next year. Poor thing, it must know as soon as December arrives it will be pulled in and out of my wallet and shoved through swipe machines at such a rate I swear its colour pales as the day goes by.

First off though, a quick chat to Steve. The question I have been dreading. "We want to take the kitchen window and wall out on Monday, is that all right?"

No, it's not. Well, ideally it's not, but as the whole project will come to a grinding halt unless they do, that is not really an answer I can give. I know this will cause mayhem and mess on another scale, and as much I think we will be prepared for it, I know we won't.

"Okay. So I presume you want us to clear everything out Sunday night for you?"

"Yeah!"

Oh. I was hoping he wouldn't say that, but I knew he would. Denial does not get any more ridiculous than this

"Okay!" I hid my despair well I thought.

Sharon and I go off to spend stupid sums of money on Christmas presents, but this is not an experience I particularly enjoy. I am sure there was a time when it was, but if so, it is a memory that has long faded. I am not a religious person and freely admit to the fact. Yet even a hard bitten detractor like me cannot help but feel that whatever Christmas is meant to be about at its real core – it was long ago shoved aside, swept up and deposited in a big grey wheelie bin, last seen groaning in the back of a dirty dustcart, heading for banishment and exile in society's growing landfill site of basic values. I may not be religious, but I would still make a pretty good second rate preacher.

It is difficult not to reach the conclusion that Christmas is the most enormous monument to avaricious consumerism. This is not the scene portrayed by so many films, TV dramas and sitcoms, of people pleasantly ambling around from shop to shop, all jolly and smiling, brass bands playing to an attentive gathering, snow falling gently, general joy and wellbeing gushing forth from the screen. The reality is, there is nothing joyous about this at all, there is not the merest shred of joy and contentment on people's faces, no feeling of happiness and ambience, and bugger all goodwill-to-all-men, women, children and dogs. There is not a smile on a single face, no social interaction, no acknowledgement and no manners. While shopping is never necessarily the most warming experience, I can't help feeling that the level of selfish, single-minded pursuit of something is perversely increased at the time of year when it is meant to be eased. It is actually pretty depressing to see people in a severe state of angst, rushing around with ever increasing burdens of shopping, hell bent in purchasing, rather than thinking and giving.

And we are no better, complete with an organised list of things of more material than actual value, to buy for friends and family. We tick off most, pile them up in the boot of the car and head home, but in the midst of all this, I can't help but find the situation at Argos of considerable amusement and dismay, in equal proportion. Argos is the High Temple of Convenient Consumerism. It is a bloody great warehouse, on one of those delightfully aesthetic retail parks, where finding a parking spot and coming away without running over a wayward child is a major achievement. It stocks everything you can think of and quite a few you could never have dreamt of (Homer Simpson Alarm Clock, golf ball tidy, personalised scrotum ring – all right, I lied about the last one, but mark my words, you'll be able to buy it soon). There is no browsing, touching, seeing, pondering, it allows you to satisfy the increasing cry of 'That is what I want, and I want it now – oh, and as cheaply as possible'. There is nothing tangible, physical or spiritual about this, it is sanitised shopping. In theory, it is the pinnacle of expediency, but in reality it is anything but – where else would you endure *three* queues? On the one hand there are scores of patient people, clearly just doing their Christmas duty, albeit in rather zombie-like fashion, getting all excited when their number appears at the bottom of the screen announcing they have only two more hours to wait until their purchase comes popping out of the unseen storeroom. On the other, countless who seem to be wandering about in a state of shoppers' shellshock, not knowing what to do, where to go, or how to empty their wallets. Then there are the spectators, like me, watching it all unfold and unravel, and wondering where it all went wrong. I imagine the end of the world might be something like this, where we will all accept our fate with a bit of a grumble, some mild histrionics and ultimately shuffle off in meek resignation, collecting our numbers on the way to the exit.

But no, let's not be morbid! The Christmas lights are flashing, Rudolph's nose is glowing brightly, and crackly carols are blasting out over speakers that have seen better days. How could I possibly be so contemptuous and disparaging at this festive time of year?

Sunday 8 December 2002

It's a Sunday in December, so it must be Hemel Hempstead. To be frank, any excuse to leave the house behind for a few hours at the moment is to be welcomed, although Hemel would not generally be my first choice of alternative venues. It is yet another cold, grey, damp and immensely depressing day, and coupled with the disarray and disorder within the house, the atmosphere tends to build to one of morbidity and bad temperedness, to the extent that Dracula might feel comfortably at home. Thankfully, we have a dance competition to attend, but I have to say this turned out to be only marginally better than moping around at home, getting on each others nerves – why not mope around somewhere else and get on each others nerves?

I used to think Hemel Hempstead was quite an interesting place, but this was when I was at University, frequently travelling through (without stopping), and can only surmise it was because my brain had been irreparably damaged by study and/or drink. Either that, or it had changed dramatically since I used to travel through and perhaps I was in such awe at traversing the magic roundabout, I did not notice what a monument to appalling 60's development it really is. For those of you who are not aware of the magic roundabout, Hemel shares this distinction with Swindon, being the only two places I know of that have within their traffic system a large roundabout which allows you to travel around in either direction. In effect, each road off has its own mini-roundabout, these being placed around the main roundabout, with two-way traffic around the whole main roundabout. If you do not understand, don't worry, you are not alone. Of course it means what was, I assume, meant to ease traffic congestion has the opposite effect. Baffled drivers who have not got a clue what this is all about drive up to it with a mixture of dread and confusion, getting slower and slower as they approach, mouths open in disbelief. At the same time, no one gives way to anyone else, and consequently cars are frequently grid-locked all the way round in a testament to traffic planning at its worst. My kids think its great fun and get a perverse thrill out of ensuring I drive around the 'wrong' way, turning right onto the roundabout, rather than left. If only they were pleased so easily with other matters.

I have to say the magic roundabout was the only thing that even faintly amused me on our visit today. The competition was held in a large Sports Hall which was so cold inside, a sled pulled by a herd of huskies would not have been out of place. Despite promises that 'the Management' were attending to matters, the atmosphere remained the wrong side of freezing all day. (The Management were probably too cold to go and do anything about it). The whole competition was downbeat and dreary, regardless of the usual excess of eye-achingly bright lycra, sparkle and sequins. My lunchtime wander into the inner reaches of the town to find something wholesome to eat merely reaffirmed my view that I would rather have played Dustin Hoffman in Marathon Man, than spend more than a day in Hemel Hempstead.

But not to worry, we would be home soon. Ah yes, home, or what was left of it. And of course there was the request by Steve and his team to be allowed to demolish the kitchen on Monday. Tomorrow. Right, that will be fun then. Remove everything from the kitchen and put it somewhere else. Somewhere else…..mmmm, now where exactly will that be, precisely? We both stood in the kitchen pondering the imponderable, as we had now pretty much run out of space. Things get very tetchy indeed when you can't think of a solution to a problem. The frequent result is to take out your frustration on those around you, and it was a close call as to whether the saucepans would fly out of the room within a whisker of my head, or whether they would simply be carried out in an enormous huff. We ended up piling stuff into the rudimentary new hall, stashed either side, so walking past could just about be done, providing you trod like you were avoiding a field of land mines, while the remainder was spread across what could still be seen of the floor in the dining-room-cum-study-to-be. This did cause some problems when access was needed to open the fridge freezer, but at least no-one was going to be able to get away with a sneaky midnight visit to the fridge without waking up the whole house. Not that we have a problem with fridge burglars in this part of East Herts you understand.

The empty, dirty, downtrodden nature of the kitchen in its vacant state was such, it could almost have been a scene from Hemel Hempstead, but without the graffiti.

Monday 9 December 2002

Bugger! I appear to have walked into an abandoned stage set from a 'B' rate 1970's sitcom. The wall and window situated immediately behind the sink and its worktop had gone completely. In its place was a large, very dirty sheet, pinned to what used to be the outside wall, billowing in and out as the rather substantial draught and very cold temperatures whipped in from outside, finding little resistance from the still incomplete rear extension. The lack of glazing in the windows was hardly well supplemented by some hardboard, and all of this meant that snow could have fallen in what remained of the kitchen without causing much of a surprise. Above the stage curtain was a now familiar big red steel beam, and at either end, wires, plaster and bare torn breeze blocks hung ragged, the result of the wall being ripped out with probably some gusto.

The kitchen itself was a very sorry state, all the units having completely disappeared from the rear wall, while cupboard fronts and tops had been removed around the other wall, which of course had now been replaced with the sheet. The whole place was *caked* in grey dirt and dust. If you had not known what was happening here, you would genuinely believe the house had been deserted years ago, dereliction having set in and demolition having just commenced. The combination of the cold, unremitting dirt and the scene of forsaken tat, was breathtakingly depressing.

The result elsewhere of all this violent activity was inevitable, thick brick dust having settled on just about everything on the ground floor and quite a fair proportion of things upstairs. The Hoover got its usual run over everything, but even its whine had a tinge of gloom and discouragement and its efforts in the kitchen were like cutting the grass with a pair of scissors. We made efforts to clean down the kitchen units and the floor with cloths and gallons of cleaner in order to keep the ingestion of dust to a minimum, but half the time it was more like spreading the problem than mopping it up. Preparing dinner was curiously in tune with the environment as it resembled a poor slapstick comedy – no longer was everything in the same room. Knives and forks were stashed in the lounge, food was in the study-to-be, salt was in the hall, back to the fridge in the study, oh bugger forgot the spoon, back into the lounge. All it needed was the Benny Hill music, scantily clad women running around the place, everything speeded up and we would be there! The final straw was the need to use the microwave, which was in the lounge, nowhere near a plug, hidden under plates and cups. We managed to stretch an extension lead across the room and gain access from the top, but approaching from the rear, like lying over the top of a barrel and reaching back inside. It was truly farcical, but in truth we were having something of a humour failure in the circumstances.

And I just know this is going to get worse.

Wednesday 11 December 2002

I have been away since early yesterday morning. Nothing has changed from the outside, but walking through the back door gave me something of a shock. While Monday's scene was a deserted and neglected drama set (displaying quite a bit of drama itself it has to be said), it was at least one I recognised. What I entered tonight I did not. The walls of what would be the utility room had miraculously appeared, while the sink and plumbing had been moved, along with the washing machine. Pipes and cables ran everywhere and it was bitterly cold. In fact, I swear it was warmer outside than it was inside. This room within a room now had the doorway into what would be the new kitchen, but for the time being led into a corridor, on the right hand side of which was the dirty dust sheet, the only thing separating us from the unfinished new kitchen extension. The corridor turned around the back of the new utility stud wall and we were in the entrance hall. Again, everything was *filthy* but I was intrigued that the inner transformation was now clearly taking place, I could see how the new plan was actually going to work, rather than simply imagine.

The lack of light, the cold, the narrow corridors and the fluttering sheet now presented the scene in a different dramatic context, as we were now in the dark bowels of a perfect horror set – I could scare the shit out of my kids if I was particularly cruel, but I figured we already had sufficient stress in the house. Perhaps I could hire the place out to Stephen King, or offer temporary accommodation to Vincent Price. Maybe I would discover that the plasterer was called Igor, and had a strange limp, or perhaps the curtain hid a dark and menacing secret from another dimension. Err….no. What it actually hid was the fact that there had clearly been some activity, including some splendid plastering of the ceiling, so even if Igor was a mad axe murderer, he certainly made up for it in his wielding of the trowel. The wiring and cabling about the place was complete, while corner mesh had been placed around all the window openings, ready for a further plastering flourish around the walls, presumably tomorrow. Unfortunately, there was still no glazing in the substantial window frames around the dining area, with big sheets of hardboard nailed up instead, together with yet more plastic sheeting flapping about in the draught still whipping through from the outside.

Not a lot else seemed to have happened, but I guess it takes a lot of time and effort to create a spine tingling set for a gory chiller. And if we don't get some windows in soon to protect us from the sub-zero temperatures outside, it could be me wielding the axe and spilling blood on the concrete floor.

Thursday 12 December 2002

We're in trouble I think, and in truth it is difficult to find any humour in this situation. It is now clear to me we should not still be living here, the conditions are pretty atrocious. There was certainly a point tonight, before I had poured myself a very large gin and tonic (but after we had played a long game of hunt the gin bottle. It was eventually discovered behind the bread maker, just by the dance trophy, under a few magazines in the lounge – of course, where the hell else would you keep a bottle of gin?) When I sat motionless on my knees, staring at the muddle and mayhem, I said to Sharon.

"We can't stay here!"

"Well you can go, but I'm staying here," she said rather pointedly.

"Oh. Okay."

She was right of course. There was, realistically, nowhere else to go. Staying with either of our parents was not a practical option, and would have tested our sanity from a rather different perspective. A tent in the garden would have at least been a change of scene, but then so is a week in Clacton, and in comparison time under canvas in a sodden plot of land might seem marginally more attractive. Hotels do not feature heavily in East Herts, but then when you can't even squeeze into the remains of your four bed house while works are going on, it's difficult to see how you can rationalise your living to accommodate yourself in one room and an en-suite bathroom. And don't even think about hiring a caravan – I can't even follow one in my car without getting very angry, let alone try and live in one for a period of weeks. My credibility, sense and well-being would be shot to pieces, with or without a gin and tonic of any size.

We decide to have a serious go at clearing as much space as possible over the weekend and shifting just about everything (possibly to include Cara if she does not start to do as she is told) into the loft. The idea will be to leave us with the minimum we need to live whilst all this is going on, but perhaps stop a little short of all sharing one fork and one plate, and timed sessions for using the only chair retained in the lounge ('Okay, times up, you can come back again at six o'clock for another 30 minutes'). In particular, I have promised the children (and, yes, myself if I am honest) that we will buy a Christmas Tree at the weekend, and as things stand at the moment, it would have to be limited to six inches high and placed on top of the television. Just how we are going to create enough space to shoehorn in a proper Christmas Tree, not to mention decorated with all the usual gubbins and lights, and have the usual 3 acres of spare floor space underneath to accommodate the warehouse load of presents, I have no idea. Find out next week in the next thrilling instalment of 'Neales and Space – Antics of the Anstey Aggregation (*n. gathered into a mass*)

Friday 13 December 2002

It was only as I drove home tonight the realisation of the day and date hit me, and reflected that although I am not generally superstitious, it had not been a good day – and it didn't get a whole lot better.

Having had a shite day, it probably wasn't the best plan to do all the removal work on a Friday night. But we'd received notice that Steve and some of his gang wanted to work tomorrow morning, which included the kitchen/utility/study/dining room/hall/confused-identity-crisis-room combo, where much of our stuff was stashed. Nerves were frayed and tempers bubbling, and this was just because it was the end of the week. Heap on top of this the need to sort out, shift, load into the loft half your wordly goods, and there is a temptation to walk off into an unknown distance, or drift gently into an enveloping sea, like Reggie Perrin.

You would like to think having moved house only just over a year ago, we would have taken the opportunity to extract and throw away all the accumulated matter which should never have been kept in the first place. But it appears we have failed to adhere to the rule that if you have not used or looked at it (or possibly both) in the last six months, then chuck it out. Why am I moving boxes of old cast off serving dishes that would look more at home on an episode of Time Team, having just been unearthed from a muddy and massive dig in Northumbria and sending Tony Robinson bouncing around the set like Zeberdee? In the meantime, we appear to have enough candle holders to start a new niche enterprise, but I can't see coach trips being organised for a major shopping trip to a second-hand candle holder shop in Anstey. And this is without the kids drawings, cards, pictures, school craft products, ornaments with at least one bit missing, rubbers with at least three corners missing, curled up photos (usually including at least one person where everyone says 'Who's that?'), frames without photos and old mugs (of the drinking variety, that is). On top of this, there are the useable things that just have to go somewhere until sufficient room has been created, and they can end their banishment to the cold climes of the loft, in favour of clean and warm cupboards in the newly refurbished Holly House.

Apart from our lack of patience, the real problem was physically moving all this stuff into the loft. You will recall, the previous occupants were not likely to win competitions for their DIY or decoration skills and while I accept their options might have been limited, the placement and operation of the loft hatch and ladder was something of a masterpiece. Okay, I am happy to ignore the hatch itself which is so hinged it stands several inches proud of the ceiling, like a badly fitting manhole cover in reverse, and opens so suddenly and viciously, you have to duck and cannot help wincing. We start to get into problems when we pull out the loft ladder, as the hatch is located right outside our bedroom door, but offset. This means the ladder fouls on the door frame almost as it hits the ground, and can therefore not be fully extended, whilst manoeuvring space around it is minimal. Oh, yes, the hatch opening appears to be designed for access only by children, as adults are clearly oversized for the entrance. So we have very little room around the landing to get onto the ladder, which itself is at such a sheer angle that crampons and climbing gear would be advisable, and a means of shrinking several sizes in order to get into the loft once at the top of the ladder would be very handy. Whatever you do, don't look at the manner of the ladder fixing once in the loft. While the screw fixing on the left looks secure (though I wouldn't bet any more than a fiver on it). The angle, size and stripped head of the screw holding it down on the right, almost causes me to make the sign of the cross in the hope someone might look after me while I am undertaking this treacherous task.

Now add into all of this the need to carry up boxes and bags of various sizes and weights and in varying states of stability (bottoms fall out of more than one, the last of which makes me shout 'shit' so loud, everyone comes running. All expect to find me and my load in a bloody heap at the bottom of the ladder) and you can begin to imagine the frustration and difficulty. Then we have to find space in the loft and ensure we do not create what some would consider a comedy moment, by placing heavy boxes on the floor of the loft that has no visible support, and so finds its way straight through the ceiling and into the room below. Thankfully, I do not do this, but if I did, it would undoubtedly be the last straw tonight, and after a few hours of not hearing from me, the rest of the family would probably find me strung from one of the beams.

We finish at close to ten o'clock and while the loft is probably creaking with the weight of items it thought it would never have to deal with, we collapse en masse onto the dusty sofa, revelling in the fact that we have created about two more square feet of living space. In fact, we have formed a nice little space for a Christmas Tree at the end of the lounge and its placement will neatly hide the remaining half board across this part of the room. Life is made of these little victories at present.

Saturday 14 December 2002

They are here again and we need to disappear out of their way for the morning. They are hammering almost before I have a chance to finish my tea and toast, but as long as progress is being made, I will not object. We leave amidst a new door-frame going up and plaster board being fixed to the ceiling at the rear of the kitchen, the latter a change at my request. The earlier plan was to continue from the bottom of the beam that now spanned where the kitchen window used to be, across to the new utility wall, but this would have made the ceiling here very low. The main reason for this appeared to be to ensure there was somewhere to run the extract from the downstairs loo to the outside. I had raised my concerns, only to be informed this had been agreed. Well, it may have been, but this plan had one fundamental problem – I was not part of the agreement. Something had got lost in the translation, but the ceiling was now being put back to the higher position. In the meantime, I had made something that is particularly rare for me – a practical and workable suggestion. Why not use the current shaft used by the soil pipe to route the extract for the loo? Brilliant, I thought, and I think grudgingly, everyone agreed. Mark this day, it is unlikely to happen again until at least 2017.

Now I have to confess, although I have become something of a cynic as far as Christmas is concerned, I absolutely insist we must have a Christmas Tree. Not only that but it *has* to be real, and it *has* to be of sufficient height and substance to ensure it wouldn't be mistaken as an extra for a Barbie House. So, off we go to the local farm shop, where there is an Aladdin's Cave, or maybe Santa's Grotto, of trees in all shapes, sizes, and breeds. Me, I'm a Nordmann Fir man, with those chunky branches and needles that only truly start to moult after about two weeks. I steer well clear of the more traditional Norway Spruce, ever since a traumatic incident some years ago – after only a few days and some time before Christmas. We had what amounted to a completely nude tree and a carpet load of dry, green needles, like a scene from a Tom and Jerry cartoon, probably with Jerry trying to hide in the tree from that delinquent, schizophrenic, and very violent cat Tom, who clearly should have been locked up many years ago. Of course these things (especially at Christmas) cost money, I think I now understand how a Christmas Tree business makes money, despite it only being able to sell its wares in what must be the shortest of retail seasons – charge as if the thing were made of platinum. But I am now immune to this, and willing to hand over significant sums of money to get a nice tree chosen expertly by Sian, taking account of its overall style, shape and ability to support a pile of fairy lights. My eye catches several trees in the corner of the yard, the size of which would rival the one they put up in Trafalgar Square, donated by those nice Norwegian people. You would have to have a house the size of the Ark Royal to get one of those in your hall. I am also intrigued by the tree wrapper, where you shove the bristling tree in at one end, and out it comes all tightly wrapped in netting at the other, and I ponder if they do a revised version for misbehaving children. I decide not to share this thought with Sian.

Having molested my car with the tree, and unloaded the other end, it then gets stuffed into a tree stand, moved harshly into the lounge and unwrapped. It springs free, doubtless gasping and very alarmed at this less than gentle transition, although you might reasonably think being cut down in the first place was probably trauma enough. Not long after, electrical wires and lights get threaded through its branches, which then glow rather hot when switched on, while strange round, shining balls get hung all over. If you were a tree, you would be screaming in abject agony and misery, so is it any wonder it loses all its needles and the will to live within a very short space of time. I am only surprised we have not seen a pressure group urging an end to this cruelty.

It has been a hard week, so I have agreed to make the family home made pizza, which are usually pretty delicious, even if I do say so myself. That's all well and good in theory, but it is not until I begin to prepare myself to make said pizzas, I realise I am lacking in kitchen facilities, most notably a surface on which to make the pizza dough. Well, the good people of Hotpoint may like to run a new ad campaign for their fridges, extolling the virtues of their tops as an excellent surface on which to make dough, although getting it off again could render the whole appliance ineffective, as chiselling seems to be the only answer. Still, who will notice the damage once its shoved back under a proper kitchen worktop.

For now, we will settle down with two large homemade pepperoni pizzas (recipes at extra cost, but acknowledgements to one time TV cook Michael Barry), a bottle of rather good Italian red wine and lemonade for the girls, all precariously balanced on the modest coffee table, being the only table left in the whole house.

Monday 16 December 2002

I am getting used to the current morning ritual, but I shall not be sad to see it replaced with something a bit more civilised. Okay, shaving and washing is much as it used to be, but in view of the lack of a toilet upstairs, I now have to hang on for a little while before making my natural morning deposit. Alright, I don't *have* to hang on, but I dare not go downstairs until I have woken up a bit, as to do so could have serious consequences. If we skip the unseemly business of using the downstairs dumping ground, it is necessary to navigate in cold, dark and disorientating conditions, the like of which may have been familiar to Scott of the Antarctic. However he probably didn't have to grope his way around a half finished wall to find his way to the kitchen.

Having done that, we now have to perform a game of organisation of lots of things in little space, balancing kettle, teapot, toaster, mugs and all sundry breakfast items on top of a washing machine of decidedly unassuming proportions. In other words, if something does not fall off by the time the kettle has boiled, it is yet another minor triumph in the face of adversity. In order to make the tea, it is necessary to find my way back around the labyrinthine utility/kitchen maze (which I am now able to do without leaving a trail of crumbs behind so that I can retrace my journey), back into the dining/study, dive under the plastic cover and hunt for the tea jar. On finding at least three tea bags, I wave these above my head in triumph and rush back to the kitchen and proceed to make the tea, being careful not to pour boiling water on either the washing machine, or myself, both of which would cause damage and substantial amounts of swearing. At this point, the bread goes into the toaster (assuming the toaster has not fallen to the floor, prompted by the activity around the kettle and teapot) and I rush to the lounge, as the only refuge of warmth. I have been known to hop about in the kitchen waiting for the toast to pop-up, but I am keen not to attract frostbite, so seek an ambient temperature above that of Siberia.

Acute hearing is an asset here, as I wait in the lounge, huddled close to the convector heater, anticipating the mechanical 'pop' of the toaster, which prompts a dash back to the kitchen, possibly only ever rivalled by Linford Christie at the 1998 Olympic 100 metres final, although he had the luxury of only having to run a straight line, and without the impediment of old sheets hung up in doorways in a forlorn attempt to keep the dust out of parts of the house. Mind you, we might have hit on a new idea for an alternative Olympic sport here, even though TV coverage could prove a little tricky. In the meantime, arriving back at the toaster in something a little longer than 9.98 seconds, the toast is swiftly shoved onto a small plate, plastered with margarine in a blur of movement between fridge and washing machine. The tea is poured rather quicker than it really is prepared for and we move swiftly, but deftly back to the lounge, which if I can manage with only three tea spillages, is another tiny conquest amidst trying conditions.

Just at the point I have thawed, tea and toast have been consumed, and it is time to dress and depart for work, although not before a final dash back to the kitchen to throw the dirty mug and plate into the sink. Given the general state of the kitchen area, these do not look out of place and can hardly be said to be making the place untidy – untidy barely does the current kitchen space justice. The rest of the mornings' effort to be ready to leave are only hindered by the need to stay away from the walls with one's suit or other formal dress, as even the merest brush deposits plaster and dust to the extent you can look as if you have just climbed out of a skip. Such an appearance does not attract admiring glances from work colleagues or clients.

Later (much later), I arrive back home to find, amongst other things, some new radiators have gone into place and they seem to give off more heat than some of the old ones. In the lounge, this has made quite a difference and while the climate is hardly tropical, it is getting closer to comfortable. Causing a little concern is the radiator in the study (its walls are plastered now, so I feel confident in calling it what it will be, rather than what it was), as the pipe comes out of the new side wall, and what was originally within the wall was the old radiator valve. I shuddered at the thought that this might remain and within time the damn thing would leak, we would then have to massacre the wall to sort out the problem. The track record of the builders suggests that I am worrying unnecessarily, but worrying in the context of all this work is something I have become, very, very good at.

Wednesday 18 December 2002
Once again, I have been away for a couple of days, and it is with some anticipation that I enter the back door, although not before looking in the garage, where the light had obviously been left on by the builders. As well as the usual stash of doors, door-frames and other sundry woodwork (not to mention the bath sitting patiently since delivery more than a week ago), we have something looking like a prop from a James Bond movie. It's bright yellow, cylindrical and appears to be sat on rails. Something 'Q' might have

devised to be strapped onto Bond's back – capable of propelling him across the countryside, whilst also turning into an Aston Martin later in the film, transforming into a wardrobe full of tuxedos shortly after he emerges from a swimming pool, and finally to be used as a nuclear bomb to obliterate the baddies lair about five minutes before the film ends. I am none the wiser as to its true function, but I suppose it's possible MI6 might occasionally use my garage as a stash site.

The first thing I notice about the utility/temp kitchen is that we have a radiator in place and it has been recycled from the lounge. It's grubby and a bit worse for wear, but nothing that a clean and lick of paint won't resolve. However, its plumbing touches a raw nerve within, as the pipes are exposed, running across the top of the new skirting and look like the botch job which all such works prompt as a perception within me. I *hate* exposed pipe-work, it is generally not necessary, it is the quickest and simplest solution for builders, but it looks cheap, nasty and ugly. Pipes serving the heating are purely functional and utilitarian, they do not need to be seen – I know what they do thanks very much, they do not need me to give them a sympathy vote by exposing themselves in front of me, cluttering up the walls and spoiling my nice clean lines. Others may get off on seeing all the services exposed (Richard Rogers again), but it just causes me to become Mr Angry of Anstey. I feel a scribbled note to Steve coming on, one made up of few words, but much emotion.

Out into the new kitchen-to-be, we are now fully exposed to the whole room, our mangy wall blanket having disappeared. The reason being, the glazing had now materialised, while the builders had thoughtfully placed a heater into the space, given its size and the fact no heating currently existed. One of the problems with the main kitchen window was always going to be its rather squashed appearance – unless you wanted the peculiar situation of the worktop cutting the window in half. The height of the opening had to be truncated so there was some space between worktop and window sill. With the sashes now in place, complete with quite fat centre bars, it looked as if someone had put it in a vice, as if the panes of glass and wood should be bulging under the tension. This is not unlike when I put on a pair of shorts I have had for too long and amply demonstrate that tightness of clothes does not fit with excess of body weight, unless you are a fan of the lumpy and squidgy look. It looks, and is, uncomfortable, and the windows look the same, only a little more dignified than me.

The glazing in the dining area looks fine, but then these are fixed, tall panes, no doubt I will get used to the whole environment, and something tells me it will all look vastly different when the room is finished and all the fixtures and fittings are all in place.

Meantime, more plastering has been taking place around the hall and inside the study. In addition, the door has gone up on the study, and this now gives a satisfying view of genuine progress towards the complete article, such that I can for the first time really begin to see what this part of the house will look like. In fact, once the new window has gone into the study, we could start the decoration, I had not thought of the prospect of being able to start to put our mark on the place while works were still going on. Unfortunately, completion of the downstairs tour revealed things elsewhere much the same as they were – dark, dirty and depressing, and that was just the downstairs loo. The lounge was its usual eclectic and grubby self – with the lights off on the Christmas Tree (not looking too suicidal I noted) and the heating off, inviting would not have been a term you would ascribe to the setting.

Upstairs lifted my spirits again as a door had emerged in the bathroom (soon to be re-christened as the landing), being the entrance to Cara's bedroom. Indeed, it even had a door handle, inviting me to enter, although whether this was in excited anticipation like some enchanted children's story, or morbid and blind fascination, like the idiot who opens the door to instant death in so many serial slasher movies, I wasn't quite sure. It seemed unlikely that Freddie Kruger had taken up residence in Anstey, so I walked in. What we now had here was a virtually complete room, all plastered, skirting boards in place, door and door-frame almost finished, window in, just a few finishing touches to do, and pretty splendid it looked too. (Providing you ignored the pile of piping, valves and strange red plastic sheeting, not to mention the store of bathroom goods along one side, all of which took up most of the floor space). It would be good to see all of this in daylight, but for the time being at least, I was starting to see just the tiniest chink, somewhere, vaguely towards the end of a long and tortuous tunnel, although there was every possibility I was deluding myself.

Thursday 19 December 2002

Progress seems to be relatively light, but I suspect this is merely as internal works are more intense and time consuming and cannot show the big gains umpteen courses of brickwork can do externally. More doors have been put on, more plastering has been done, but the most obvious sign of work has been the installation of more windows and their finishing touches, unfortunately some of these have not left me terribly pleased.

I have a pathological hatred of plastic in windows. If god had meant windows to be plastic, he would have created trees made of polyethylene or polystyrene or polyputthekettleon, but he didn't, and quite right too. So, I was a little shocked to see parts of the windows, the internal 'runners' to be precise, to be clean, white, antiseptic, soulless plastic. On top of that, some of the finishing was not of the highest standard, the painting was poor, and I positively flipped at the sight of a real cheap and nasty, must-have-fallen-out-of-a-cracker, catch on the window in the new rear bedroom. I will no doubt be vilified as a pedant, but attention to detail is likely to make or break this whole project and possibly the windows more than anything.

In truth, I am not so bothered about the plastic, I can see the logic of these in making the sashes run smoothly and being easier to maintain, but it would have been nice if someone had told us. The painting and the joke of a catch I am not prepared to accept, but I am too tired and going down with a cold (just before Christmas, fabulous timing!) to do anything other than pen a note of concern for Steve to pick up in the morning. Having done this, and left strategically placed where I know he cannot miss it, I have a pang of guilt. To date, the builders have been better than I really could have hoped and they have endured some dreadful conditions, yet pressed on as best they can. I have no desire to spoil any goodwill, but I don't feel I can remain silent on these matters. 'Bastard!' I can almost hear them shout.

I am then reminded, Sharon and I had agreed we would buy them all a bottle of wine to show some appreciation and that could be arranged tomorrow. Of course bearing in mind my note, we might find a nice red stain in the lounge and a broken bottle outside the back door later on.

Saturday 21 December 2002

I had expected half the crew to turn up today, but instead it was left to Eddie to carry the burden of weekend working. Eddie is one of the more mature members of the building team and fairly quiet, but he is a master at the art which baffles and fascinates in equal proportion, that of plastering. How you can turn the roughest, undulating and most unkempt piece of wall into a perfect surface, as smooth as the proverbial babies bum, is beyond me. How you can do it with a board, trowel and a gloopy pile of pink sludge which would appear to be the last thing to stay put, is even more remarkable, still further that it should be done with such quiet calm. I stand behind and marvel at what Eddie is doing, but this seems to unnerve him – I can tell this, as he keeps looking at me with increased frequency, while remaining silent, as if to say

"Yes, was there something?"

"Yes, how the hell do you do that?" is what I want to ask, but it's not a terribly intelligent question, and to be honest, he is unlikely to break off in order to give me a master class in plastering skills and technique. So, mildly embarrassed at my ineloquence and curiosity, I slope off. Eddie continues, humming quietly to himself, safe in the knowledge I am unlikely ever to be a competitor in his field.

During Friday, some more little jobs had either been started or were nearing completion, including more doors in place, and commencement of the balustrade at the bottom of the stairs. This is a slightly odd concept for us, as we have been used to a rail on the right, but not on the left. It's not exactly a grand staircase in the style of Gone with the Wind, but it's good to have the real impression of a proper hall, rather than the previous matchbox proportioned circulation spot. Work on this has banished the rather insecure temporary wooden prop that sat at the bottom of the stairs, and with it the light switch for the study, lashed with gaffer tape. As the electrics were not complete, this did not mean, as you might think, the switch was now where it should be – in the study. No, in fact not only did the switch remain outside the study, but in order to make it particularly entertaining, it was not even on a wall, or indeed on a vertical surface at normal switch height (you know, somewhere around chest height, unless you happen to be Michael Jordan, in which case you would struggle to get into the house anyway, although quite why Michael Jordan would even contemplate a trip to Anstey would be the greatest mystery). No, the switch was on the ceiling in the hall, just above the stairs. I am pleased to say this was entirely temporary, although you could have an awful lot of fun with someone else's house, wiring switches to rooms in different rooms in odd places (Well, you could if you were Jeremy Beadle).

One other problem for me. I have been in disgustingly good health all year, but now, just as Christmas draws close and I am looking forward to relaxing and stuffing my face, the lurgy strikes. Headache (indeed, most things ache), cold and cough like a seasoned smoker. The sort of cough which at the end of a fit feels you are about to eject your throat on to the floor, and takes you a little while to recover your breath and composure. Not very dignified and not the sort of thing to make you full of the supposed joys of this festive season. Good news however for pharmaceutical companies and chemists everywhere. I cannot help a wry little smile when earlier in the day, I find my way to the shelves in the supermarket marked 'Coughs & Colds'. I discover there is at least a common theme to transcend baked beans and toilet rolls, as all that remains are a few packets of Beechams, a pile of Paracetamol caplets (you try and swallow them) and blackcurrant throat sweets. Tell, a lie, one bottle of 'All-in-One' (I kid you not, that is what its called – sounds like you should be able to spray it into your car engine or onto your furniture). It promises a miracle cure for all my ills and being the gullible/desperate (delete either, or more likely, neither), I purchase. As ever, I live in hope.

Monday 23 December 2002

My 'All-in-One' cure has failed to live up to expectations, as I still have all my ills in one disgusting human package. I decide to spread my seasonal germs around the office for part of the morning in order to tidy up some work before the Christmas break, but then head back to home, which will have the benefit of speaking to Steve on the builders' last day before the break. I had left a note warning him I would be back about lunchtime, but had left out the bit about him and his team being in danger of catching the plague in my presence. As it was, I wanted to raise some questions about the quality of some of the finishes, so there was, for the first time, enough potential for a little bit of conflict without me suggesting that if he came within a bricks throw of me, he might find his Christmas would go with rather less of a sparkle, more of a cough and splutter.

Over the last week I had left a number of notes raising some queries on the detail of some of the finishes, especially on the windows, and when I arrived back at the house and met Steve, there was a detectable bristling. Given this atmosphere and the fact that I was outnumbered on site by about seven to one, full-on confrontation would not have been a good strategy, and in any case, we were talking about detail rather than the overall quality of the works. In addition, the house was a bustling hive of activity, with people working everywhere on everything, in order to restore some semblance of order and space before Christmas. I had already employed a favourite pre-emptive strike by buying bottles of wine for all members of the team, but still, I started to feel a bit mean spirited about launching into criticism. In fact, the first thing I said was a heap of praise, but this can be a little bit like saying, 'With the greatest respect' – often this means 'You are an arse, but I cannot say this to your face'. I told him, genuinely, I thought the standard of work and the work rate was exemplary, and I could not have wished for a better firm of contractors, *but* (tension builds again), I want to make sure the attention to detail is as a good as it can be. I wait for a withering look, but it doesn't come. In fact, we take a good natured tour around the house to have a look at some of problems, which it turns out he knows all about and will attend to them when it comes to finishing off. Classic defence, always successful – admit the problem, recognise you already know it exists and commit to its rectification. If only all others who provide me with a service were so communicative and committed.

    I bid Steve and his team a pleasant Christmas, and then leave them to it for the rest of the day, while I retire to my mothers and the kids who are most of the time looking after my parents, rather than the other way around. Feeling fairly grim and sorry for myself, I collapse into an armchair with a nice hot cup of tea and then realise something that leaves me horrified. The radio is on, nothing desperately unusual there, but it is the station to which it is tuned which almost has me spitting my tea back into my mug. I am of an age where Radio 1 finally lost me about three years ago. I hung on and hung on for as long as I could, but I ultimately had to admit, I could not listen to rap, hip-hop, garage and music that simply had me furrowing my brow any longer. It was a painful experience, this was a station I had listened to since the early 1970's. For god's sake, I grew up with such DJ luminaries as Dave Lee Travis, Jimmy Young (on Radio 1!) and 'Diddy' David Hamilton and if you can endure those, you can live through most things. In truth, Radio 1 started to lose me sometime before, but I felt a curious duty and warped loyalty, that I should not falter. I had flirted with the commercial stations, but there are only so many adverts for shampoo, Land of Leather, and Smiths Electrical store ('just off the by-pass, turn left at the Fox and Goat, and meander 17 miles along a country track, you can't miss it!') you can take in a day. So finally, with trembling hand one day I had gritted my teeth, closed my eyes and tuned to Radio 2. I know, once on the gentle green sloping pastures of Radio 2, it is only a short shuffle to slippers, green striped pyjamas, and a wardrobe full of beige and cream, but there I was. It was not, and is not now, a fanatical listening, but it keeps me comfortable on long journeys, usually in the afternoon. But horror of horrors, my parents are listening to Steve Wright on Radio 2, in their house! They can't do this, this is the preserve of forty-something's driving in their cars to appointments, it is not a programme or a station for parents of 76 and 81 years of age. I suddenly feel very old and very sick indeed.

Just to make my day complete, I am filled with humbleness when arriving back home that night, I find Steve and his brother have left two bottles of rather nice Australian wine for us as a Christmas present. It is truly a curious time of year.

Tuesday 24 December 2002 (Christmas Eve, as if you didn't know)
I am sitting in the lounge with my laptop, not unusually, on my lap. Sian and Cara have e-mailed Santa (doesn't quite have the romance of writing a letter, putting it in the fireplace, and swearing I saw it taken by a breeze to disappear up the chimney), and we have watched 'Muppet Christmas Carol', which still ranks as my favourite Christmas film. Why? Well, whatever you may think of Dickens, he told some belting stories and this is no exception, while the moral also serves as a timely antidote to my current overdose of cynicism. I also grew up with the Muppets and while they could never be said to have got it right all of the time and like most good things they continued past their sell-by date, I had loved the characterisation and the humour, combined with just a little dusting of pathos and probity. Add to that a super performance from Michael Caine, an actor who you just can't help watching as he invariably gets it either very right or very wrong, (clearly the former in this case) and you have one and a half hours of considerable entertainment. Which is just as well, as there is not a lot else to entertain in the Neale household.

Indeed, someone had remarked the scene within Holly House might resemble one from 'A Christmas Carol', particularly that within the Cratchett household, all members crowded into one room, huddled around a meagre fire. I could see the point, but in fact the Cratchetts had a bit of an advantage on us, because unless Dickens had made them more wretched and poor than I remember, they at least did not have their windows boarded up. True this gigantic pin-board at one end of the room could be put to good use as a place to hang cards and paper chains, except it was so hard, all the drawing pins we tried crumpled and bent in defeat, so we had to revert to Sellotape. Indeed, we used tape to stick cards, and some additional decorations, all over parts of the wall, but unfortunately the board and the grossly painted anaglypta walls had the last laugh, as they clearly had an impregnated non-stick surface as part of their finish, but with the comedic quality of only kicking in over a random period of time. So first off, it all sticks fine, but the clock is now ticking.

There I was last night, sitting in the armchair watching television, quietly minding my own business. Suddenly a stream of ten cards all stuck together and anchored at the top with a wedge of tape sufficient to wrap an elephant, collapsed and fell onto my head like a heavyweight streamer. More than that, it all fell perfectly, while several of the cards sat atop my head, the rest formed an almost perfect chain running down across my forehead, nose mouth and onto my chest. Understandably, this brought howls of laughter at my expense, until the next one fell, although this time, narrowly missing both myself and Sharon as it fell equidistant between us, we looked at each other as if to say 'Phew! That was a close call!' I suggested we could have a bet on which one would fall next, but the odds would be only marginally short of the National Lottery.

As I recall the Cratchetts were rather squeezed into one downstairs room to include the kitchen, so I suppose we do have a slight advantage on them, as we do have a separate kitchen area, albeit a little crowded into the utility-to-be. Our work surfaces are limited to none at all, so stuff is piled onto the top of the fridge (now released from its primary function as pizza dough surface), while the top of the washing machine is used to house the toaster, kettle and teapot, so at least breakfast can be prepared. Of course, the washing machine also has a job to fulfil in its own right, but this then has implications for the items that are currently relying on it for stable support. Unfortunately, this fact had escaped my attention, when earlier in the day I thought it would be sensible to wash the rug we have been placing onto the floor in our temporary kitchen. This has been serving to collect as much dirt as it can before people trail it around the rest of the house. (in fact, it had become so laden I had thought I could shake out its contents into a pile and sell it as top soil). Now, don't try this at home, because if you put a single bulky item into the washing machine, and it is also one that soaks up water like a sponge, it's a bit like putting a large rock inside. This creates serious imbalance in the machine when it spins, and the resulting violent jerk as it commenced its first spin cycle almost demolished the sink to its left, as it then began to waltz across the utility, shedding from its back first the toaster, then the kettle. I entered just in time to catch the teapot, but was still able to witness the washing machine about to attack the fridge.

It seems a wise move to have arranged Christmas lunch at my parents. The sight of food may have moved the washing machine into a fit of jealousy, and provoked a serious case of GBH on the cooker.

Sunday 29 December 2002

Thank goodness for friends and family at this time of year, but especially *this* year. My parents hosted us on Christmas Day, and no description of the day will be necessary from me, if you cannot picture this scene well enough by now, you are without doubt, an alien from a distant galaxy. Some good friends then hosted us on Boxing Day and very splendid it was too. Both of these had given me an impression of normality, being away from the pit of despair that is Holly House. On top of this, the vast majority of the weekend has been spent with Sharon's relatives, so the mirage of familiarity, space, tidiness and cleanliness had been perpetuated, only to be rudely shattered on returning home tonight.

As always happens on these occasions, we have returned home with armfuls of presents, and whereas in previous years we have pondered where they can go, this time there was no need for such deliberation, as there is only one area of the house with more than a cubic micron of additional storage space – the loft. I did feel a bit like The Grinch, the slightly sad faces of my children at the bottom of the north face of the Eiger, otherwise known as the ladder into the loft, as they handed me their Christmas gifts to be rather informally stacked and shoved into any available space amidst the piles and piles of existing household items, squeezed onto temporary boards across and between the rafters. It would have looked like Aladdin's Cave, except none of it shone and sparkled, and the underside of a felted roof and heaps of crossed timbers and spilling insulation do not do a good impression of a magical place hollowed out of rock. And I bet Aladdin never had to take his life in his hands in order to get in and out.

The rest of the house is much as we had left it – cold, dark, dirty, chaotic and half-finished, but thankfully, the washing machine had not run amok in our absence. What particularly shocked me was the state of the living room carpet. Over the last year we have accepted that buying a light cream colour carpet in a room taking the most amount of traffic was about the dumbest retail decision in the history of purchasing. Add to this the building works producing a constant storm of more dirt and dust for the past three months and a recent acceptance that the carpet would have to be consigned to the bin come the end of the works, (Which, I ashamedly have to admit, meant we became less and less bothered about the odd spillage), and the carpet was beginning to resemble the one it replaced when we first moved in. It may not have smelt like a dead dog, but visually, it was starting to do a good impression of one. Indeed, I was so ashamed of its state, I cringed, went over to the dimmer switch and turned the lights to the not-quite-able-to-see-the-carpet setting, which produces about as much light as half a candle, but made me feel a little more at ease. Well, they do say what you can't see can't hurt you, which is of course a load of bollocks, but at least what I can't see, won't be able to turn my stomach.

Wednesday 1 January 2003

Have you ever had one of those Wiley Coyote moments? You know the sort of thing – that pesky Roadrunner has beaten you for the seventh time, and by now you have been flattened by a seven ton weight dropped off a cliff, run over by a speeding train which appeared out of nowhere and blown up by an unfeasibly large stick of dynamite. Quite reasonably, you think this cannot get any worse, that you have reached your nadir, that there is a ladder just around the corner that will start you on your climb back up to some good fortune and enable you sneak up on this rather annoying (but rather fast) little bird. Errr...no. It doesn't. That bastard Roadrunner has rigged the ladder so it comically collapses as you are half way across a ravine, and like Wiley, you turn your head to wince out of the screen in resigned despair, a second before you drop into oblivion. Just once it would be nice to wipe that smug smile off the Roadrunner, and bring an end to that irritating 'meep, meep'.

For one thing, it continues to rain, just like it has been raining since, it would seem, October. Previously, I had mused Noah would have been called out of retirement in order to assist with matters. I think it likely in these conditions that he has probably capsized, and as I write is bobbing up and down, clung to an elephant, or some other such large beast, by now not giving a toss about saving any species, much more focused on saving his own arse. The front garden would frighten even the likes of David Attenborough, as it is both a pond and a marshy bog, the latter terminology rather more apt, given the fact that our septic tank also resides in this area and has spewed its contents around the vicinity. In fact, were it not for this, it would not have been a surprise to see it frequented by water skiers and windsurfers, although in Britain you might reasonably surmise they would be used to avoiding the odd floating turd and discarded paper. For whatever reason, despite the fact Anstey is more than a few metres above sea level, water seems to hang about everywhere, refusing to drain, indeed half the village seems to be draining in our direction. Water from the field at the back is running constantly through the site, so much so that the builders have created sink holes into the new drains (both foul and surface), in order to encourage it to run through the site, into the front garden and preferably out the other end. However, as described, at the moment it is just creating the reservoir from hell, but at least the grass has rarely looked greener.

We have all woken up at about ten o'clock this morning, a legacy of rolling in through the front door at two o'clock earlier in the morning, following a New Years Eve soiree at friends. This was all fine and splendid, but it was I who volunteered to drive, hence it was I who remained sober through the whole evening. Again, this was all fine until about eleven o'clock, at which point two things happened; Firstly, I discovered I will never, ever be a World Champion Pictionary player. This could be because I am not a lateral thinker, or am unable to unravel the intricacies of the cryptic clue, but more likely because I am plain shite and cannot shout louder than nine other people. Secondly, it was at about this time there was a shift in dimensions, as everyone else moved into the realms of being pissed, while I remained in the land of the temperate. There are few more disturbing experiences in life, it is a little bit like watching the last train of the night trail off into the dark, leaving you all alone, except for the bunch of French exchange students having a riot on the next platform. There is plenty going on, but I am buggered if I can understand any of it.

Unfortunately, there is much to be done today, as we have promised Steve we will have moved out of our bedroom and into Cara's new bedroom by tomorrow, when they return to start work again. Failure to do so will not only incur the wrath of the builders, but will also probably result in all the stuff in our bedroom being distributed in random piles in other parts of the house. Now, this is not the work of a moment, once more it requires a combination of both logistical skills and the ability to juggle. This time, I make a fatal error when I move a good deal of clothes, boxes and a moveable wardrobe into Cara's current bedroom, in order to able to move other stuff out and around. The fatal mistake I make is to pull the wardrobe into place, only to realise that in doing so, I cannot get out.

"Sharon!" I shout rather ashamedly, as both Sharon and Sian's heads pop around the door, which I can just see from my distant vantage point.

I struggle to sandwich myself between the wardrobe and the computer desk, lift one leg half over the end of the desk and thrust my hand as far forward as possible.

"Can you pull me out please?"

A small burst of mirth ensues as I am pulled like the end of a piece of rope in a tug-of-war contest, until finally I stagger out. You could almost hear a 'pop' as I emerge from the self-created constriction, like the proverbial cork from a bottle.

When everything has been suitably moved to clear the floor in the bedroom, the exposed state of the carpet is nothing short of disgusting. I am not so much bothered by how so much dirt and dust can accumulate, but am rather more troubled by all the hair and fluff. If you gathered it all up, you could probably knit a few jumpers for the whole family and still have some left over for a scarf for my mother. These sort of mysteries rank with the ever multiplying numbers of coat hangers that appear in your wardrobe (they must be at it all the time in order to breed so quickly), and the great odd sock conundrums, although in my case this can usually be tracked down to theft by the tumble dryer. I can only surmise there is some strange process of physics by which fluff is created from nothing, which takes place in such diverse environments as my belly button and the underneath of my bed.

Eventually, we manage to clear enough space to transport the carpet from our bedroom to the new room. Once it has been shorn of all its rather unpleasant cargo, we move all our (and those of many others) items in, including bed, wardrobe, chest of drawers, games, puzzles, excess fluffy toys, three mirrors and enough hair dryers to probably evaporate half the surplus water that lies in the village. It is with some surprise, we discover Cara's new room is bigger than our current bedroom, and although there was certainly not enough spare space to host a party, you could at least walk all around the bed without having to take avoiding action, or turning sideways. And despite the grotesque weather outside, the large single sash window created a splendid frame for the view across the back garden and the fields beyond, or in the case of today, the large grey, looming mass pervading every scene, that sat rudely and gloomily over the landscape.

All in all, this was not a pleasant day and once again tempers frayed rather badly, always signified by shouting at the children for the smallest of indiscretions, all punctuated by long, tense periods of total silence between all. By the end of the day, virtually no-one is speaking to anyone else, save Cara, who has not yet developed the prejudice, resentment and all round antipathy of adults, and in these circumstances rather perversely acts more like an adult than the adults, who are being far too childish to notice. Just before bed, she sends me back into the land of the living, and makes me feel desperately ashamed, by giving me a big, warm soft hug, the type that only your children can give you, and generally only up until the age of about ten.

"You're the *best* daddy that *anyone* could *ever* have!" she says with genuine feeling.

I am unable to say anything, but hug her back, gently stroke her hair, kiss her on the forehead, and bid her good night.

There is a reason to live after all.

Thursday 2 January 2003

A call from Richard, who in turn has had a call from Steve, who may well have been shouting 'Man Overboard', and asking for inshore rescue. It is *so* wet this morning, a river is virtually running through the site, and it seems there are genuine concerns we ought to do something about it very much sooner rather than later. Putting a mast on the roof, and setting sail is one option, but far better is a plan to improve the drainage by putting in a land drain down the eastern boundary, running this right down the front garden, putting in another cross drain to catch the current 'weepers' from the septic tank (finger drains from the last chamber of the septic tank system, rather than a group of pitiful Anstey residents in group mourning, hanging around the garden), and then into the ditch in the road. That's all fine and I give the go ahead, although I cannot help thinking, the land should be doing this job itself, rather than need an expensive helping hand from me and the builders. I also fear this will merely create a simple transference of the new lake from my front garden to the road, but perhaps we can see this as my gift to the village.

At this time of year, as it has been for more than two months, it is dark by the time any of us get home, indeed, it is dark when I leave in the morning, so I never get to see the house in daylight until sometime on Saturday morning. This means it is very difficult to gauge what has been happening externally, we have to revert to enacting the cliché from so many detective stories by prowling around the outside with a torch, peering around the house and into every nook and cranny. I feel I should be dressed in a cape and deerstalker, but I suspect Ever Ready batteries and a Pifco were not invented in Sherlock

Holmes's era, and I am buggered if I am wandering round with a bloody candle lamp. The inspection later today reveals a distinct change in the water level at the back of the house, at least along the side by the garage, which generally only needs a bucketful of water to form a large, immoveable puddle, but tonight is (almost) clear. Around the other side however, water is running in a constant torrent along the side of the extension, then down into the new foul drain, then of course goes to the septic tank, which at present simply appears to be bubbling merrily all over the front garden. I assume all the water *must* be going somewhere, and I attempt to inspect the front garden, but have to abandon this plan from the first step, when my foot almost disappears amidst a squelchy concoction of water, grass and mud. As far as I can tell, no additional drainage works have been done, although clearly something is assisting the water on its quest to get from back to front.

Inside, more doors have gone up, more plastering has been done, but most excitingly, they have ripped out the daftest shower cubicle known to man from our bedroom, which I can now see in all its stupid glory. I had not appreciated what a disgusting beetroot type colour it was and not just the shower tray, but also the tawdry plastic side panels and revolting shower 'tidy'. I rejoiced at its dismemberment, as it lay in several pieces strewn across the bare bedroom floor and pondered for a moment whether I should ceremonially carry it downstairs and hurl it into the skip. It may then be questionable as to whether the skip lorry would refuse the load, deeming it to be far too toxic and heinous to be transported to a common landfill site, but requiring specialist treatment and destruction. Either way, I was glad to see it dismantled and close to obliteration, although this was a little tempered by the site of some preliminary work in the adjoining airing cupboard. The works would require relocation of the hot water tank, and some fairly complicated and time consuming plumbing, the result of which we had been warned about – up to three days without hot water and possibly no heating. In the middle of winter, this is not a pleasant prospect, and I am already thinking about emergency measures when this happens. It seems likely we will have to impose upon my parents a few miles away, although the very serious downside of this is a second bout of group Radio 2 listening, and I am not sure I am up to that sort of embarrassment. However, the alternative of wrapping up in blankets, washing in cold water, and generally doing a much more accurate impersonation of the Cratchetts in A Christmas Carol is marginally less appealing.

Friday 3 January 2003
It has now turned rather cold, so it is good to see some progress with the under floor heating, scheduled to be installed in the kitchen and dining area. Or at least I assume that's what it is, even if it does look like an enormous model train layout on a vivid red base. Actually, on closer inspection, this is in fact an adult version of those children's puzzles I used to love – You know

the ones. Who is flying the kite at the end of the string, is it Johnny, Mandy or Jimmy? Well, bearing in mind they have all got themselves in a right state by getting all their strings twisted together in an almighty mess, I don't think anyone's kite is going anywhere, but I always had great fun tracing the lines. Yes, it was usually the last one I tried, and they always seemed to have a bit of a smug look about them. Why then I didn't just simply look for the smug bastard, I am not entirely sure, but these were more innocent times.

There is what appears to be two very long continuous runs of grey tubing looping round and around from the middle in wider and wider circles and if you look at it long enough, you will probably fall over in dizzied disorientation. The impression of something weird is accentuated by the red plastic sheeting on which it is laid, or rather *within* which it is laid, as this has regular 'bubbles' that protrude across its area, and the piping is held in place as it is wrapped around these. To the rear of the dining area, four pipe ends disappear into the wall, and on checking the other side, emerge rather rudely in the downstairs toilet, where piles of excess pipe are coiled up and sat against the wall, but in such a way that if you go to extract your coat (only place left in the house where coats can be hung), you end up in a bit of a skirmish with the piping as it seems to fight to retain your coat, presumably thinking it would make damn good lagging. Personally, I prefer to wear my coat myself, rather than see it wrapped around some grey plastic tubing.

Outside, I gather some serious work has been in train in digging out the land drain, but frankly it is far too bloody cold and dark for me to start foraging in the front garden. I will wait until morning arrives rather than do another Sherlock Holmes. I do not have a Watson I can send out instead. Besides, I suspect devastation has been wreaked and I am not sure I am up to such a revelation this evening.

Saturday 4 January 2003
Oh my god! There is one of two things happening in the front garden, although a third is a remote possibility. It could be construction has started on an Anstey bypass, and this is scheduled to run right in front of the house, as it is not difficult to believe such mess, and particularly the brutal gouge running the length of the garden is in fact a serious work of engineering. It could be that Tom Hanks is in the country again, looking to shoot a sequel to 'Saving Private Ryan', and on spotting my garden, decided it would be a splendid location to re-enact a trench warfare scene. Or maybe, just maybe, this is the land drain dug to pass water through the site by the quickest and most efficient means possible. But since it looked as if the worlds biggest JCB had been trampling across the garden, digging a channel deep enough and so full of water, that Jacques Cousteau might have found it of considerable interest, I was very tempted to dispel the final theory. In my imagination, I had thought we might have seen a fairly discreet little trough along the very edge of the garden, barely disturbing the shrubs and lawn, gently coaxing the water away,

and shyly discharging it in a tiny trickle into the ditch alongside the road. What we had was a great big fat bastard of a trench, blasted all the way down the garden, from underneath the gravelled parking area all the way across and through the lawn, beds, plants, trees, women, children and small animals. It was a rather massive slash across the grounds and was pretty shocking at first sight.

Since the weather had also been very wet up until today, it was no wonder to find a boggy, muddy mess around these works, although they had done their best to keep this to a minimum by putting down planks on which to walk and run their wheelbarrow. However, in the circumstances, this had merely limited the damage to dreadful, rather than unbelievable, and general obliteration was the order of the day. But this was no fault of the builders, merely a reality check for me and a reminder that whatever you imagine to be necessary in these circumstances, multiply it by a factor of at least five. Of course, there was a serious upside to all of this, in that you could walk on the front lawn without the need of a wetsuit, while there was no longer the prospect of having to construct a rival to the Hoover Dam in the back garden. Most gratifying however, was the moment I lifted one of the manhole covers over the foul drain run, which only a few days earlier had been bubbling and spewing its less than pleasant contents all over the place, but was now completely empty, bar a modest trickle towards the septic tank in the very bottom. On closer inspection of the dug trench, water was in constant flow, partially from its top (where it ran from the soak-away), but also from its sides, taking water from the garden generally, but also (clearly signalled by the ripeness of the odour) from the weepers of the septic tank system.

I made my way around to the road at the front and found a constant flow from the garden, discharging through a pipe about the size of a normal drainpipe, into the ditch. This had also been helpfully cleared by Steve and his men, and seemed to be running relatively freely. For the first time, I spotted the flow along this was in the opposite direction to the way I thought it went, but since I had never seen it flowing, only stagnant under a jungle of nettles and weeds, this should not have come as a surprise. I discover what small pleasures man can derive from the gentle murmuring of filthy, stench and debris filled water in a grubby roadside ditch. I am sure there are unpleasant names for men like me.

Sunday 5 January 2003
Today is another one for some internal reconfiguration, otherwise known as moving things to places that do not exist. Well, no, not true, space does exist, it's just getting access to it, whilst carrying the load to be moved, is about as practical as doing the London Marathon in a diving suit…which is of course what someone did, so who am I to complain? We now have to move all the remaining stuff still sitting in Cara's old room (soon to be bathroom) out, and the only place it can go in, is the loft. I take a deep breath, and having

sorted out some of the books, clothes, broken toys, dolly's clothes without a dolly, and even a dolly without any clothes (sadly, one did not match the other), we have umpteen piles to go in the loft, and only one pile to find its way into the nearest wheelie bin. The piles that wait patiently to be hoisted aloft are not your regular little boxes of ordinary, light objects, but include (amongst several others) a bag of assorted books, the weight, instability and extremely bulky exterior of which would have made a good prop for a Worlds Strongest Man competition, a plastic toy-tidy whose diameter was a match for the dimensions of the loft opening, thereby making its (rather forced) journey through a rather distressing (and expletive filled) affair, and a desk. Getting this latter article through the loft opening was relative child's play compared to the contortions necessary to get it over to the other side of the loft (the only space left in this increasingly clutter filled area), through, under and over a multitude of beams and cross beams. It was like a contorted Krypton Factor challenge, only without the lurid and unpleasant jump suits they used to wear.

Talking of which, I have to confess to a moment of over exposure. Lifting ridiculous items over an assault course can be a hot and sweaty experience, and very soon in these proceedings, I had shed my T-shirt, and was continuing with my tasks *sans appareil* from the waist up. While I was completing this exercise, Sharon was busy tidying up the lounge, in particular, banishing Christmas from every corner for another year, including pulling down the Christmas Cards and simply binning those having found their way onto the floor days before (see previous entries). The Christmas Tree remained, only now denuded of all decoration, lights and wonky angel. The tree was by now bone dry and petrified, so needed a decent burial, but instead was shoved out of the rear French doors, unscrewed from its base, dragged rather cruelly and un-ceremonially around the side of the house and thrown dead trunk first into the skip. Having then slapped my hands together to get rid of the needles, I realised I was outside the front of the house, in sub-zero temperatures. My hair looking like it had been used as the proverbial floor mop, ripped and dirty jeans that would have been rejected by any self-respecting tramp, and semi naked. I looked around furtively to see if anyone had spotted me, then darted back around the side of the house, rushing in through the back door as though being chased by a pack of hounds.

No police car has yet arrived to ask searching questions about my less than appropriate appearance, but there is still time yet for a knowing knock at the door.

Tuesday 7 January 2003

Seemingly slow progress again over the last few days, in particular the puzzle on the kitchen floor remains unsolved and unfinished. Apparently (and I know this sounds a bit like leaves on the line), the sand needed to do the work has been frozen, thereby preventing its usage. It is a statement to which I really have no answer.

They have at least been completing some finishing works involving piles of architrave, whilst preparing the bathroom to take the essential trinity of bath, bog and basin. There has also been some liberal use of plasterboard to fill in what was the door to the bathroom when it was a bedroom and to replace the ridiculous and very 70's obscure glass top-lights above the door frame into Sian's room. The rest of the works will ensure these are completely banished from the house forever, but I confess to being completely in the dark as to why they were installed in the first place. I tried to think of a synonym for this situation, and all I can come up with is putting a hat on an elephant. Okay, it has a head, and some people wear hats on their head, but for an elephant, it is the definition of superfluous, and moreover, just looks plain stupid. Not ideal, I know, but you catch my drift.

Wednesday 8 January 2003
The puzzle has disappeared below a sea of very sandy concrete, so I assume they must have solved the problem of very lumpy sand caused by the Arctic conditions. In fact, I am alarmed to hear from Sharon that before she left this morning, they were using what appeared to be a flamethrower.

"What!"

"Yep, a cylindrical thing with flames coming out of it!"

There was no paint stripping to be done, no impenetrable jungle to blast through, and certainly no alien running amok tearing people into gory pieces (just reliving a scene from one of my favourite films there, although in the right light Eddie the brickie did look a little like John Hurt).

"They were using it to defrost the sand...although in the process, nearly got a bit close to my car!"

Ingenious, and presumably very effective, but a tad dangerous one feels, especially with the proximity of wood all over the place, not to mention one not very old and rather loved Citroen C3, even if it was finished in a bright flame red colour.

Elsewhere, we now had a new front door, although the old one still remained, and since the front extension, which includes the new, larger hall was far from finished, it would be a little while before we could dispose of the old. It was however not only getting dirty and damaged, but was getting subject to increased abuse, as we so longed for its dumping into the skip. Partly, this was because the current front door was configured to open out (inner hall could not possibly have coped with a door that opened in). It was only when you went to open it for the first time, you discovered that holding the handle while doing so meant your knuckles were removed without the benefit of anaesthetic. This was followed by vehement swearing, jumping up and down and finished off with a brutal kick to the door. Indeed, over time, the door was becoming less well fitting (which is a bit like saying Patrick Moore was becoming less well dressed, but there you are) it actually needed kicking hard to open and a damn good pull to shut. However, about a week ago, I had been in the process of pulling the door as hard as I could, when an incident straight out of a well-worn sitcom occurred. The handle flew off, I flew backwards with it, landing in a heap on the stairs, arms still outstretched, crappy handle, plate, and screws dangling still in my hands.

"Bastard, bastard, BASTARD!" was all I could shout at it.

So, when the door has to be opened, I now take great delight in going outside and kicking it shut, as hard as I can, with considerable feeling.

Talking of doors, another has been replaced, this time the one into Sian's room. This is yet another of the poor quality doors the previous residents had painted in a rather foul off-yellow. Sian had become so disgusted with it, she had decorated it virtually top to bottom in order to hide its foulness and had written on it at the bottom

'This Door Smells and is Rubbish!"

Okay, not the most withering insult, but it had a simplicity and directness that seemed appropriate somehow. Her old door was now propped in her bedroom, as the builders had rather thoughtfully surmised she would want to take her pictures and cards from it before it was dumped. This she did, but it was then with much acclaim and celebration that the door was heaved out of her room, manhandled down the stairs, then out through the front door to be rudely and loudly discarded into the skip. I put my hands aloft in triumph.

Saturday 11 January 2003
Bit of a toss up a to whether this entry should be in Friday or Saturday. But as the first drip that assaulted my shoulder was a few minutes past midnight, I suppose I should stick with the actual time of the event and record it as the very, very early hours of Saturday morning. This being despite the fact I had not yet gone to bed for the night.

So, there I was, standing in the downstairs loo, having emptied my bladder before retiring for the night, washing my hands by the deep burgundy basin, made marginally less attractive by the grey layer of dust that I reminded myself I should wash off in the morning. (That's the sink was marginally less attractive you understand, rather than me – I tend not to stand still long enough to gather a coating of the stuff, although some would doubtless suggest this could be an image enhancing move for me). It was then that I felt something lightly drop onto my shoulder. I looked round, nothing there, I looked up, nothing there. As it was gone midnight and we had consumed a good bottle of Italian Rioja a few hours before, I gave it very little further thought. Then, as I was drying my hands, another light drop, this time I did not bother to look round. Lets face it, other than the Ghost of Competent DIY, it was very unlikely some supernatural spectre was wandering around the halls (sorry half finished hall), of Holly House, seeking reprobation on those who had created such a ridiculous monstrosity in the first place. Indeed, if he was, I should think he would want to lavish substantial praise and satisfaction on the work in hand, perhaps hastening a release from his shackles to coincide with completion of a useable entrance, saving him the bother of having to come up through the downstairs bog. And even if he was trailing around, he would be falling over boxes, heaters, toolboxes and dumped shoes, so either I would have heard him long before, or he would have given up to return for a bit of peace and quiet in the septic tank.

Looking up, at the same time just pausing to note there was not a see-through hand on my shoulder, I tried to focus first on the ceiling, but then my eye was caught by a little glistening drop of water about to fall from the light, which itself was dangling and wires exposed from a hole. Lets see now... water and electricity....if my rather sketchy knowledge of science is correct, not to mention general health and safety, I recall these are two elements that are best not acquainted with each other, as the result can be a bit of an unpleasant punch-up, followed by a messy conflagration...oh, yes, and death is also pretty likely. I move myself out of the toilet and hurl myself up the stairs at some velocity. On arriving I realise this is not a reoccurrence of the leaking tap at one end of the bath, as the downstairs loo sits directly below the other end...which is boarded in with tasteful green panelling. In fact some of the pipes in the vicinity have been exposed, but as there is no evidence of water around these, this is clearly not the problem. I also know that Wally the electrician has been working in the vicinity of the toilet (purely in an electrical capacity you understand) today, so what price a misplaced drill coming together with an errant water pipe. I sigh. What do most people do at just gone midnight between Friday and Saturday? Generally, pissed, still getting pissed, or beyond both and fast asleep. Me, I shall be attempting to rip out some bathroom cladding and floorboards – can't see this as an activity that would readily transfer to pubs and clubs across the UK. There is a small access door at the right end of the bath and I see on opening it, some holes have been made in the floor and I also spy a load of wires running in different directions. The finger starts to point at Wally and his wayward drill. I can also just about see (with the aid of a torch the size of a Ford Mondeo, but with the light issuing capacity of a damp match) that it is wet on the underside of the ceiling. Kneeling right by this hateful hatch, I stretch out my arm, loop it underneath the hole in the floor and wait to be electrocuted. This doesn't happen, so I flail my hand and fingers about, until I happen upon a pipe from which water is dripping rather profusely. Of course, I can't see any of this, I am just looking pained, staring into the middle distance, trying to imagine what it is that my hand is fondling. This must be a bit like James Herriott with his hand up a cows arse, only I don't know what I am really looking for, and he has the pleasure of being able to do this during normal working hours.

Given the amount of moisture, I stuff an old towel into place, in order to try and prevent any more dubious meeting of electricity and water and then proceed to rip the cladding off the end of the bath. Of course, this is partially to get a better position, but also as a way of venting my anger at my less than desirable situation. This in turn disturbs Sharon, but at least this means we now have some practical application on the project. However, if you were to take a step back from this scene, and stand just outside the bathroom, what you would see and hear might make you turn and run out of the house. Both of us are on our knees facing away from the door, and slightly upturned in order to manoeuvre around the scene and into the hole. This means both our arses are in the air facing out and the conversation, rather breathless and angry is something like

"Can you feel it yet?"

"Yeah, its all rather wet down here!"

See what I mean? Where else could you get such priceless innuendo in such trying circumstances?

We decide we must turn off the mains water at the stop cock, and drain the entire cold water tank in the loft if we are not to awake to a collapsed ceiling and an almighty mess in the morning. So, Act 2 is waiting in the bathroom, bath tap on full, waiting for the tank to run completely dry, wandering around aimlessly. It takes an age and by the time it seems to have run down completely, it is nearly one o'clock in the morning and of course we have no water. The latter realisation does not truly dawn until next morning, when I am about to use the toilet, but stop *just* short, as it occurs that what I now deposit cannot be flushed, and I *really do* want to deposit. Oh, shit, quite literally. I cannot wait, I *really*, cannot wait, so I hit upon the idea of turning on the stopcock for a moment to enable me to fill up a bucket, which I can then use to flush the contents of the toilet post-action. It is not a recommended process, but the subsequent relief is a little like the Irishman who, when asked why he was hitting his head against a wall, replied because it felt so good when he stopped. Life in Holly House feels a little like this at present.

Wally is due back this morning and we also make a call to the builders, who promise to fix the problem. In fact, it transpires we have done poor Wally something of a disservice; it is the curse of the previous owners that has struck again. Apparently, the act of putting up the tasteful cladding around the bath had included nailing the thing down to the floor at certain points, and at one of these points they had rammed a nail into one of the pipes. Quite how this had not leaked before is a mystery, but the work in the area on Friday had caused it to be disturbed, hence the leak.

Disturbed, indeed – this would be a very good adjective for our state of mind at the moment.

Sunday 12 January 2003

Winter can be a bit of a cleanser, and this morning a very sharp and penetrating frost has left the landscape a dusty white, and sitting quietly beneath a clear azure sky, it is a vision of tranquillity and calm. Around the garden, it helps to hide some of the disorder and destruction, particularly out front. Given the trials and tribulations of last night and early this morning, I resolve to get out for a walk, and drag the girls along with me. After a bit of cajoling, they agree, so wrapped up in thick coats, scarves, gloves and boots, we make our way down the road and past the pub.

Cara delights at jumping on the frozen puddles, Sian joins her, whereupon the ice collapses and much giggling and shouting ensues. We continue on our way to the church, just before which sits a solitary bench, with a view across open, gently rolling farmland. Years ago, this scene would have been dotted with trees and criss-crossed with hedges, but modern farming is no respecter of such natural barriers, and only a few remain. Still, if hardly exhilarating, the picture is pleasant enough. The white frost sitting like a soft, milky veil across the fields, smoothing out the scene like a soothing hand, the silence adding a dose of real serenity and the appearance of a few wispy clouds give some real depth to the view. We stand and stare for what seems like a good few minutes, but I suspect is a matter of only a handful of seconds. The cold and quiet is seemingly distorting the passing of time.

We continue to the small village playground, where we find the stream that passes to the side is flowing, but does so in part underneath a crust of sparkling, spiky ice. At one point by the small bridge, it looks as if this crust is made up of thousands of long, white glass shards, almost a sculpture of a thin delicate bridge, under a bridge, over a stream. The girls play around on the swings and climbing frame, whilst I simply survey the scene and marvel at the power and beauty of nature, and the way it can cloak its body in all manner of weird and wonderful guises. I then decide to write my name on the grass by shuffling over the frost, and the girls do the same, only with a bit more style, while Cara, as usual, goes over the top by developing hearts and kisses as part of her message to the world.

When the chill starts to penetrate, we head back, but on a different route, beside the church, and across a field, then beside a large, mature woodland area through which there is no public access. All remains quiet, save a horse galloping across the other side of the field, and a dog, trailing obediently behind, working hard to keep up with owner and steed. Halfway along this part of the route, immediately alongside the wood, we suddenly face up to a herd of deer, all Does, about fifteen metres into the trees. Deer are common in many parts of Hertfordshire, and despite a fair bit of destruction of their natural habitat, it is not unusual to see packs of them. At times they are passing the time of day, gently nibbling at grass on the edge of woodland, at other times ambling across fields and frequently bolting along, usually desperately heading for cover. Despite this apparent familiarity, they still fascinate me and fill me with some wonder and excitement – it's still one thing to be amused by a load of sheep, cows or horses, but these are kept and farmed. Deer are truly wild, striking and very grand creatures, and unless you do come across them in a farmed (or heaven forbid zoo) environment, you won't get close to them, so you have little more than a tantalising or distant glimpse. Their shyness adds to the mystery, if you ever have the pleasure of seeing a fully grown stag, you will appreciate they are truly magnificent beasts. This group of modest females, about ten in number, stopped, and eyed us suspiciously, as if to say 'what do you want?' Moments later, they had decided we were probably trouble, turned ninety degrees, charged through the wood and across the field from the direction we had just walked. They disappeared from view almost as quickly as they had materialised. A small, but memorable encounter, on a morning enveloping us in the richness, beauty, peace and quiet excitement that was this little patch of England.

Later in the day, we decide we should get ourselves out of the house, and propose to meet my parents at what is locally renowned as a very fine tea-shop, in a village a few miles away. Despite having lived in the area for more than ten years and passed the shop more times than I could possibly recall, we have never ventured inside. The village is a typical, old linear coaching point, set on what at one time was one of the main routes from London to Cambridge. It has a number of old, timber framed cottages and unpretentious houses, although has also suffered from some ridiculously inappropriate development, all strung out along one long road. The village is quiet, but The Old Swan Tea Rooms are busy. Even before entering, you get a sense of history, and not just from the somewhat dilapidated but grand double frontage of this large former public house, with its twin, towering gables. The door latch is a large, heavy, gnarled iron ring and you have to pull and turn with some force to open the door. Inside, the smell of freshly baked cakes and smoky oak beams wafts on a meandering haze of gentle conversation and clanking tea cups. The heavy, blackened beams and whitewashed walls, the sturdy ingle-nook and the red carpet help to give the place a sense of total ambience. Even the small floral patterned tablecloths, the terracotta sugar bowls, and the slightly dog-eared menu, which in normal circumstances might have had you turning to exit almost as soon as you had entered, added to the atmosphere and feeling of welcome, a gentle invitation into hospitality and warmth, where just being and experiencing, was rather more important than appearance and show.

The service was friendly and courteous, the tea was flavoursome, the fruit-cake was mouth-watering and the whole experience again seemed to slow the passage of time. You could have sat there for hours, as we nearly did, during which time my father consumed a bowl of soup, two rolls, three cups of tea and half a scone. Staring out of the window across at another handsome timber framed house, and musing over the contents of a little leaflet extolling the virtues of wild boar (although I was a little disturbed they seemed to name all their animals, oblivious to the fact that within time, they would become a jar of rather tasty pate), I was again reminded for not the first time today, what a splendid and rich country England can be, if only we took the time to see, rather than look, listen rather than hear, and feel, rather than just touch.

Back at the house later, a little obsession seems to have begun. The plastering of the hole where the door through to the kitchen used to be is wonderfully smooth as usual, but unfortunately, it has been done up to the point where the wallpaper stopped, rather than peeling this back. The result is, the height of the new plaster is above that of the existing and an unplanned textured wall with a great long crease down the whole length now marks the old from the new. I am sure this can, and will, be put right in time, but this has prompted more peeling back of the wallpaper. Apart from confirming the atrocious taste of our predecessors (the wallpaper seemed to be one big sheet of ugly, textured polystyrene, the sort of thing that would be far more at home wrapped around a precious vase rather than slapped incongruously on the wall), it then incited a frenzy of wallpaper peeling in other places. Before I knew it, Sharon and Cara had a mad wide-eyed look, and were knee deep in paper peelings in the hall. This threatened to get out of control, but when these two are on a mad mission, it is best simply to stand clear, close the doors and let them get on with it.

Some while after, they had peeled the whole hall and had thankfully run out of steam. Of course, all they had managed to do was peel off the top layer, the paper backing remained resolutely stuck to the wall. I knew from previous experience, this had been stuck on with a wonder-paste otherwise unknown to humans, and getting it off the wall would require at least a swimming pool load of water to soak, possibly a blow torch, even a handful of dynamite. But I am used to the fun bit being done by the women, leaving the interesting bits to me.

Monday 13 January 2003
'Baby & Children
New and Nearly New Sale'
I do not often double take when I am reading a paper, but I had to for the above advert in the local paper. These are difficult times, but how desperate must these poor people be to sell their new, and nearly new, offspring. Or perhaps they weren't theirs, perhaps this was the most overt display in human traffic yet seen in rural Hertfordshire. I did wonder what sort of guarantee these might come with, whether they came boxed and wrapped, and of course just what this might look like on your credit card bill. I don't think (and I fervently hope not) that the world is yet, or will ever be, ready for a 'Children R Us' store. In any event, the two I have is plenty, thanks very much.

Back in the house, the new bathroom is almost installed. Almost installed, in as much as the waste pipe has not been connected to the basin. This is a fact I discovered after I turned on the water, only to gaze down at the resultant dribble onto the floor, having found its way straight out of the bottom of the basin, which of course is not supposed to happen. It does if the waste pipe has not been connected.

Elsewhere, I opened the door into our bedroom, only to find a scene from a disaster movie. The entire front wall and both windows had gone, and an abyss had opened up, the whole room and roof above kept in place by a couple of grubby, rusty metal props. The room was littered with debris, but I ventured forward, edging close to the point where the floor ended, peering over and down into the unfinished ground floor below. I am getting used to dramatic film sets as part of this whole experience, but this was as realistic a scene from a natural disaster epic as I was likely to witness. I felt a pang of guilt, as I am sure those who suffer terrible storm, earthquake or falling small aircraft hitting their houses, would probably recognise the vista before them, it really did look quite devastating.

I turn and exit, leaving the cold and picture of near Armageddon behind me. I make a mental note to ensure the children are banned from the room, otherwise we are likely to have a real life disaster on our hands.

Tuesday 14 January 2003
More plastering, and more exposure of just how bad are the existing walls. Any attempt to peel off paper in some parts merely brings half the current plaster layer with it, leaving a pock marked and very unattractive surface, like a magnified poor teenager's once zit ridden face, only without the messy puss bit beforehand. Mind you, this was all pretty messy stuff and where the plaster did remain fixed to the wall it was all very tenuous – a mild sneeze would probably have sent big chunks tumbling.

This problem and the act of plastering, had created yet another coating of thick dust on everything. And when you have spent half the weekend clearing it all up only 48 hours before, you feel as if you are not so much treading water, but in fact have found you can't swim. Or have lost your life-belt and some thoughtful bastard also seems to have tied a concrete block to your legs. We have however, discovered an additional source of this problem, and a rather perverse and ironic one at that – Eddie's dustsheets. Sharon looked on in some horror this morning when he unfurled these, shook them out and placed them on the floor. In the act of doing so, the sun dimmed and the microclimate of Anstey rose by several degrees as a veritable canyon full of dust, dirt and god knows what else billowed out and was set free onto the rest of the world. There was apparently no truth in the rumour that she had also spotted both Shergar and Lord Lucan lurking in the folds, but one suspects there may be other long lost treasures within the other world that is Eddie's dustsheets. Apparently, on seeing this, Sharon offered to wash them for him, but he laughed rather manically – perhaps he is all too aware of what lurks within.

Meantime, I venture again into the Disaster Movie Film-set and find it looks much as it did yesterday. Except for the fact, there are now two familiar red steel beams, one across the top of the room where the wall and window used to be and one sitting across the floor of the opening. I decide on a little, rather precarious, experiment. The en-suite off the bedroom is housed, sorry squeezed, into a space under the extended roofline of the main house, above the hall. This means headroom is going to be limited, and of course part will be inaccessible, unless you are Cara's size. We have been hoping Richard's plans have been correct, in as much as they predict we will *just about* get a sink in this area, and be able to stand up by it, without developing a stoop, or a permanent 45 degree angle for your head, but I know Steve has serious doubts. With this area now all open and the wall gone, I reckon I can test out this theory, but it will need me to balance on the new wall that has been created from the ground floor and currently stops at first floor height. It also requires me to step on the new floor beam, and it is not until I do this, I realise it is not secured – the resultant wobble, makes me do the same and also causes the word 'shit' to issue forth from my lips. Indeed, I was probably not far away from this coming out of another orifice, as I momentarily fought to keep my balance.

Having got this far and cheated serious head injuries, I decide to continue the experiment. I stand on the wall, position myself where I think I will have to stand and rather stupidly, motion as if I was washing my hands. I must have looked a total arse, but there is always a wicked pleasure you get out of doing something totally stupid, when you know (or at least hope) no one can see you. I conclude that the sink in this position and the act of using it is possible, which is a bit of a relief, as an en-suite room without any en-suite facilities is a bit pointless.

I decide this is enough danger for the night, but then returning to the aftermath of Eddie's dustsheets in the rest of the house can hardly be classified as being without hazard.

Wednesday 15 January 2003
This seems to be the week for animal encounters, perhaps I am becoming Anstey's answer to Johnny Morris. While driving to work this morning in pitch dark, I catch two sizeable deer in my headlights in the middle of the road, but expect them to take fright and scarper off into the gloom. In fact, as I get closer, I have to slow, until I have stopped. The leading doe gently wanders across the road, not even acknowledging my presence, and pushes her way through the hedge on the side, into the field. The second one stops and slowly and deliberately looks at me. I can almost hear her saying:

"Do you mind, I have right of way here! You drivers are all the same, you just wait until I have found my way across."

And with that, she turned her head back in the direction she was heading, sauntered through the same hedge as her companion and was gone. I think I am starting to know my place in this environment.

Sunday 19 January 2003

The Nadir. The bottom of the pit of despair. No, in fact, I have found a shovel and have dug even beyond this, and have found it to be cold, dark, wet, unpleasant in the extreme, and full of disgusting bacteria. This could be the explanation for my very close acquaintance with both the downstairs toilet and the upstairs basin.

It all started quite well. I spent most of Thursday morning at Heathrow Airport, due to fly out at lunchtime, coming back on Friday night. Airports fascinate and intrigue me in equal amount. They are truly small towns in their own right, except the major form of transport in and out is by air. They contain everything you find in a small town (and plenty you don't), except that it's all internalised – the shops and cafes (and god knows there are enough of them) open out onto you with no discernible shop fronts and doorways, no real demarcation. Toilets, banks, first aid points, security and more policemen than you can shake a truncheon at, are all within close proximity at every turn and trip at the end of an escalator. Transport, meanwhile, is very externalised. Everything (as far as possible) is brought to you, rather than you having to pour over an A to Z to find it. It is as if someone has taken a major town centre, picked it up, turned it inside out, stuck all the people inside and plonked it down again. This makes it warmer, and generally rather more agreeable and comfortable than your average High Street. And since it also seems to adhere to the principle of giving the customer what he wants, rather than the customer running out of patience when no-one seems to have anything that he needs, it can be a pleasurable experience. My theory is vindicated when I find the small WH Smith in my part of Terminal 1 not only has Thursday's copy of 'Autosport' (unheard of apparently in most of East Herts), but also has a sales girl who looks at me when serving, smiles and says thank you. Now, bearing in mind that Woolworths Girls generally go to the WH Smith School of crass service and customer denigration, this was a revelation. Perhaps I should do all my shopping at Heathrow.

And in true cliché form, all human life is here, particularly, it would seem, in Terminal 1. Every conceivable age, colour and nationality is milling around, sitting, reading, chatting, ambling aimlessly, talking on mobile phones, drinking coffee, eating doughnuts, checking in, checking out, changing money, changing planes or waiting – there can be an awful lot of waiting at Airports. One very obvious element of Terminal 1, which you do not generally find in your average British Town (unless you live in Mosside) was heavily armed policemen and women. I could not quite make up my mind whether this made me feel safe or nervous, but it had the curious side effect of making me worry about the waste bin I was sitting next to. Hadn't they taken bins away from these environments for fear of some deranged follower of Bin Laden making a McDonalds look like a bomb, and placing it neatly into such welcoming receptacles? Was this a good place to sit? Hang on, did that rather swarthy middle eastern looking chap just put something in there? I actually shifted in my seat, and stood up pretending to be looking for something in my coat pocket, so I could peer down inside, presumably half expecting to find two sticks of dynamite with a clock attached with the words 'BOMB – PROPERTY OF AL QUAEEDA' written across it. In fact, the bin was nearly empty and there were just a few pieces of paper lurking not very menacingly at the bottom.

A little later, I checked through and made my way to the departure gate, passing countless people talking on their mobiles. One in particular was getting very animated, a tallish man, dressed very simply in black trousers, jacket and white T-shirt, with long dark hair and a very American accent. He was gesticulating wildly, saying:

"Honey, now listen very carefully to what I am going to tell you."

Honey then obviously speaks.

"Okay, yeah, I know, but listen now to what I am going to tell you."

I wanted to hang around and listen myself, but that would not have been appropriate I felt. It could have been anything, he could have been talking to anyone and that was equally as fascinating as what he was about to say. I was out of earshot by the time he started talking again. There is always something going on at Airports.

Passport photographs are of course a wonderful fund of humour and derision, and mine is no exception. It was taken some eight years ago when I had less grey hair, but a substantial amount more brown hair growing across my top lip. But since I was not travelling with a group of friends all of whom would unquestionably have asked to see each others passports for the sole purpose of taking the piss, I had considered the likelihood of someone pointing at my passport and guffawing loudly was pretty slim. Coming back through Heathrow on Friday night, I had failed to account for passport control who clearly had too much time on their hands, and a propensity to ridicule.

Having got through one official with no problem, just as he was handing the passport back to me, it was snatched away by another who was standing behind, looking over his shoulder.

"Are you sure that's you Sir?" he said with a chuckle

No, I am not. It is actually a doctored picture of Judith Chalmers during her particularly hirsute phase, and I get great fun out of impersonating her at Airports. I stopped myself saying this, thinking that to upset an immigration officer, especially in the current climate, would not have been an advisable career move. I decide to humour him

"Well, my wife still recognises me." I say, with just a hint of sarcasm.

He hands it back to me, already in search of his next victim.

I arrived home far too late on Friday night to investigate what had been happening in my absence, but Saturday morning brought it back into focus. The kitchen and dining area had been pretty much finished, while the hatch that previously existed from the kitchen into the dining room (now study) had been obliterated from memory. This was courtesy of some blocks, render, and a nice smooth finish of plaster – it was now a deceased serving hatch and all the better for it I thought. More woodwork had been finished in the form of architraves and skirting, while upstairs the new bathroom had its full complement of fittings, now all connected and working. This was together with a functioning heated towel rail, the output from which might quickly see the bathroom converted to a sauna, unless we had a means of adjusting its volume. In the front bedroom, the bones of the en-suite were in, beams were in place, and flooring had been completed. All of this had however created a veritable Sahara load of gritty, crunching, penetrating grey and red dust over everything.

This caused me to go into clear up overload, I simply had to do something to make life at least a little bearable for the remainder of the weekend. I then proceeded to spend most of Saturday vacuuming, wiping, dusting, changing, swearing and shouting all over the house. This in turn caused an increase in tension and tolerance levels, which led to yet more shouting and swearing. But this all stopped about five o'clock, and the events thereafter prevented us from attending a party at night. I had begun to feel nauseous and put it down to a bit of indigestion, caused by my obsessive quest to rid the house of every last speck of builders' shite. Yet by six o'clock, It was clear that my stomach was rebelling against something having been imposed upon it.

I doubt that in books on relaxation therapy, the position of being on ones knees in front of a toilet, arms crossed across the seat, head slumped on the arms, is considered one of great comfort, but believe me, in the situation where the Battle of the Somme is being replayed in your innards, it is the most blissful position possible. Of course being in the toilet also helps in taking the product of this battle, each time it erupts, although the trick is to identify which orifice to place over the toilet. Early skirmishes had seen a rear end action of some ferocity, but as time passed, I was getting very tired of pacing up and down the stairs to reach the only toilet. The climax of the tumultuous internal battle saw me stagger, in just about sufficient time, to the bathroom basin, whereupon a full frontal eruption exploded in a number of violent volleys. Thank god there was not a rearward attack at the same time, although once in France, I did have to constantly juggle my position between toilet and basin since, as the saying goes I was 'burning at both ends'. Unfortunately, both could not be fully accessed for the purpose of deposit at the same time, which rather added to the already miserable situation.

By this morning I was still a bit sticky, but the worst was over, although I was completely shot. If there is an upside to these circumstances, it is that it forces you to do absolutely nothing and I am not used to doing absolutely nothing. However, for most of the day, it was all I could do to get up off the sofa for a glass of water and watch hour upon hour of inane Sunday morning television. Although I was mildly entertained by 'The Englishman who went up a hill and came down a mountain', with Hugh Grant playing – well, Hugh

Grant really. I did also cringe at a film I remember going to see at the cinema when I was in short trousers, HG Wells 'First Man on the Moon', starring a completely over the top performance from Lionel Jeffries – which I suppose is Lionel Jeffries. By Sunday night, apart from being bored and televisioned out, I was at least very relaxed. Perhaps I should do this 'absolutely nothing' thing more often.

However, one last thing to do tonight. Friday had brought warning of the builders bringing down the last remaining boarding at the front on Monday, breaking through to the extended lounge and new bay. We should have moved everything in the lounge down to one end, and covered with sheets, but I had neither the strength or the inclination and Sharon volunteered to do the honours in the morning. Thank god for wives, I say.

Monday 20 January 2003
I have an office of a reasonable size, perhaps about twelve foot by ten foot. It has a nice, but bland, clean blue carpet, big windows, and a clear clean white wall. Access is by a large full height beech door, with a shiny stainless steel handle. I have a beech desk, which despite the fact it is frequently covered in paper and folders, not to mention laptop and printer, is kept sensibly clean and tidy. It is nothing special, but it does me pretty well. Compared to the state and space of our main living accommodation at Holly House it is a veritable palace, a cornucopia of luxury, freedom, opulence and pristine wholesomeness, a vast chamber of obscene wealth of room.

First, the good news, the boarding at the front of the lounge has finally gone, and to be able to look out over the front garden again (although we will not see daylight until the weekend) is a great relief. However, nothing is finished and where our carpet ends, here begins bare floor, block walls, exposed ceiling beams, nailed down windows, trailing wires, dangling pipes and a mini workshop of builders' tools and benches. All the furniture is shoved down one end, and covered with a combination of plastic sheets and old curtains – oh, yes, and the dust covering these. The carpet is even dirtier than I thought it could possibly look, while plaster is coming away from the walls like they have some insidious disease. We have an area immediately in front of the fire into which I might be lucky if I could fit my desk from work, and that is our living space for the time being. It is pointless retrieving all of the furniture to rearrange – not only will we have to put it all back at the end of the evening, but the act of doing this will simply release a cloud of dust of biblical proportions.

We at least want a little bit of entertainment. Although the plan is, this should be provided by the television, in fact the act of liberating the television from its hiding place at the wrong end of the room provides probably sufficient entertainment to keep a bus- load of pensioners happy. The television is wedged between the second sofa and a rather immovable bookshelf and squeezing me in beside it threatens to create a terminal blockage. I consider the prospect of being stuck in this position for the remainder of the evening and into the next morning, then waving to the builders as they enter at seven thirty the next day and asking them if they can get hold of a crowbar in order to get me out again. I manage to manoeuvre in order to get a hand under the television, but find that the video and half a dozen tapes are still sat on the lower shelf. Eventually, I manage to disconnect the video, and shove the tapes in any spare space I can find, which allows me to manhandle the set and rather ungainly thrust it over the top of the sofa, where it is helped on the remainder of its journey by Sharon. What makes this all particularly comical is I have removed my suit trousers, but nothing else. This serves to protect the trousers well being, but does nothing to preserve my modesty. I emerge with tie wrapped around my neck, shirt now a rather fetching combination of yellow with grimy grey swathes of dirt. My dark blue underpants sporting plaster skid marks on the *outside*, bare legs and black socks that have turned almost totally grey, partially out of attraction to the dust, but I suspect partially out of shock at the proceedings.

We wheel the set around to the other end of the room, and pull out the main sofa from underneath one of the dust sheets, and there we have it – instant accommodation centre. Thinking back to Christmas, I feel maybe Bob Cratchett and his family may well have found themselves in a position of considerable comfort and convenience compared to us.

Tuesday 21 January 2003

Electricity. You do not realise how much you rely on it until you haven't got it, and when you do not have gas as an alternative means, it's a real pain in the arse. At ten o'clock last night, the power rather strangely dwindled off, rather than the usual flick-off-a-switch type off you normally get with a power cut – unless of course this was not a power cut. Perhaps the whole of Anstey relies on a herd of hamsters turning their wheels, and someone had forgotten the food, so they had gradually ceased to produce enough revolutions to keep the village lit. On the other hand, our cheery friend Wally the electrician had been rumoured to have been on site Monday night, so perhaps he had mixed his positives with his negatives, or got so depressed and decided to pack it all in. Of course it could just be there was a fault and we could expect rectification within minutes.

At half past four this morning, the power returned, but the way the lights were flickering, you would not want to bet on the thing lasting much beyond half past five. At half past six, I was on the road, but Sharon rang the electricity board, who professed to be completely unaware of a problem, but promised to send someone out. I in turn rang Steve, who in turn scrambled Wally to investigate. Several hours later, the electricity board were digging up half the village, no-one had turned up at the house, and no-one had informed us that in fact, yes, it was a supply problem. So, thank you the wonderfully named TXU, which may well stand for Totally, Excruciatingly Unhelpful, which would be a much better, and more accurate slogan than there current laughable, and totally untrue, effort of 'Extraordinary Service' – extraordinary in what sense? Extraordinarily useless, I suspect.

On returning home on Thursday night, half the village (why did it have to be our half?) was in total darkness, while the air was filled with the sound of a generator assisting the good TXU people to repair the problem that apparently did not exist. Finding the way around your house without lights in normal circumstances can be a tricky business, doing so when the internals of your house have been completely rearranged is a bit of a circus act, complete with comical falls, trips, bumps and bits falling off. Moreover, when we eventually got back at nine o'clock (having taken temporary refuge at my parents), on a mid January night, the temperature was less than balmy. And there was no television. Or radio. And no light, although having fumbled our way around the place with a torch which kept going on and off like a distress beacon, we managed to find some matches to light a few candles. Nothing left to do but go to bed.

Wednesday 22 January
I thought someone had lobbed a grenade into the bedroom, such was my perception of the bright flash that occurred at about five o'clock this morning. I managed to just about stop myself from leaping out of bed and seeking refuge underneath, but you know what it's like when you are woken very suddenly, your brain reacts and passes messages to your limbs and mouth before it has had time to assimilate the reality. Whether the latter is quick enough to counteract the former is a matter of circumstance I find. So, being in my bedroom, my brain was sufficiently primed to stop me shouting

"Fuck me, the bastards are chucking bombs at us, get down!" whilst simultaneously pulling Sharon across with me and manhandling both of us under the apparent protection of the bed. This was of course a great relief, as Sharon would surely have done far greater damage to me in the event that this occurred, than any stray incendiary device might have done.

In fact, the power had snapped back on, and so had every light in the house, not to mention the clock radio, the fridge, boiler and almost every other domestic and fitted appliance in the house. Whilst for most of the past twenty-four hours we had consumed no electricity at all, we were making up for it big time now.

Returning home this evening, the kitchen fitters had made serious progress with (oddly enough) fitting the kitchen. They had started yesterday, but owing to the complete lack of illumination, we had not been able to properly survey the work thus far. However, over the last couple of days, all the base units had been fitted, the new oven installed, and some of the finishes had been completed, notably many of the doors, cornices and pelmets. My eye however was drawn to a corner wall unit and the work done to install the cornice above. One part of the cornice was clearly split, whilst the end panel immediately below was badly cut, such that the edge was littered with chips. Most disturbing though was the rather contrived looking configuration of the cornice, which should have been a simple 'external' corner, but in fact was made up of three pieces, with an odd triangular section in the middle. Either they were trying to be artistic, in which case they had failed, or they were trying to hide a cock-up, in which case they had also failed. The fit was poor, but since the simple cornicing was never meant to perform such intricate party tricks, it was hardly surprising, and it had all been badly cut and measured. Here we go again, my blood pressure rises at what is, in reality, a relatively small problem, the rectification of which is probably quite straightforward, but I just *hate* it when this happens.

We decide we will write a note, but a) no-one can read my writing at the best of times (not even me) and b) I am so cross, the pen will probably pierce the paper. I know I shall sign off with a death threat unless they get it right, so we also agree said note will be done by Sharon. This she does on luminescent yellow paper, whilst I decide I will make absolutely sure they know *exactly* what the problems are and where, by tearing off strips of the same paper, writing the defect analysis on each, and sticking in close proximity to said defect. By the time we have finished, the kitchen looks as though we had a particularly violent duel. This seems to involve the shredding of those luminous jackets worn by railway workers and policemen and I dare say if you switch the lights off, you could probably find your way around courtesy of the glow from the aftermath. I think they will probably get the message.

Saturday 25 January 2003

I am beginning to wonder if Wally has a home. Granted, if you imagined what a refugee seeking asylum from a building site might look, you would probably come up with Wally. He sports long straggly, grey flecked hair, a permanent hang-dog expression on a face fighting a losing battle against gravity, blue grubby sweatshirt, trousers of indeterminate colour, but vaguely matching the sweatshirt, and a gait that has resignation written all over it. You do feel each time you see him, you want to offer him a comfy seat and a cup of tea.

In theory, he likes to work alone, saying it's much better not to have people milling around all over the place, and there is of course the need to constantly switch the power on and off. In essence, lots of people doing lots of things with drills, saws, chisels and other sharp pointy metal instruments is not conducive to being mixed with wires with electricity coursing through. But, I like to think he also appreciates the slightly different company he gets on a Saturday and despite him telling us he will only be there 'a couple of hours', invariably he is there for most of the day. When I get back a bit later this morning, he is in usual pose, mug of tea in hand, puffing on a cigarette, looking as though he has to wire Buckingham Palace on his own and only has until eleven o'clock to do it.

"How you getting on Wally?" I chirp

As usual, I get a bit of a shrug, a knowing look, and a sigh that tells me the answer is 'not very well'.

We have a brief chat about the cooker hood now installed, but which thus far won't do an awful lot other than blow its contents back into the kitchen owing to the fact there is no flue installed through the wall. I get a slightly uneasy feeling that the kitchen fitters think the hole is going to be made by the builders, and the builders think the kitchen fitters are going to do it. The question of just who is going to break through the wall has rather more drastic implications for the sink and dishwasher waste, as failure to do anything about it will have us paddling in dishwater in very short order. Wally is wise to this:

"I've been watching this and I just knew this would happen," he drawls and cracks one of the first smiles I have seen from him. He then takes great pleasure in demonstrating that where the kitchen fitters ideally want to put the hole will foul externally on the tile hanging, and I am rather uneasy at the increasingly perverse pleasure he is getting from this unfolding difficulty. This then prompts a bit of an assassination of kitchen fitters generally ("They'll turn you over if you're not careful") and ends with the sentence:

"They just haven't fuckin' looked have they?" I note this is the first swear word I have heard any of the builders utter.

Still, he gets on with what he is doing, disappearing into all parts of the house and spending a lot of time in the loft. Now, I have not been into the loft since we loaded some additional stuff more than a week ago, and I revisit my thought that Wally might be looking for a home. Okay, he has his van, but this in is the sort of state only a builders van could be. Whether its natural colour is white or rust, I am not sure. Externally I am worried that if you try to use one of the handles in a conventional fashion, like a clowns car from the circus, explosions would happen, smoke would burst from various points, and everything would fall off rather ungraciously. In the meantime, every conceivable space within is crammed with boxes and bits of electrical fitments and wires, all seemingly coated in a large helping of grease and general dirt. In short, I am surprised it can perform its primary function of transportation, let alone considering the prospect of being transformed as a part time caravan. So, perhaps when I next make the trip up the ladder of impossibility, I will find a magical loft conversion and a tatty sign reading 'Chez Wally'.

Meantime, I can report that the kitchen has moved on, with the worktops now largely in place, although intrigued by the long row of crocodile clips down one of the exposed sides of the breakfast bar. These turn out to be clamps, holding on a very thick edge piece which is being stuck all along one side. At the same time, blue adhesive is squeezing out along its length, as it is where the three worktops join at the two corners. The colour and texture of this looks strangely like Sian and Cara have been at work, let loose with their paint tubes, and indeed the overall mess on the floor left by the fitters would do justice to either bedroom. Still, I can't deny it is starting to look good, although I am reluctant to suggest that I can see light at the end of the tunnel – this could simply be, in the words of David Brent, some bastard with a torch, bringing me more work.

Sunday 26 January 2003
Our friends have come to the rescue again, and have offered us food and clean shelter as a welcome respite to the troubled environment of Holly House. These friends, my very good friends, are those whose kinship dates back to school days, and, not for the first time, we got onto the subject of early gallic experiences.

Madamoiselle Prunerais was a French bit-of-stuff who didn't even speak particularly good English. She was short, trim (up to the point that her stomach began to bulge as a result of impregnation – who was responsible for that?), dark haired with omnipresent dark glasses to match, strict and a total exhibitionist.

Ask any of my old school friends about her even today, and their reactions will all be the same – knowing chuckle and grin, barely concealed twinkle in the eye, followed slowly by a quizzical 'if only' look. Their abiding memory and vision will be a duplicate of my own.

Scene: Classroom – the usual assortment of gnarled and hacked wooden desks in neat rows, attended by a dishevelled and amorphous grouping of the schoolboy species – odorous, maybe odious, but generally oblivious. The ways of the world, let alone female French teachers, had not yet permeated the chubby pink flesh of these naive pupils.

Atmosphere: Tense – fear and anticipation is a heady and emotional cocktail, but when Mme Prunerais stood erect (unfortunate adjective) at the front of the class, tapping her knuckles with the board duster, spitting instructions with a rasping French accent, you knew if something wasn't happening then, it sure as hell would soon.

Players: The aforementioned assembled menagerie of pre-pubescent youth and Mme P herself. My thesaurus suggests I call her an indelicate pedagogue – I think gallic sadist with a penchant for short skirts and the most ridiculous frilly knickers would be a more apt description. And all of this in a boys' school.

Act 1: Mme. P is spouting forth in her usual sharp manner, with the rather flawed intonation that some continentals possess when speaking English, probably about the use of masculine and feminine nouns. While doing so she is walking slowly and deliberately up one of the aisles between the desks.

At this point it is imperative to appreciate the average level of an 11 year old boy's head while sitting at a desk corresponds quite neatly with the level of a short female French teacher's bum. Some may be at a higher level, but mercilessly none were below (unless your name was Gibson, in which case you deliberately sought to adopt this position, despite the fact that retribution was swift and painful)

The result of this obscure equation was a ripple effect, starting from the front row, of heads turning in unison, eyes transfixed to Mme. P's nether quarters, craning until the crack of individual neck bones was audible. Simultaneously, the scribbling of French prose onto exercise book was a secondary, but continuing function, resulting in entries looking as if they had been made by a drunken spider. Many a 'merci' or 'bonjour' trailed inadvertently onto the desk itself. The odd pen nib even went so far as to exit both paper and wood, spearing the unfortunate child's leg, accompanied by a barely stifled yelp of anguish.

Act2: Mme. P halts her progress and surveys the scene, her punishing diatribe continuing. Her gaze darts around the room for a suitable victim, but invariably it falls on the poor wretch at whose desk she stops. Given the height differential in this situation, other people would stoop to converse with (or in this case berate) the hapless boy. Not Mme P. – her upper body would crank down to form a perfect right angle at her waist, the effect of which was to perform a barley latent act of self exposure, especially given the factors of short skirt etc. This display was often accentuated by inexplicably engaging with the pupil furthest from her, access to whom would have been more easily gained from the next aisle.

Snap! Picture of frilly-knickered French bum atop pair of short legs, in a crowd of sweaty boys, framed and hung on the wall of our memory banks. The impression still is timeless and palpable, and it is one of the most vivid memories of the earliest days at secondary school. And it never fails to produce the most enormous collective sigh.

Where once a toilet sat, a new mysterious doorway has materialised….

…and once opened reveals a pandoras box of drying plaster and washing

Looking into the new kitchen extension, which thankfully no longer gives you a queasy picture of yellow and green. The strange item wrapped in foil is the obligatory Christmas Turkey, which gives you an indication of the ambient temperature.

The dining area of the rear extension, prior to any underfloor heating, hence the rather forlorn little convector, doing its damndest to keep temperatures slightly above Arctic conditions

Sian in the utility, which was the kitchen, and at this point still was. Using the washing machine as a worktop was a challenge that required skills and dexterity only known to world class jugglers, particularly if it was on a fast wash programme.

The new kitchen area – minus kitchen

Christmas 2002 – the tree stands defiant against all the odds, not to mention the sheets of polythene

Sharon looks remarkably chuffed by one of those presents you never knew you wanted – she must have been on the gins particularly early. Notice the novel use of the plywood wall for decorations

….and a closer look at the at the most novel use of plywood ever conceived – if you can tear yourself away from the site of Cara exploring her nasal orifice

Both Sian and I have reached the conclusion that Cara has finally been tipped over the edge by our plight

Cara looks perplexed, I look totally out of it – which about summed up Christmas Day

Shabby Chic a la Anstey – another doorway appears

Arthur, the Trojan worker, and all round good guy – not sure if he is surprised at having his photo taken, or just shocked at the colour of the walls

Believe it or not, this did eventually become a working toilet in a usable bathroom

Daylight breaks through as the original external wall from our bedroom comes down, and the old window awaits its grisly fate

**The (maroon) big plastic thing is the remains of one
of life's mysteries – the unusable shower**

**Oh how we mourned the passing of the plywood barrier – not!
The new bay is opened up to the room – note Winnie continues to look
rather depressed and somewhat comatose on the settee**

**And we have light at the other end, which in this shot allows you just a
small view of the crazy paved fireplace – any more than this would be
hazardous**

A hall with (some) space, light – and exposed joists and blockwork

The new kitchen, and a new use for bulldog clips

Snow comes to Anstey – it would be Christmassy if it weren't for the fact that it's well into January

The old well looks suitably picturesque – as long as you don't pan left and catch Holly House in mid build

East Hertfordshire is calm and tranquil in a coat of white

Banished from the lounge this now becomes the builders workshop, the floor soon to become an ideal place to mix plaster

There's that bollard again – men at work, or drunk in charge?
Look carefully at the prophetic message on the small sign propped
by the stairs

June 2003 – builders have gone, but dancemania continues. The school wins the overall competition in Guildford, but I stay sensibly behind the camera (unlike the wife)

We're done – the back

**The front – unfortunately, the garden now needs some attention.
Any volunteers?**

Monday 27 January 2003
We seem to be back to marking time again. The kitchen looks no different to how it looked this morning, while the rest of the house has seemed in suspended animation for almost a week, although we have another layer of dust, so I must surmise something has been happening today. I am told by Richard he expects the builders to be gone within two, possibly three, weeks, but I think on balance, it might be safer if I place any money on Wally being the Messiah.

A recap perhaps on where we are may either persuade me that we are not so far away from completion, or it may drive me to spend the next month in habitation in the shed behind the oil tank. And in some parts of the house there are similarities in décor and ambience.

The utility has remained pretty much unchanged, and continues to be the only room in the house where we can cook and wash, all within a space large enough to swing a cat, providing it is tucked firmly under one arm. One wall remains delightfully unplastered and pock marked, like the inside of a somewhat insalubrious cave, while a thick grey wire continues to trail across the back wall to the cooker. The very 1960's fluorescent light has gone after it developed a fit about a week ago, during which it flickered on and off like a manic disco system, or at least like the manic disco systems that used to be all the rage when I frequented discos. Thankfully, I managed to stop myself from seeking out my flares, platform shoes and multicoloured tank top, giving my own, very personal, rendition of 'Staying Alive', and anyway, I always find the presence of a sink, cooker and fridge rather cramps your style when attempting to boogie. The floor of the utility is constantly filthy owing to the large amount of traffic, owing to it being the only realistic route in and out of the house. Indeed, the amount of activity during the day can often be roughly judged by the level of grime implanted on the floor and the length of time it takes us to restore to some degree of cleanliness at the end of the day.

The kitchen and dining area are pretty much finished as far as the builders are concerned, although we wait to see how effective our under-floor heating will prove to be. I have to confess, the concept of this worries me a little. As one who has on more than one occasion, become externally scarred by overzealous radiators, but still marvelled at the fact that unless you are standing within two microns of it, the general temperature of the room still requires you to wear seven layers of clothing, I am baffled as to how the room can be generally warmed through a surface I must walk upon. Unless the system comes with instructions on how to walk across hot coals like a mystic tribal leader from the Amazonian rainforest, I fear I may be in a bit of trouble. That aside, the kitchen itself remains tantalisingly close to completion and we also await the arrival of G. G can only be described as a Geezer, and I swear Paul Whitehouse must have studied him when looking to research his take on such a character for The Fast Show. G is our floor tiling man, who has 'done us a bit of a deal' (in which you must pronounce the 'l' in deal like a 'w') on the tiles of our choice, and promises he will come and fit them as of tomorrow. He can not only talk for England, but could happily take on the role for the rest of the UK and Europe. About G I can say no more, other than the anticipation of his activity is at fever pitch.

While the study remains as it has done for many weeks, the hall has now been extended, as, joy of joys, the front door has been consigned to what I hope is the furnace from hell. And we are now open to our new improved space and door – except in this extended area, no floor exists, the walls remain in exposed block and there is no heating. It also seems to be a useful storage spot for piping, pieces of wood, and what looks like an evil new weapon the Klingons might have added to their armoury in order to finally rid themselves of the intensely irritating Jean Luc Picard (bring back Kirk I say). A long plastic pipe and nozzle, backed by a hefty steel shaft and brace, it might be just as effective if you simply slapped old Picard round the chops with it, rather than fiddling about and setting it to super stun. I suspect in reality it was a mastic gun, used to seal annoying little gaps – can't quite make this match the crew of the Enterprise, but I am sure there is a gag there somewhere.

The lounge is an unremitting shit-hole. While the French windows and door to the dining area are in at one end, all the other walls are a pretty awful confection of peeled wallpaper. Wallpaper that simply won't shift (largely in view of the fact it seems to consist of industrial strength blown polystyrene stuck on with Super-glue). lingering lining paper, plaster dangling precariously from the wall, gaping holes and marks where the plasters desire to cling has been overtaken by the simple physics of gravity, substantially aided by the fact that the walls seem to have been plastered by someone who probably had skills and application, but sadly not in the art of plastering walls. The carpet now looks worse than the one we pulled up and threw away in disgust, before we moved in. But this runs out at the point of the new extension at the front, which, like the hall, is in its raw state and is also used as a staging post for all manner of tools and materials. If you were to pan across with a camera in the lounge, you would finally see this area revealed, like the back of a stage set, not meant to be seen in shot, complete with workmans' bench and floodlights. The latter is necessary as we do not have any light in the lounge, which could have something to do with the piece of wire dangling from a hole in the ceiling, just above the current light switch. Meantime, most of the furniture is pushed down to the end by the French windows. This is covered in a variety of plastic sheets and old curtains, leaving our little grubby patch between, where the grotesque crazy paved fireplace chuckles at us as we sit grim faced in the only living space we have at present.

Upstairs, the current bathroom remains as an obscure adjunct to the entrance to the new bedroom, where the window frame sits in place still waiting patiently for a window to fill it. The grubbiness of this room is demonstrated by the aftermath of taking a bath, where, once the water has struggled its way down the plughole, you are left with a pile of silt large enough to make your own sandcastle. Next door, all the fitments for the bathroom are teasingly in place, but cannot be used. Partially, this is because the new window has not yet been formed, but is also because we have discovered the pressure available from the hot and cold water tanks would be hard pressed to move a ping pong ball, let alone fill a bath or make the shower work. Indeed, the pressure is so pathetic, the little diverter that you pull up to move water away from the spout to the shower head will not stay up, and even if you hold it up yourself, the resulting dribble out of the shower head wouldn't even do justice to a teething baby.

The new bedroom remains occupied by Sharon and myself, but is a multimode space – in other words it has more personalities and uses than a Swiss army knife. As well as sleeping space, it is games storage space, clothes storage, ironing and general laundry room, Cara's dumping ground, and general contemplation arena, staring across the fields at the back and wondering if life will ever return to normality. It remains in its complete, but unfinished state, and Cara is already planning her décor, which in its intended pinkness, might even make Lady Penelope choke a bit.

Sian has a knowing smirk, as her room has remained pretty much untouched, save for some plaster falling off the wall around her window, a result of preparation work externally in readiness for her new window. However, the smirk was rather wiped off her face this evening, as she came home to find an apology note from the builders, who had taken up her carpet and floorboards in order to access and move the light in the study downstairs into the middle of the room. The apology note was in view of the fact that either they could not, or would not, reinstate her books and other personal paraphernalia, all left rather rudely dumped on the floor. This merely attracted a very teenage "Hmmppphhh!" together with a bit of mumbling, but no lasting damage appears to have been done, either physically or mentally. I think she realises her privileged position in matters of personal space during the last four months.

Cara remains shoehorned into the spare room, but I still cannot work out how someone so small can create so much mess. Indeed, if you did not know where Cara resided, it would be a very simple exercise to discover. Simply follow the trail of clothes (mostly, but not exclusively of the worn and dirty variety), Paper (dead give away this, as it usually has hearts, or pictures of what Cara perceives to be a 'cool girl' drawn on it), Pens, the odd bit of jewellery, crumpled pyjamas and (usually at one or other end of this trail) Pooh Bear. Other than this, the overwhelming pink hue that emanates from her room is also a rather large clue. In truth, she is in the most unsatisfactory of conditions, sharing her room with a computer and its desk, a keyboard, and a shocking red colour painted on the windows and door, both of which will thankfully be banished to the skip in the very near future. This clashes dreadfully with the harem like crimson coloured bed canopy.

As for our bedroom, it has now been for some time an internal building site. Again the front extension has been opened up, preceded by a large beam that dips alarmingly below normal ceiling level, but at least the walls and ceiling of this area are close to completion, with plastering almost complete. The en-suite is largely formed and having now genuinely stood at the 'virtual' basin, I can confirm, I will be able to stand up, although my head will become extremely intimate with the sloping ceiling in the process. There seems to be some head scratching on the position of the shower, and what to do with the hot water tank, which is now exposed to reveal all the pipes and valves surrounding it. In fact, the whole room looks like they spend a lot of time in here scratching their heads, a room for builders' contemplation, amidst boxes of sockets and light switches, pipes and pipe connectors, wood of all shapes and sizes, doors, cables, benches, bits of plasterboard. And still neatly wrapped in their boxes, the shower tray, the shower system and the shower door. We should, however, not mention the shower door, as it caused me to swear at the suppliers and incited me to write a very snotty fax – twice. It took eight weeks from order rather than the four promised, and please someone explain to me why it is *me* who has to chase *them* to find out what the hell is happening, and not just once, but *five* times. The last straw was when the dozy muppet at the sharp end, aka 'Daayve' *promised* (honestly he did, he *promised*, I even wrote it down), he would phone me back at ten to five that evening to let me know when I could definitely expect delivery. When this did not happen (and this was not the first time that 'Daayve' had been less reliable than a rail timetable), I fired off a fax to the Manager of said store, to inform him a) his staff were crap, b) his store was crap, c) his concept of customer service seemed to fall short of normal expectation. No-one seemed to know what a customer was, and almost certainly could not even spell 'service'. Surprisingly, this produced a phone call from 'Mick', during which I kept my hand close to my mouth for fear my brain would force my mouth to swear. Two days later, the shower door arrives, but why does it have to be this painful?

So there we have it, a comfortable, spacious, pristine abode -sorry, there I am again, living in fantasy land.

Tuesday 28 January 2003
G the Geezer. What shall we do with him? Well, if he were here right now, Sharon would probably head for the kitchen to find the biggest, sharpest knife she could, in order to separate his body from his limbs. Actually, no, she would get more pleasure from physically tearing him apart with her own hands. Her fears about his reliability and lack of propensity to do what he says he is going to do, seem to be materialising. Without replaying the saga of the tile supply, he had promised to start today. In fact, he phoned me yesterday to enquire if he could start a day early. No problem, I say. But we have no sign

of any activity whatsoever. It is not often that Sharon gets cross and shouts through gritted teeth, so I surmise she really is not very happy with his non-appearance.

Somehow, this has an air of inevitability about it, so I am calm. We will have words with the Geezer tomorrow. We might also have words with the kitchen fitters tomorrow as well. They should have been finished yesterday, and although the kitchen has the look of completion, this is not the case. Neither have they rectified the problems so kindly pointed out by ourselves in unmissable fashion. But perhaps most irritatingly, word from the builders that they are both lazy and very untidy, seems to be borne out by the mess. Fag packets and half empty drinks bottle in the study, sawdust and general kitchen fitters crap all over the kitchen floor and worst of all, evidence they have enjoyed a nice few cups of tea, leaving clues the size of the Albert Hall. I have no objection to them making a cup of tea, but when they leave the sort of mess to even shock my kids, you begin to wonder about their general attitude, demeanour and ability. We can deduce this from the sugar packet left wide open to the elements, ditto the box of tea bags, but more telling are the four empty and dirty mugs on the top of the washing machine, across which is a rather large slick of spilt tea, nicely congealing over the surface.

Having lived with my builders for four months, I know this is not their work. I just hope it is not an indication of the thought and application gone into fitting the kitchen.

Wednesday 29 January 2003
"Hello" I say, as straight and stony faced as I can muster, which isn't very difficult as I am feeling very stony faced. "Where's G?" I continue, in a manner which clearly says I may not know where G is, but I definitely know where he is not. He is not at my house.

"Is he not at yours?" says the lady behind the desk in a pretty unconvincing display of innocence and confusion. I fix her eyes.

"No."

What I really want to say is that G is a shister, a liar and has the business acumen and customer service skills of a retarded hamster. Indeed, he and my shower supplier would make a wonderful combination, blitzing the market in a whirlwind of broken promises and overall uselessness. They would go far.

"I'll give him a call, and see where he is?" The quizzical look she now had was marginally better than the original flannel, but it was hardly an Oscar performance. Nicole Kidman has nothing to fear from this particular Hertfordshire resident. She picks up the phone and dials, G answers.

"G I've got Mr Neale here, wondering why you are not at his house?" Some conversation follows, after which she turns to me and says, "G didn't think he was due at yours today."

"What bollocks!" Okay, I didn't say that, but it was a close call as to whether the rational signal from my brain reached my mouth before the emotional one, but the former did so by virtue of a brave overtaking move at the final bend, that saw the 'bollocks' word crashing off before the finish. Shame, it wouldn't half of shaken up the staff and customers.

"G asked if he could start on Monday, but was in any event due to start yesterday and here we are at Wednesday." I am remaining calm. Terse, but calm.

"G," she says to the phone "Mr Neale says you were due to start yesterday." Pause. He is probably telling her to stall me, or perhaps spin a line that his dog ate his overalls this morning, and what with his piles playing up as well, he just has not quite managed to make it today. "Do you want to speak to him?" She hands me the phone.

"Hello Alan," he says in his geezer voice "Sorry about this, but I think we might have a bit of a mix up." I replay the story of his statement that he could start a day early, but was due to start yesterday.

"G, if I am cross, it is nothing compared to Sharon who would have torn you limb from limb last night." This doesn't quite seem to have the impact I thought it would. Either he is thick, or thick-skinned, I suspect both.

"Well, we decided on balance not to start Monday as you thought we might be in the way of the kitchen fitters."

"G, they are gone."

"Well, I thought my team had finished this other job and might have started by now, but we seem to have a bit of a communication breakdown."

"It's a bit of a cock-up all round really isn't it?" This was of course a rhetorical question.

"Bit of a communication breakdown between us." No communication breakdown on my side G, just a simple case of a tosser trying to get the best of me. "We should be able to get up there tomorrow."

" I certainly hope so." I say on terseness overdrive.

"Yeah, that shouldn't be a problem." Many proverbs cross my mind, including one involving pigs and flying. But I try and quell my cynicism.

"Right, we'll see you tomorrow," and I hand the phone back before he can think of another excuse. "Thank you, goodbye." I say to the lady and walk purposefully out of the shop. "Tosser!" I mumble under my breath.

This was the climax of a bad lunchtime, having dropped in at the house to find no G, and no kitchen fitters. On the kitchen front, Steve then showed me what a poor job he thought they had done, done being the operative word, as they clearly thought they had finished. None of the faults had been corrected, whilst I was also shown that without much effort, it was possible to lift the worktop underneath the window – handy if you can't be bothered to open the drawer underneath to place things into, but it was not the preferred means of access. Steve's view of the kitchen fitters was clearly on a par with their propensity to create a mess. Thank god for Steve and his gang, as I do not think I could have stood a trio of tossers at this point. I phone Terry to advise that his fitters appear to have buggered off without finishing the job. He listens dispassionately and says he will visit tomorrow. Please Terry, do not do a G impersonation, as violence will almost certainly be the end result and we really do not want blood over what I hope will be nice new tiles as of tomorrow. Whatever the God of Hope, they receive our fervent prayers.

Thursday 30 January 2003

A call from G, I recognise the number before I answer my mobile. I draw a deep breath. What excuse is he going to give me? Floods in Buntingford, specifically outside his shop, preventing him getting to any appointments? I don't think he has the intelligence to be quite so inventive.

"Hello," I answer with deep anticipation

"Hello Alan, it's G," in usual geezerese

"Yeah, I've been up at the house where the boys are laying the tiles in the kitchen and its looking good, but I wanted to talk to you about the floor in the utility."

I put my hands up to my mouth. I so really want to say something biting and rude, but I decide to listen

"Mmmm?"

"Well, you know the wooden floor behind the new screeded floor in the kitchen, well it has a bit of a spring in it, and Steve says he was waiting for the Architect to give him a solution, but I asked whether they could put a bit of a joist support, sort of thing, underneath, but they don't think that can be done, but I don't think its too much of a problem. We've got some flexible adhesive, I just wanted to see if we could do anything to make absolutely sure, but I don't think it will be a problem, you know."

I feared this. The old floor is a strange construction of floorboard on top of polystyrene, on top of concrete, which means it does indeed have a bit of give and immediately behind the new solid floor in the kitchen, there is a clear difference and a bit more movement than seems healthy. This has been pointed out by me (twice), the builders (at least twice), and the architects. I *really, really* want to say something rude now. I am also certain he is lying about Steve telling him that Richard was meant to come up with a solution. G has said previously it is not a problem.

"You are a liar, a tosser of humungous proportions, and breathtakingly eloquent in your command of bollocks-talk." I *so* want to say this, it pains me to know I can't.

"G." I start, very deliberately, "you have seen and surveyed the floor on at least two occasions, the problem with the floor has been pointed out to you a number of times and we have asked you to confirm this does not present a problem. You have confirmed that it doesn't!"

"No, it should be okay, I just……..." I lose interest, we simply replay the same conversation three times. Why he thinks telling me what he has already told me will suddenly make me change my mind, I really do not know. Perhaps he really thinks I will say, "You know, G you're right, it could be a problem and you could not possibly have foreseen it. You do the best you can, if it all goes horribly wrong, well C'est la vie."

After we have agreed he will use his magic flexible adhesive, all will be fine and the kitchen area will be pretty much done by tonight, I phone Steve.

"He is a shister," says Steve, so we're in perfect harmony there. "Lovely bloke, but he does talk bollocks." A man after my own heart is Steve.

Later, very much later, I get home. The reason for my late arrival is a natural phenomena that only the British seem to regard as calamitous and for which we are always so badly prepared, you would think it only happens about as often as a nice letter from the Inland Revenue – snow. While the rest of Europe and probably the world, take it in their stride, disruption to a minimum, for us it's like putting a stick through the spokes of your bike and the resultant arse over tit accident is replicated on every road. It is both a mystery and a wonder. Cars abandoned in the road, across the road, back end stuck out of a ditch, people wandering around while in queues of traffic vainly expecting to see into the distance as to the cause of the hold up. More than likely the cause of the hold up is some idiot who got out of his car while sat in a queue of traffic. It takes me two hours of careful driving, allied to some neat slalom skills between discarded cars, vans and even, bizarrely, a breakdown truck.

When I do get home, apart from the temperature requiring even brass monkeys to put on an extra layer, I discover to my surprise G has indeed been, or at least some of his tilers have been. Even more to my surprise, it looks rather good. Unfortunately for us, if we are to be certain of getting him back again (that is discounting the tactic of re-entering his shop with a shotgun under my arm), we must clear the utility. While on the one hand, this is a simple job of moving out the appliances that have made it their temporary home, on the other hand, it also requires us to rip up what remains of the repulsive and badly laid laminate floor. Given the time, we are not going to make much progress tonight, but we start to have a go, just to see what sort of job we have on our hands tomorrow night. In fact, the stuff turns out to be totally plastic, with a dreadful little plastic veneer of fake wood, and while it might be dreadfully tacky in style and quality, it was also particularly tacky in a literal sense, as the glue used to stick them down would probably have held a Sherman tank dangled from the ceiling. Having ruined an old kitchen knife and found even a paint scraper whimpering at the exertion, we give up for the evening. The side benefit of this effort has been to make me warm, even start to sweat, but somehow, I can't quite see the upside of this at the moment.

Friday 31 January 2003

It may be disruptive, but there is no doubting the beauty snow can bring to a landscape. On one level, just coating everything with a liberal layer of pure, brilliant, sparkling white seems to calm and smooth even the most jarring scenery, urban or rural, like a metaphorical dose of tranquillisers. On another, it is nature's inspirational sculptress, forming voluptuous arcs and knolls, perfectly tapering swells and swooping hollows and peaks, regardless of topography or barrier. Trees and hedges are transformed into statues of gleaming petrified jewels, fields have a sugar coated frosting, and all is still and peaceful, shimmering this morning in a dazzling sun set low within a delicate, clear sapphire sky.

Amidst this backdrop, I venture to try and make my way to work. My first attempt sees me slithering my way towards Buntingford, only to discover around one bend the aftermath of a special effects scene from a blockbuster disaster film. Two cars are in the ditch to my left, one at forty-five degrees, its back end and wheels dangling helplessly above the road. Just beyond there is a car and a van at strange angles, sprawled across the road, but somehow in harmony, as if they lost traction and skated along in unison. Adjacent is a bus, at a slightly tilting angle, which I suspect has edged itself into the ditch on the other side of the road. All vehicles have been long since abandoned, and in the meantime snow has built up all around this impromptu car park, creating a ghostly road block, with just a few wisps of white blowing off the top of the bus. Thankfully, a small access road leads off to my left at this point and gives me just enough space to turn around and try a different route. I eventually make it in nearly two hours later, passing innumerable vacant, half buried, rather sorry looking cars.

Back at the house, putting aside the difficulties of tilers and kitchen fitters, a lot of work is being done as we enter the home stretch of maybe the last two or three weeks. The new bathroom window, or at least the opening for it, is formed, although at present this consists of a bloody big hole, some sheeting and a couple of cross timbers to keep everything in place. While the new bathroom door is on, it still means on a bitterly cold night, the new bathroom would double as one of those large butchers walk in fridges and the arctic conditions in here are tending to permeate the rest of the house. Steve has also completed what he freely admits was the job he was anticipating with the least relish – moving the hot water tank, and reconfiguring the piping. This has actually been less traumatic than imagined, as it has only been necessary to move it all a relatively short distance, and has been done all in a day, so the prospect of no heating or hot water for a few days has not materialised. My god, something has turned out to be better than expected!

However, the nature of the walls in the lounge and an aching desire to get rid of the artex wherever possible, has led to a very expensive decision. Whilst the original contract anticipated finishing of the new works, this would have left us in a situation where we had good plaster finishes solely in the front extension and around the new doors at the rear of the lounge. This would have been the wholesome bread in a sandwich of unedifying shoddiness, as more and more plaster fell off the walls. I did not fancy the prospect of only showing guests into either end of the lounge and them thinking we were complete nutters for keeping them away from the middle, for fear at any given time, a chunk of the wall might come crashing to the floor. And I certainly did not have the skills to do any repair work myself. There was also the problem of extreme embarrassment caused by a probable botch job on the plaster, and the horror that may ensue should people think we actually wanted to keep our artex. This may finger us as some weird 60's retro freaks and have friends scurrying out of the house as quickly as they could. So we had agreed to allow the builders to completely strip off the old plaster in the lounge, tack the ceiling with plasterboard, and re-plaster both walls and ceilings, while they would also work to do the same to the ceilings in the hall, landing and two of the bedrooms upstairs. This all came at a price, and one a bit more than a few tins of beans, or even a few tins of paint.

Saturday 1 February 2003
Wally is back with us again, but we are beginning to feel quite comfortable with each other now, while I am also appreciating his desire to do the job right. Having already put up the lights for us in the kitchen and dining area, which he clearly had no need to do, he is now doing the same in the utility. In order to do this, he is also moving the position of the light, as in its original state it was in approximately the middle of the old kitchen, but given the complete change to the internal layout, it now sits almost hard up against the side wall. That's fine if you want to do all your laundry and other utility type things (in my experience, the utility becomes the dumping ground for things that appear to have no discernible home) squashed into the far corner. It would also be very disorientating to see the light in the rear corner of the room when entering, I can almost see people stepping back and losing balance while they figure out if the room is some optical illusion. Wally is also busy sorting out extractor fans in any room that might have even the merest hint of moisture in the air, so this particularly covers the bathroom, downstairs toilet and en-suite. Now, I can see the need for one in the downstairs loo, or rather my nose will often bear testimony to the need to get air out of this room as soon as possible, the alternative being the issuing of gas masks on entry. My family seem to indicate I am the greatest perpetrator of this need, but Sian is the undisputed champion in the foul smelling gas stakes – how someone so small can produce something so momentous, is a little scientific conundrum that I tend not to dwell upon. However, removing moist air (or indeed air carrying anything remotely undesirable) from the two other rooms can be accomplished rather quicker and easier by another means – opening the window. This is however far too simplistic for Building Regulations, something I think must be dreamt up by a roomful of people with a strange obsession to make life as difficult and rigid as practically possible. I think they must be remunerated on the basis of how many obstacles they can put in the way of a straightforward and commonsense route.

A little later in the morning, I receive a telephone call from Terry, he of the Kitchen suppliers and fitters. I have already reached the conclusion that much of what Terry does is subcontracted to others, which is fine, unless your subcontractors are untidy, work-shy morons. Given my experience with G the Geezer, or indeed the Shower that supplied the shower, I expect a bit of an argument, perhaps a suggestion I am imagining the problems, or I am exaggerating. At least my lungs are getting a good workout, as, yet again, I draw another deep breath before conversing. But in fact, Terry runs through our list of problems and details they will all be sorted, he wants to ensure it is all cleared up next week. Oh, okay. What, no story, no fib, no deceit? I am almost disappointed, and a little stunned, so much so it is not until I have put the phone down I realise I did not get an apology. Perhaps that is expecting too much.

Cara was insisting I be dragged out for a walk in the afternoon, we witnessed snow can disappear almost as quickly as it can materialise, with ditches, streams and gullies all over the village becoming mini raging torrents of dirty water and debris. But still much of the snow remained, and at some of the field edges, drifts deep enough to see most of Cara and my legs vanish, causing hilarity with daughter, and wet foot for father. Melting snow is in the starkest contrast to a new fall, there are few things more ugly, invasive and utterly inescapable than dirty, brown rivers of slush. Thank goodness for wellies.

While otherwise occupied this afternoon, I discover the remainder of the family on hands, knees and arses, trying to wrench up the remainder of the floor covering in the utility, with a variety of paint scrapers, pallet knifes and grunts. I venture in to find out progress, only to discover that whatever glue stuck this hellish stuff to the floor, has remained wedded to the floor rather than the tiles, and now threatens to trap the entire family in the room for eternity, such is its ability to hold on to its prey. I am sure the last time I witnessed an adhesive substance like this was on the floor of the cinema at Harlow. As it is, Sharon has considerable difficulty removing backside from floor, while Cara and Sian eventually remove their feet like extracting themselves from a floor laden with thick sticky toffee. I make the mistake of kneeling down in shorts for a while to survey the scene, only to discover the floor makes a wonderful hair remover, nearly taking the skin with it, as I yelp on standing up. It would not surprise me in the least if we were to discover the tiles had been laid with Immac.

Tuesday 4 February 2003
Today has a certain symmetry about it. It's my birthday, and I am 44, that's pretty symmetrical. It has also started to snow again, like last Thursday, and like last Thursday, I am having a shite day, so that's a bit more substantial symmetry. In the first part of the day, the trouble is all down to work, but I have vowed not to feature my job in this tome. So I will park those problems,

although I will do so in the style of someone crashing into the back of their garage in a fit of rage.

Related to the house, we have had bestowed upon us a matter which I consider to be the cruellest of irony, which had me putting my head in both my hands, and saying over and over again:

"Shit, shit, shit!"

You will recall, I fought the equivalent of Custer's last stand in finally getting the shower door sourced and delivered within anything approaching a reasonable timescale, and breathed an enormous sigh of relief when it finally found its way to Anstey in one piece. Since then, it has been sitting quietly in the new bathroom, awaiting its triumphal transference to the en-suite. It also, incidentally, cost more than you can imagine a simple glass shower door should cost, but simply seems to have been a function of the amount of effort expended to get it delivered.

However, it doesn't fit. The width, which I have to confess was the only dimension I had concerned myself with, was fine, but it had not crossed my simple brain that its height would be a problem. In fact, it would not have been a problem if there had not been a dirty great beam that now crosses the bedroom and en-suite, in order to support the new extension. The height of this, and its position dictates the current door will foul and will therefore bar entry into said shower. Ergo, current shower door is about as useful as the proverbial chocolate fireguard, only a damn sight more expensive. I want to cry, I *really* want to cry, but this is not an edifying site in a man, particularly one sitting in a meeting at three o'clock on a Tuesday afternoon. So having increased my blood pressure to danger levels in getting the door conveyed and into my position, I have now got to suffer the ignominy of sending it back again. Not only that, but as I have already accepted it, returning it will cost me twenty five percent of its cost. That will be the most expensive piece of ridiculous masochism I am ever likely to suffer.

Driving home later, there is a perfect crescent moon playing hide and seek behind the tall gangly branches of the trees lining my route as I cross back into Hertfordshire. The sky has a faint but deep purple tinge which blends into orange as it meets the horizon, while a number of feathery clouds scuttle silently across the scene. A little further on, a car is stopped on the other side of the road in what seems to be a strange position and as I get closer, I have to swerve to miss what looks like a flapping carpet on my side of the road. As I do this, I realise it is a large Deer, struggling to get up, but clearly unable to do so, I wince in realisation that car and Deer have had a probable fatal coming together. There is nothing I can do but feel sorry, and I continue on my way. What a terrible juxtaposition of beauty and tragedy. Just a minute later, the news comes on the radio, and recounts the sombre memorial service for the crew of the Space Shuttle disaster. Immediately following the news, an Elvis Presley song is played, and he met his maker more than twenty-five years ago. My problems seem pale and insignificant next to all of this, my own little negatives add up to very little.

On top of all of this, I am heaped full of positives as I get home. The lights are all off and as I walk in, I am met with a resounding chorus of 'Happy Birthday', and a bucket load of hugs. I barely notice the fact that more tiling has been done on the kitchen floor, as a bottle of wine is opened and a glass shoved into my hand. Dinner has been all prepared and I have just enough time for a bath before eating. At this, Cara disappears, I find her a few minutes later running my bath, and as I am ready to enter she stands in best attendant's pose, towel over arm.

"Your bath is ready Sir!" she pronounces. I cannot help but chuckle.

In the meantime, candles have been lit around the perimeter of the bath and in the glow, you could almost forget this is little more than a temporary and very shabby lobby off the landing. Suddenly, Sian appears with my glass of red wine, and shortly after, this is followed by a bowl of peanuts. I do not think I have ever consumed aperitifs and nibbles while soaking in a nice warm bath, but I am sure I could get used to it. We all have a laugh, but none more so when Cara reappears with another towel, a bottle of some lotion, and a very French twirly moustache drawn above her top lip.

"I am monsieur le masseur!" she says emphatically, and proceeds to rub the lotion into my back.

"Ahhh, merci monsieur." I reply in suitably satisfied manner.

I quietly rejoice at all the things I have, and the best of them are nothing to do with material goods. I suggest to myself, perhaps this is all I really need – at least for today.

Wednesday 5 February 2003

What a difference a day makes, as some American song-stress, whose name completely escapes me, once warbled very irritatingly. Firstly, I drive into Hertfordshire in a very circumspect fashion, I do not want to be the cause of the next unfortunate and violent meeting of car and deer. More disappointingly, but inevitably, no pampering this evening, not even the whiff of a crisp, let alone bath oil, romantic lighting and tasty canapés. Normal service has been resumed.

In the house, we have a shower tray installed, but I can now see the full extent of the problem associated with the shower door. Unless you have the physique of Olive Oyl, the opening that would be available to enter could not be accessed by any normally built human being. Even if you were Olive Oyl (apart from having a very annoying voice and getting sick to the back teeth with two arguing oafs along with more spinach than could possibly be good for you), it would still require unfeasible contortions to squeeze between wall and door.

In the meantime, we have a pump installed to finally ensure that the bath and shower attachment in the new bathroom can do the job they are supposed to do, rather than attempt them rather apologetically and fail dismally in the process. The bathroom seems to be nearing completion, with everything installed and plumbed, window inserted and lights working, but we are not quite there yet. The big round hole in the outside wall stuffed with a dirty rag is the extract, and unless we are to have the most primitive means of extraction (i.e. remove the cloth to work, put it back in again to stop), this is yet to have the fan unit installed. The other issue surrounds our perennial problem with the plaster. In putting in the window, it has been discovered the plaster on this wall has all the stability of a pile of candy floss, except that would probably stick a bit better. It is currently all peeling away like the rind of an orange, so it will all be taken off and we will be left with the render underneath. Not pretty, but pretty firm and apparently, better for sticking tiles onto.

The kitchen and utility remain in their tantalisingly semi-useable state, but tomorrow we expect to be revisited by a 'remedial' kitchen fitter (i.e. man to correct the mess of previous fitter, or 'irredeemable' fitter as I have tagged him), and G's Gang to finish the tiling. Every digit inside and outside my body will be crossed.

Thursday 6 February 2003
Much to my relief, I am pleased to report the difficulties encountered in uncrossing ones digits have been worth the small trauma, as both kitchen and tiling operatives seem to have done something worthwhile and valuable today. Reports indicate that Kitchen Rescue Man was not enamoured by the quality and execution of work undertaken by the previous dork, and although he has to make another visit to finish the job completely, we are nearly there. Meanwhile, the vast majority of the floor tiling is now down, and if I can bear to cross my fingers again, they could return tomorrow to complete the project.

The en-suite has also continued to move on, the shower system is now in place, together with sink, although from what I can gather, the latter has caused much wailing and gnashing of teeth. As headroom is limited, so then, is the space and the position you will have to adopt in order to wash without incurring minor head injuries. We have therefore, had to try and find a basin of limited width, yet one that does not look like it has come from a Wendy House. There was also the problem of getting something delivered within a few days, which did not require me to threaten violence in order to ensure its arrival. We also have to admit to a moment of weakness in the fashion victim stakes. We plumped for a round basin that stood away from the wall on a steel pedestal, this had a rather funky tap with its own wall mounting, so there was no actual physical connection between wall and tap. Sounds odd, but in the words of Sian looks "Coooool!" However, funky and cool are not words in a builders dictionary, or if they are, the correct translation is 'Bastard!' and 'Double Bastard!' Suffice to say, fitting and plumbing all this in was not as straightforward as Steve would have liked, but he seemed to take it all on the chin.

Much later, I am lying in bed reading, when I hear the boiler fire up. As this is eleven o'clock at night, the whole thing should have shut down at least an hour ago. I surmise the power must have been off for a while today and so the clock on the boiler has got itself all out of time with reality. Mind you, the nature of the boiler clock and programmer is such that even without a loss of power it probably struggles to keep up with modern life. It is a purely mechanical system with a twenty four hour dial which chugs around rather noisily, two little fiddly tabs clicking the boiler on in the morning and early evening, and two more clicking it off later in the morning and evening, and that's it. However, it is about as precise as cutting bread with an axe and loses time as if it is drifting into another dimension, and none of this is helped by its dreadful brown colour and nasty plastic fake aluminium dial. If it were a car, it would be an Austin Allegro. So, I fling back the covers and prance downstairs, stark naked, heading for the boiler, tucked away as it is under the stairs, but accessed via the toilet. On pulling back the door to reveal the workhorse of the heating system, I stop in my tracks as I discover that the Austin Allegro has been replaced with a Nissan Primera, all white, sleek and digital, with buttons and a display that makes no sense at all.

"Ah- Ha!" I say, trying to convince myself this should present no problems, but knowing my grasp of these matters could ensure I will stand here with not a stitch on for quite some time. I must try and figure out whether I am programming the boiler, or setting course for Alpha Centauri on the Millennium Falcon.

I think I might know where the instructions are hidden, and, by a minor miracle, I am correct, as I find them in one of the kitchen drawers. Let's see now…. To set the time of day, press this button until it flashes, and then hold that one down, while scrolling through with this one…….now press that one again to set……then set the 'on' time for heating zone 1……now to set the off time…….then it has three times for each day of the week, so………press that button, squeeze this sprogget, copy that widget, turn around three times, clap your hands and shout "Shit!" This thing has so many permutations and configurations, I am more likely to win the bloody National Lottery than get it right! Despite being clothes-less, I am now getting both hot and bothered, and in desperation I look for the override. I think I have found this, and my fingers are a blur as I tap and scroll away until I have the words 'OFF' displayed all over the place – but the bloody thing keeps going, merrily burning oil and pumping hot water. I have had enough.

"Bastard!" I shout at it, but strangely, that seems to leave it unmoved.

For the time being, I make do with turning the boiler and main room thermostat down, but to my chagrin, it does not seem to have much effect. Perhaps the whole system has taken umbrage at my display of naked flesh. I throw the instructions down on the stairs, and stomp back up to bed. Clearly this needs a dose of true practical application. In the morning, this will be a job for Super Sharon, High Priestess of All Things Practical. As a mere man, I must admit defeat.

Saturday 8 February 2003

The fifth member of the Neale Anstey clan is with us again this morning, as Wally trundles in through the front door with his usual "Morning!"

"I'm going to be a bit noisy and dirty today," he says. The mind boggles. "I've got to channel out all this wiring for the light switches in your lounge before Steve gets in on Monday."

True enough, we have been asked to make sure we clear the lounge completely on Sunday night, as they plan to obliterate the old and put up the new during Monday. This means we are going to have to squeeze most of the lounge contents into the new dining area, but for now, we need to move it all out of Wally's way, so he can hack away at the walls. At this precise moment in time, we have nowhere else to put it all, so we make do with piling it up in various areas, away from where he needs to work, and cover it all up as best we can with dust sheets. On turning one of the armchairs upside down in order to put one on top of another, a clanking and rattling issues forth from its bowels, like someone has dropped all their change on the floor.

"Bloody hell, what you got in there?"

While it is not unusual to find the odd comb and five pence worth of change down the back of the chairs, this sounded more akin to the contents of an entire salon and the Bank of Anstey, AKA Sians money box. We looked at each other rather quizzically, and for a moment I wondered if he was going to suddenly rip open the bottom of the chair in expectation of finding some ancient lost treasure, but we both shrugged and continued with the piling of furniture. The problem with our concept of piling was, on this occasion it made the middle of the room look like a bonfire. And after I had finally stuck some magazines and the coffee table on the side in a rather precarious position, all it needed was a box of matches and some petrol.

However, all it actually got were a few dusty old curtains and a long discarded brown and red stripy sheet thrown over the top. The origins of the latter article are something of a mystery, but I think there might be the touch of an heirloom about it. All I can safely say is that I did not buy it and cannot think such an article could be bought. No sensible retail outlet could possibly stock such an item and retain high street cred, not even any self respecting charity shop would contemplate letting such an item adorn its display of old, but useable, goods. It would make an excellent prop in an Austin Powers film, but apart from that, it was reaching the height of its abilities as a dust-sheet.

Shortly after the bonfire building in the lounge, work started and there was no missing this. I am sure Jules Verne gained some inspiration from Wally's large masonry drill in coming up with his tale about journeying to the centre of the earth. Whilst the noise was as if this was exactly what Wally was doing, a peek around the door later on revealed merely some serious gouging and channelling of the wall to take light and switch cable, in order to relocate the room thermostat. This had been dangling rather despondently over the new side door, occasionally swaying back and forth, for the last few days and if it was transmitting messages to the boiler, then it was a minor miracle – I am sure I could not do my job while hanging by my innards.

Having been out for most of the afternoon (a course advised by Wally as the best bet in the circumstances) we returned to find Wally had gone mad. Well, okay, he may have retained some sanity, but the degree of destruction wreaked in the most unexpected places, did leave me just a bit surprised. All the channelling and wiring had been done, and, bless him, he had cleared up rather well and put our furniture back in place. But a look up to the ceiling led to gasps as bloody great big holes had been formed and large parts of the ceiling had been destroyed all along the far wall and a couple along the near wall. It was like inspecting the damage caused by huge rats, except not only would they have had to have been impossibly big, but strangely adept at climbing walls and hanging on upside down while munching away at the artex and plasterboard. I know strange things are apt to occur in Anstey, but this would be beyond any twilight zone.

I surmise, in feeding wire through in various places, it might simply have been easier to do this, rather than fiddle about lifting boards upstairs. Good job the ceiling is going to be replaced.

Sunday 9 February 2003
We have been putting it off all day, but we can no longer ignore the fact, we have to move everything out of the lounge tonight. After we have manhandled a few general bits and pieces from the lounge into the study (or the warehouse as it is becoming known) it's time to move some of the bigger pieces from lounge to dining area. This can only be done by opening the French doors of each, transporting them briefly outside before moving them back in again.

However, just before this, we enact a scene that would have been at home in an Ealing comedy. We have a very tall bookshelf, which is greater in height than the door frames and getting it through entails tipping it first one way to get the front end through, then tipping it back to get the rear part through. It is also cursedly heavy, and apart from being likely to sustain damage to most protruding parts of your body, carrying it requires small, scuttling steps, like a demented ballet dancer. As you would expect, lots of swearing can also be heard. We shuffle it out of the lounge and into the hall, with the expectation that we can shove this particular piece of furniture into the study. However, when we reach the door into the study, there is an obvious problem. It won't, of course, go through the door unless we tip it, but as the hallway has somewhat limited dimensions, we can't even turn the bloody thing, let alone tip it. Looks of resignation ensue, followed by murmured profanities, as we lift again, and simply continue all the way down the hall, tip it back and forth again, into the kitchen and finally into the dining area, to push up against the far wall. In geographic terms, we have gone from Cambridge to London via Edinburgh.

While we are in a bad mood, we may as well continue with the unpleasantries, so throw open the French doors to the elements, move the secondary sofa and two armchairs, staggering, and shouting to each other like a couple of removal men. All we needed were some brown overalls and a couple of flat caps. Sian looked on in warped amusement, but neither her nor Sharon were able to resist the lure of the rattling noise coming from one of the chairs, so arms were wedged down the side in an effort to remove the offending articles. In no particular order these were about twenty-four pence in change, two pencils, one pen, a pair of tweezers (I knew there would be something related to female beautification) and a long lost belt. Not a haul whose value would prompt early retirement, but it's better than a furry sweet and half a cheese sandwich.

Once this is completed we are left with just the main sofa and the telly, which now sits alone in the lounge, and is our resting place for the remainder of the evening as a not very fond farewell to the décor and finish we long to see erased. By half past ten, Sunday evening viewing has run out of steam and preparations must begin for Monday morning. The television is switched off, wheeled out into the hall and into the study without a hint of reluctance. The sofa is lifted and shifted out through the elements and back into the house to join its mates in the dining area, this will just about leave us enough room to sit on it and stare at the wall about two feet away. Doors are locked, lights switched off, and I have one last look at the lounge, as its fate awaits less than twelve hours away. The Condemned Room. I feel a pang of guilt at the little smirk weaving its way onto my face, and then shut the door.

Monday 10 February 2003
The scree slopes of Anstey are alive and well and piled up in our lounge. Their related dust piles are thick over everything else in the house. The scene in the living room provokes a combination of surprise and resignation – all the old plaster has been hacked off the walls, the ghastly stone cladding to the fireplace removed and on the face of it this has given the impression of a little more space. However, the floor, or rather the carpet, is littered with piles of the stuff from the walls and dust is hanging in the air, to the extent you can see and taste it. In fairness, we had indicated we had admitted defeat with the carpet some time ago. We had got used to its gradual desecration, including oil, ingrained plaster and thousands of grubby shoes. Even before the builders it had suffered from every conceivable soft drink spillage, chocolate milk from countless bowls of coco-pops, several accidents with cough syrup, and enough tea, if you boiled up the carpet, you could probably give the whole of the building gang a nice cuppa. Despite this, I had not expected all the rubble

and rubbish to be dumped on top of it and if it wasn't ready for the skip before, it certainly was now.

The dust was one problem, but morale in the house was made lower by the fact, we now had to live in the kitchen, plus a tiny section of the dining room. This allowed us to just about sit on the sofa, even if it did mean facing away from everyone else. In an effort to make things a little more bearable, we pulled in a portable television from out of the study, but it is questionable if this made things better. For one, this is a portable television, of an age that potentially John Logi Baird himself might have had a hand in its production. In addition, it has a volume control seemingly completely unrelated to the volume control button on the front. It is also so covered in dust and looks as if it has lain undisturbed in some ancient time warp electrical store for years. Added to all this, it has a small little external aerial, as we have no facility to plug into the aerial in the roof from the kitchen. The result of all of this is a grubby little box, which sits on the corner of one of the kitchen worktops, with infinitely variable volume that shouts at you when you least expect it. Not to mention a picture, which switches at will from black and white to colour, with most scenes being done amidst a serious blizzard – family entertainment at its best!

The amount of room we have available is also causing some frayed tempers, as usual the children are on the receiving end of some of this. Cara, in particular, has been driving Sharon into fits of apoplexy by constant dawdling and generally doing things, or rather not doing things, twenty minutes after she is asked. This includes putting on pyjamas, getting a drink, getting undressed/dressed and switching off, physically and metaphorically, the television – her trance like state while watching the Simpsons is almost eerie. Unfortunately, she has performed (or not, as it were) up to standard on all these counts tonight. So at the time she is really meant to be in bed, she is open eyed at the second-rate goggle box (quality of viewing does not seem to matter) picking slowly at a piece of bread. She gets the proverbial rocket from Sharon and walks off in that wounded and sorry way only small girls and dogs can do.

I fear our overall patience and wellbeing is going to be tested to the limit over the next few days.

Wednesday 12 February 2003
A magic transformation of the walls in the lounge has taken place, and the chimneybreast too has been dragged into a new dimension, as new plastering is complete, wet and dry patches around the whole room testifying to the freshness of its application. It is a revelation to see such smoothness and firmness on the walls and the fireplace is now a joy to behold. Okay, it's not something I would write a poem about, or dedicate a song in its honour, but to see the old stone cladding gone, and the grim, grey, ugly hearth banished,

brought a real sense of relief – perfectly even, pink and unblemished, ready for a new, rather more accommodating hearth and mantel treatment. Bliss! The carpet had all but disappeared and merged into the rest of the floor, while the rubble and debris of the preparation work still remained in heaps and piles, but it did not detract from the real progress in the room.

Meantime, we now finally also have some radiators up and running in areas where the cold was starting to penetrate rather pointedly. While this included our newly extended bedroom, the en-suite and the very front of the lounge, the most pressing need was in the new hallway. A combination of lots of glass, a door that had all the draught-proof qualities of a wind-tunnel, and bare cold concrete floors, made the hallway a zone whose ambient temperature differed very little from the world outside. Indeed on some of the sharp mid-February mornings of late, I would not have been entirely surprised to have found a friendly Polar Bear taking refuge. Thanks to a radiator of such impressive proportions it could have been a striking entrance sculpture were it not for the fact it was too obviously a bog standard radiator, normal standards of internal comfort were being approached.

The problem of the omnipresent dust however remained, to the extent we all now had what appeared to be permanent colds, or more particularly sore throats, stuffy and runny noses and steadily hoarser and hoarser voices. However, none of us were feeling particularly ill, just suffering the symptoms as if we were, not to mention getting through enough paper towels and toilet roll to make a tree hugger weep. It is rather peculiar having all the indications and effects of illness, without feeling ill – I can't make up my mind whether I feel a bit of a cheat, or a bit cheated. ......

Friday 14 February 2003

A sharp white frosty morning and a child vomiting at 6.15 am – it's not my ideal combination of events to open the day, but if nothing else, it breaks the routine. There I was, padding about the kitchen (cum only-living-space-currently-available room) juggling with the logistics of making tea and toast, whilst ensuring my usual Valentine mementoes were in place for the three main women in my life, when a commotion ensues upstairs. This is always witnessed by rapid and loud movement on the floor above and a shouted enquiry, in this case:

"Sian, are you all right?"

No, in fact Sian was not all right and neither was her bed, but I will refrain from a better explanation and description. I join in the rapid and loud movement and run upstairs to find said oldest child looking pale, but then so would you if you had deposited half the comments of your stomach onto your bed. But as I said, no descriptions – I was rather glad I did not have my lenses in and even more so when Sharon offered to do the clearing up. For whatever reason, traditionally this task seems to have fallen to me, but I cannot recall ever having obtained a GCSE in Puke Disposal. Mind you, the amount I have successfully cleared up in years gone by, I could earn a tidy living as a touring lecturer in the subject.

The turmoil of all this has understandably disturbed the whole house and within a short while all are up. Sian continues to look a little pale, but says she feels better for having got out whatever it was causing problems within, even though doing so has not done the health of her bed, bedclothes or poor old mattress a lot of good. Cara is bouncing around in the knowledge it is Valentine's Day and wants to start creating cards for her harem of admirers at school as soon as possible. Sharon sits quietly sipping a cup of tea and no-one says very much about the three single red roses sat in glasses on the kitchen worktop and the cards adjacent. The humorous romantic little scene and its impact has been a bit spoilt by the fact it served as a background to Sian being ill and lost all element of undisrupted surprise. Besides which, it's all a load of commercial twaddle, but as ever, I do my bit to try and play along.

On returning home later, I discover work has begun again outside. Perhaps the last three months had been a Bobby Ewing shower moment, I had dreamt they would soon be gone, when in fact they had only just started. That would all be fine if a young and voluptuous Victoria Principal were to appear with an alluring look, but then such thoughts would merely get me into serious trouble with the good lady wife, especially on this St Valentine's day. In fact, as one of the last serious acts of building, they had begun on the concrete slab for the conservatory. Money prevented this actually being built, but we could just about stretch to the base being put in, so at least getting the really grubby bit done while we had on site those best placed to do it. No doubt this will get curious looks, and we shall pine to be able to finish it, not entirely unlike the feeling we have had with the kitchen over the last few weeks.

Remedial Kitchen Man turned out to be a bit of a disappointment. All right, he had fixed some of the worst bits and put in a cupboard to house our fridge freezer, something that Mr Irredeemable had strangely forgotten all about. But I still objected to mitres and joints where the gaps were big enough for me to stuff in a piece of toast, but my biggest gripe was that even after the worktop had been polished for a second time, it looked like Torvill and Dean had performed Bolero on it, including a lengthy encore. Some of the scratches were so deep and obvious, you could catch your nail, but it was the wealth of swirly scores at various points in various patches that had made me rather cross. Earlier in the week, for the second time, I had made the call of complaint to Terry and this time he was less than accommodating, even a touch aggressive:

"It's your builders," he barked

"They've been gone from the kitchen for more than two weeks." I said tersely

He then started to blame the tilers and while they were probably less than models of tidiness, I didn't think they had put their ice skates on and danced all over the worktops. After some pushing, he said he would send another 'team' along, but they would need a 'finishing kit' and would not be able to get there until Friday -today.

So Sharon was earmarked to be in all day. And did they turn up? Answers need not be submitted on a postcard.

Although Steve & Co. have not finished the lounge, we have the expected request to move Cara out of her temporary room, vacate the bathroom, so they can do the final phase of obliteration and remodelling, to create our new room, the new spare room and the landing. This we will have to do at some point over the weekend, but the upside for now is that the new bathroom is just about useable. I take advantage and have my first long relaxing soak in the new, rather deep, bath and muse at the finish currently greeting visitors to this room. It is not so much the rough render wall surrounding the window, or even the now grey, bare, unkempt plaster of what used to be the outside wall. It is probably the 'shabby chic' (a ridiculous phrase I heard the other night, but I think is an apt description) of the splintered plywood boards that box in the pipe work. These generally don't meet or match, possibly the overall décor combining the best of pink paint and plaster. Or even the patchwork chipboard floor, that has been cut, pulled up and replaced to do wiring and plumbing so many times, I could probably box it and sell it as a 500 piece giant jigsaw.

The other problem with the new bath is the presence of a pump, although upon turning on the water you could be forgiven for thinking a diesel train was about to arrive and come crashing through the wall. The overall water pressure had necessitated its introduction, but I had not dreamt it would sound as though it was being powered by Concorde. Of course, it wasn't helped by sitting in an empty wooden box, being the new airing cupboard, open to the room and with no contents to deaden the sound. But even after this, I had the feeling it might have the potential to cause some severe disturbance in the future, should anyone ever try to take a bath in the middle of the night.

No matter, for now, it was good just to have a bath that I didn't have to share with half a kilo of dust and potentially get out dirtier than I had got in.

Saturday 15 February 2003

If I remember correctly, on moving Cara from one room to another, we had taken the opportunity to dispose of a fair amount of accumulated rubbish. In the course of doing so we had just about condensed matters to ensure she fitted into the spare room, knowing this would also be home to the computer and its desk, not to mention retention of a few other bits and pieces. Pulling all her stuff from underneath her bed again, I can only assume, like Dino from the Flintstones, who jumps back in through the window having been put out for the night, all the junk had promptly removed itself from our wheelie bin, crept back upstairs and thrust itself back under the bed from whence it originally came. In fact, I am not sure it has not multiplied and reproduced in the process. How can one little girl create so much crap?

At the same time, heaps of dust works like life's negative photo, leaving imprints all over surfaces and floors where articles and obstacles have sat. Apart from emphasising just how many articles and obstacles sat in Cara's room, it also graphically displayed just how much debris was falling from the air and onto every exposed surface. The contrast between box on floor and the floor adjacent when box was removed was breathtaking, it was as if a volcanic cloud had deposited its unpleasant cargo all over the room. God knows what has been making its way into our lungs.

The biggest conundrum of this exercise was the logistics of moving the computer, not to mention the printer, scanner, piles of CD's and the rather hefty desk it all sits upon. Where to put it? Placing it into our room was out of the question, unless it was to be the third inhabitant of our bed. Personally, my sexual proclivities do not extend to gaining satisfaction from an intimate moment with a rather worn wooden desk, although I have no doubt someone within this weird world would get a kick out of it. Putting it in Sian's room would have meant her eviction, in which case the desk would have its own room, although it might have found the tongue and groove cladding to two of the walls a bit upsetting. Downstairs, the lounge was out of bounds, the utility was virtually inaccessible, and the study was totally inaccessible. That just left the kitchen, but more likely the dining area. On inspection, it seemed if we moved the sofa, so the bar stools were rammed up against the breakfast bar (and providing there was no one sitting in them at the time) we should just about be able to squeeze the desk behind. And so this is what we did, accompanied by the PC and all its kit, which took no more than five minutes to dismantle and disconnect, but unsurprisingly took more like fifty minutes to wire and connect back up again (even then I managed to plug the mouse into the keyboard slot and vice versa).

The final act in this mini comedy was the process of getting the whole lot plugged in, with the nearest sockets located on the other side of the dining area, behind two upturned armchairs on top of the second sofa, in front of a bookcase, already rammed hard against the wall to give us more space. We could feed the extension lead under one of the chairs, but then getting to the lead the other side, to then pull out and plug into the socket was a problem I felt did not have a solution. With some assistance from Sian, I finally managed to clamber past one of the armchairs, perch myself on the back of the sofa, squat rather dangerously and increasingly impermanently, so I could stretch my arm out towards the floor. Unfortunately there was a clear mismatch between the position of the plug and my ability to reach down, which succeeded in nearly suffocating me against a cushion, but sadly failed in getting my hand to the floor or the plug. My balance was also now getting ever precarious, I started to ask Sian agitatedly to pull the plug back and try and throw it down the narrow gap, in the hope it might hit my outstretched hand and I could grab it. She tried this several times and failed, by now I was sinking into oblivion and possible permanent damage. So, what else to do in these circumstances but shout, it's the tried and tested British way to ease circumstances of frustration. The French person can't understand you? Well, just shout at them, that will do the trick – it was the same idea.

"For Gods sake Sian, COME ON!!"

"I'm trying," she said, and seeing my predicament, simply started to giggle – which just winds me up even more

"SIAN!"

She giggles even more.

Just as I think I will be stuck here for the rest of my natural life and will simply become blended with the back of the sofa, I catch the plug. In an almost seamless superhuman move, borne out of total desperation, I twist, mate the plug with the socket, push in, switch on and scramble out of my personal hell hole, like a tarantula was crawling up my leg.

Whatever you do, don't try that at home.

Monday 17 February 2003

Immediately I step in the front door and look up the stairs, I can see things are not as I left them this morning. Rather than the dark vista of the small unlit landing and the blank view of the wall that formed the bathroom, I can now see Sian. That in itself is not too unusual, given the fact she lives here. However, whilst previously the room for manoeuvre would be such, she would have to be perched at the top of the stairs, she is now stood some way back. Behind her I can now see the window that was in the bathroom, but clearly now sits in the back wall as the rear of the new landing. I am lured up the stairs by this scene, but don't worry, there are no spooky staccato strings accompanying my movements and no prospect of a knife wielding scar-faced maniac leaping out of the shadows, although it is true the stairs are now strangely creaking.

At the top of the stairs, the view is one of complete openness, as walls have been torn down. The first few timbers of new ones have been put in place, while one is complete and now defines the rear of our bedroom. The rest is just one big, dirty empty space, with what was the bathroom and the spare room completely devoid of partitions. The feeling of room is quite liberating, and finally gives us some sense of what will be a much more sensible and useable order on the first floor. However, this is currently tempered by the state of the floor, the gaps in the plaster where the old walls used to be, and the presence of orange traffic cones. Aha, you say, Monday 17 February 2003 is the date London Congestion Charging came into force. You would be forgiven for thinking that Ken Livingstone's influence had extended far further than central London, ensuring traffic also flows freely around the landing of Holly House, and no impatient builder parks his cordless drill within this zone without paying the obligatory £5. Not a bad idea, although no spy cameras here to help, but in fact these were in place to try and ensure small, or indeed large, individuals did not step into gaping holes in the floor. Or onto exposed pipes (probably then through the ceiling) causing general chaos and calamity, not to mention serious personal injury.

The other strange anomaly remaining is the light and light switch for the old bathroom. The former sits quite neatly in the middle of this new enlarged area, but the latter is a long pull switch that dangles in the middle of nowhere. This means in its new function, it is not best placed for access as you enter the 'room', as on reaching the top of the stairs, it is necessary to grope around rather aimlessly. If this does not work, walk tentatively forward until your forehead collides with the light cord. Or, if you are not thinking and not bothered about the light, you can merely give yourself a bit of a fright on walking across the landing, and as the cord strikes you unexpectedly and for a spilt second your brain alerts you to possible spider attack, arms flaying in repellent mode. Not for those of a nervous disposition

Wednesday 19 February 2003

Like the final furlongs in a horse race, or perhaps more appropriately the last minutes as you approach closing time in the local pub, the pace seems to be hotting up and things seem to be being done all over the house. The partition walls are now all constructed upstairs, the one remaining wall in our bedroom plastered, the new window in the spare room complete, all the ceilings tacked with plasterboard, a door on the new airing cupboard and a canopy has suddenly appeared over the front door. I had rejected the first drawings of this, as its size and depth looked as if you could have landed a Jumbo Jet on its upper surface, while its overall dimensions would have had you constantly wondering if it was all about to collapse. The newer version is still of some substance, but then as it is covered in substantial amounts of very shiny lead, it needs to have a degree of strength to support its own weight.

There really was rather a lot of lead needed for this. I thought of tales from years gone by, when lead was regularly stripped off churches and other roofs in view of its value, although bearing in mind weight and density, leaves a bit of mystery as to how the perpetrators got it home. It is not the sort of thing you can realistically stuff into an old swag bag, heave over your shoulder and saunter home whistling innocently. The act of having to drag it, sweating and swearing would have been a bit of a give away to the local constabulary. Either way, while I was not aware of lead having any great value any more, I did wonder if we might wake up one morning and find we had a canopy with a strange translucent quality. We might then witness an old style robber complete with flat cap, wobbling away from the scene on his old bike, heavy bag over his shoulder being rapidly followed by an old style policeman, blowing his whistle and shouting 'Stop! Thief!' – rather disturbingly, this sounds like a scene from 'Heartbeat' a programme I cannot abide and never watch, but somehow seems to have infiltrated my psyche. Must be all the dust.

In the meantime, Kitchen Man the Third has made a visit in order to effect a final finish to the worktop, I am pleased to say there is now no evidence to suggest it has been used as the local ice skating rink. It is very smooth and very shiny, so much so it is almost dazzling and I am afraid to place anything on it. Firstly, it seems a shame to sully its pristine appearance; secondly, I won't be able to see myself in it; and thirdly, I am frightened of damaging it. While the first two are just silly, the latter is plain stupid – this was a kitchen worktop. If I remember rightly, worktops are generally meant for work across their top, rather than for admiring the shine and their general aesthetics (although judging by the latest Turner Prize efforts at the Tate, I could do worse than try and exhibit the worktop as a modern masterpiece). Granted, the kettle and toaster may well have slightly padded feet, but past experience suggest they are more likely to be dropped than placed, along with countless knives, pans, plates, bowls, bottles, cans not to mention the odd backside courtesy of one or other, or both, of my children. As a worktop, if it cannot take this sort of abuse, then it is a true wuss of a worktop, a feeble fop in the cauldron of contemporary cuisine, a limp larry in the maelstrom of modern machinations and a total waste of time and a lot of my money.

Back in the land of reasonableness, I am hoping we are truly near the end, particularly as in just over a week I am planning to take time off to try and blitz the decorating. This will not be possible if they are still messing around inside, as paint and dust don't mix. Or rather, they do mix, but the result is an unintentional textured and uneven finish to walls and ceilings. In theory, they could be gone, but looking around me, I think it more likely that Michael Jackson is a sane and stable human being.

Friday 21 February 2003
Being half term, I have taken today as holiday, but there is no intention for us all to spend the day getting under the feet of the builders. In any event, staying purely within the confines of the all purpose kitchen for the whole day is neither feasible nor advisable. Whilst in normal circumstances it might be possible to play a board game, spend a bit of time on the computer, do a little reading, even watch a modicum of children's television, this would be done in various parts of the house at various times, giving some break in proceedings and crucially able to do something different with each child in order to avoid the outbreak of inevitable hostilities. We are all, of course, restricted to one room, which itself is half filled with furniture and kitchen fitment cast offs (having replaced the corner cupboard and several miles of cornicing, they have either forgotten, or couldn't be bothered to take the removed bits away). Therefore, forced together like castaways in a dinghy, spending the whole day together doing things in this environment will merely lead to a criminal act,

involving near murder of at least one, or likely two, of the assembled gathering. Anyway, I can't bear the thought of another game of Mousetrap. This game lost its novel appeal and attraction after the very first game, when it took half a day to reach the cheese, the rubber band kept flying off the crank for the boot, the ball kept coming off the contrived ramp, and the sodding diver kept missing the tub. Or, more often, even an earthquake couldn't shake the bloody trap from the top of the stupid pole to catch the brainless mouse.

So you will gather, we planned to be away from Holly House for most of the day. Before doing so, it gave me the opportunity to remind Steve that in less than a week, I would be an omnipresent pain, as I would be commencing my marathon redecoration while Sharon and the girls flew off for five days. This was not a forced evacuation, but its timing was pretty much spot on as it looked like we would not have the majority of the house back within the next week – for the second year in a row, the dance school had been invited to the Irish National Championships. Now, this sounds like a tag line for a joke, but to the best of my knowledge this did not consist of lots of people standing in sinks professing they were doing a tap dance. Nor was this a parade of thousands of Michael Flatley look-alikes, but since I did not go last year, I can't be one hundred percent on that. At the very least, it had to be better than a Sunday in Hemel Hempsted, so prospectively, they were getting the better deal. My conversation with Steve commenced thus:

"You're not going to be gone by next Thursday are you?" I said with a very straight face.

"Er...no," he said.

"Right. You know I am taking time off and need to be able to get on with decoration big time, concentrating on the kitchen, new bedroom and bathroom!"

"Yep," he said as if he meant no.

"So we need to try and make sure all the snagging is done by then – cracks in plaster, nail and screw holes filled etc."

"Yeah, okay." He was almost as unconvincing as my friend in the tiling shop.

Later discussions with Richard seem to suggest that this sort of finishing is associated with decorating. My simplistic view is, if you do a job, you don't leave holes behind for others to fill before you can do what you need to. Think of the havoc if your friendly highways contractor built a new road and left umpteen holes and crevices for you to dodge in your car. Hang on though, I think the M25 may well have been built in this manner. We shall see what transpires.

Part of the day is spent ten-pin bowling, something we all enjoy, although none of us excels. I was much amused and significantly cheered, when I had booked this the previous day. This was owing to the lady on the other end of the phone who, on taking down my details, insisted on confirming each piece of information with either 'Okey Dokey' or 'Lovely Jubbly' in a very upbeat, happy, smiley way. However, I resisted the temptation to ask if she was on any medication, or whether she would share with me exactly what it was that she was metaphorically floating upon. More amusement followed, as we went through our games, the children's good humour upheld by the presence of bumpers, which prevent the ball falling into the gullies. While Sian seemed to perfect the science of multiple angles, bouncing the ball off the bumpers several times before knocking down virtually all the pins, Cara went for a strange combination of the brutal and stealthy. This consisted of a small run up, a swing back that threatened to send her flying backwards (the balls momentum only marginally less than her inertia) and a throw having rather more upwards than outwards trajectory, sending the ball crashing down to the lane with a noise making me wince. The ball having landed only a few inches in front of her then proceeded to trickle slowly down the lane, gathering a little pace as it went, almost invariably homing in on the middle of the rack of pins and pushing most of them over. Meantime, I heave away and hurtle the ball down the lane like an exocet, only for it to dive off and smash just one pin off to the side. No matter, we have lots of fun.

Back at the house, the reconfiguration of the upstairs is moving on at good pace, with walls, door frames and doors all in, and some significant plastering completing the scene. At the same time, for the first time in the house's history, we have natural light to the landing. The (very) mouldy piece of board that has sat across the outside face of the new window frame has finally been prised away and the two small sashes have been slotted into place. I fondly imagine the impact must be like the opening of Tutenkhamun's Tomb, only he had untold treasures and hordes of jewels, gold and priceless artefacts, while all we have is a few grubby green floor tiles, an old traffic cone and a hideous loft hatch. Still, he'd been dead for rather a long time and I'm still here, so perhaps he got the raw end of the deal in comparison.

Saturday 22 February 2003

Chris is our resident chippie and has been responsible for much of the cutting and fitting of frames, doors and skirting and anything else vaguely wooden throughout the house from the beginning. He is a chirpy character, but being self-employed relies on job following job and needs to be gone from Holly House by this weekend. Personally, I have wanted to be gone from Holly House for the past five months, but have been stymied by the lack of any alternative accommodation, so at least he has the upper hand on me there.

His arrival is what might seem to any casual observer as a very bizarre scene, but to us all is perfectly normal within our current circumstances. We, as the family, are sitting in the kitchen, dressed only in pyjamas, save me who is dressed in a fairly well worn dressing gown, radio on, in varying stages of munching toast, eating cereal, drinking tea, reading, or likely doing all four. We look as if we have just got out of bed, which of course we have, so dishevelled and bleary would be both apt and accurate, complete with my now common place morning hairstyle, which looks like a crushed Mohican. That would be fine on a teenage boy, or a wayward geek, but not so convincing on a forty-something Dad. We hear the front door open, but no-one even looks up. It could be the Anstey Maffia looking for retribution following the builders slight indiscretion when the van ran across the small green by the old pump, leaving some rather obvious muddy tyre marks in their wake. It might have been a Police raid, CID in search of dubious substances, reasoning no family could possibly tolerate our living conditions for five months without some form of illegal medicinal support. No, for just a few seconds later Chris wanders into the kitchen.

"Morning," he chirps

"Hi, Chris," we say, and do so with the faintest of acknowledgements, but otherwise continuing with what we are doing, totally unfazed by his apparent intrusion.

"Just need to unlock your back door so I can get on with that."

"Yeah, no problem." I say through a mouthful of brown toast and peach jam, waving a hand in total acceptance.

Trust of these people has become endemic.

The afternoon does not go quite as planned, thanks to an inept member of staff at a tile shop – what is it with us and tile shops? Do I have a sign on me saying 'Treat this man with contempt and provide him with a level of service that would shame Attila the Hun'? Now, as you will have gathered, we have not ventured forth to G's local Tile Emporium, owing to the fact that if he were the last Tile Shop on earth, I would more happily dig up my own clay and make and fire my own tiles than buy from him. Judging by the problems I am encountering at the alternative retail establishment, this could now be a better option. This is the equivalent of a Tile Superstore, on yet another bland retail park, but its whole demeanour and atmosphere is all a bit shoddy and downbeat. There are various displays and heaps of tiles in rows and aisles, but it is not particularly organised or inviting, but then I suppose making a tile shop inviting is a bit like making cough mixture tasty (although I was always rather partial to a drop of Galloways, even though it didn't do much for my cough). Not a lot caught our attention, other than some nice deep blue ones we thought would look nice in the en-suite. Okay, I look for the nearest assistant and it's just my luck to land Darren, the one with a mildly vacant look, who when standing still always has his mouth open and eyes open a little wider than seems natural. Still, I give him the benefit of the doubt and I tell him how much we want. Unsurprisingly, they don't have much in stock, but we can take what he has and he can order the rest.

First off, he disappears for an age looking for a sack barrow, and in doing so walks backwards and forwards past us, still looking vacant, at least four times. I worry even at the first hurdle, he can't find what must be one of a dozen barrows in the shop. He finally returns, loads up the boxes and wheels them to the checkout.

"Right, so that's seven boxes, and you need........" he is now concentrating and it looks painful. I cringe with him and after a little while we conclude we are going to have to tell him the answer. This is like being a teacher in a maths class at primary school.

"Twelve more."

"Is that right?" He's thinking again and I fear the consequences.

"Yes, it is, believe me."

"Okay." He seems happy, returns to his till and punches all the relevant information into his computer, only this is obviously a particularly difficult task, as his eyes are opening dangerously wide and his mouth is open sufficiently for me shove my fist in should I be so inclined.

He taps away rather deliberately and it is sometime before he emerges from his somewhat trance like state.

"Okay, so in total then that's £442."

I hand him my credit card, but continue to think about this. It is not until he returns with the slip for me to sign, I point out, his maths would not qualify him for a place at the local nursery.

"Hang on, 20 tiles in a box at 85 pence per tile is £17, and 19 boxes is £323."

Oh bugger, I think this level of information given at such speed will send his brain into meltdown. He is staring at me in a very scary manner as if he is about to go into a fit. I grab the calculator on his desk as a means of demonstrating that it is he who is talking bollocks rather than me

"See?" I perform the calculation and show him the result. A huge furrow develops on his brow, and he returns to look at his screen. He taps away, and then starts hitting one key progressively harder, clearly frustrated both with his computer, and his own inability to comprehend the situation.

Of course, what happens in these situations is that gradually all the rest of the staff in the shop are called in to offer advise and assistance, but each one of them seems to have a similar vacant air. Sharon even offers to go round to other side of the desk and point out what a complete pillock this man is. But instead this just confirms that whatever this moron has done, he has somehow contrived to try and charge me for a shed load more tiles than I am planning on buying. Inevitably, the manager arrives, but this is even more troubling as he looks about fifteen years old. Meantime, the shop has become very busy with lots of other customers, many of whom seem to be having problems of their own. In a blur of dealing with our problem and those of the rest of the staff, who clearly see him as some Messiah, he points out that Darren has replicated part of our order, must cancel that, refund our credit card, run through another charge, and apologises profusely for the problems and the time taken to sort it out. By this time, I am looking away from the counter, as I do not know whether to laugh hysterically at this scene, or threaten physical assault, but there are more of them than me, so I opt for very tight lips and a withering stare.

As a final gesture, Darren decides he must help us wheel the barrow and tiles to the car, but in the process comes very close to dropping one of the boxes off the barrow. How I resist the temptation to stop dead in my tracks, spin round and shout:

"For fucks sake, will you just piss off you useless tool," I really don't know, but I send him scurrying back to the shop with the barrow trailing behind him as quickly as I can.

On returning home, we note Wally has also been in residence with Chris, and I am sure they have both been very happy together. More switches, lights and sockets are in, together with an extractor fan to the downstairs toilet, a blessed relief to all occupants and users. However, the downside to this is the exposed new piping that runs up through the landing and the fan which seems to run on for ever, long after the toilet has been vacated and by which time I am sure the air inside will have been changed a hundred times. This would not be a problem if it were not for the constant droning that comes up from the loo to the landing and sounds as if a light aircraft is getting ready for take off. Perhaps we should decorate the toilet in the style of an in-flight w/c, although unlike my experiences with such facilities, ours has more than enough room to turn around without crushing parts of your lower body on the basin.

Tuesday 25 February 2003
For the first time since just after the builders started, there is light and in more ways than one. As I exit the house this morning, dawn has most definitely broken and the glow of the early day is almost enough for me to drive on sidelights. It is a most calm and beautiful morning, with just a hint of mist lurking around the trees and hedges and the handsome graduated late winter sky, from pale orange at the horizon, blending seamlessly to a hazy powder blue at the sky's zenith. The odd aircraft trail shoots across the sky like a fluttering ribbon, and within ten minutes, an iridescent ball of orange peeps over the edge of the landscape, as the sun starts to stamp its authority on the scene. Spring is not far away.

Later in the morning I receive a call from Richard who has been on site this morning and, prompted by my stabbing reminder last week, has discussed with the builders both works to tidy up and a timetable for departure. The latter, to my complete surprise, is set for this Friday. Knowing they still have two new windows to put in, a heating system to fix (again), rather a lot of plastering and some odd, but fundamental finishing touches (like having a letter box, before the postman finally decides he is fed up with guessing where he should dump the post each day), I am rather sceptical. I am also faced with the prospect they will not be doing the plastering in the lounge until Thursday, which rather clashes with my need to clear the kitchen on that day, having planned to do so by moving the lounge furniture back from whence it came. Unless I particularly want a new textured, pink finish to the armchairs and sofa, this will not be a good move. I point this out to Richard, but this gets me the usual 'Mmmm...yes....well' which translated means 'can't help you there.' I proffer the hope that the weather is as sunny and calm as it has been for the last week. In which case we might just be able to pile up the furniture outside, although since what space is currently available on the patio is just about enough to stand up on, doing so will present merely the latest in logistical gymnastics. I think when this is all over, not only will we be lost in all the apparent acres of space we will suddenly have to use, but I will be the worlds expert on cramming lots of big things into very few tiny spaces. The Tardis principle becomes reality.

When I get back to the house later, I find, at least one of the bigger jobs has been done, courtesy of a new window in the study. While this looks pleasing from the outside, it is all a bit ugly inside. It looks like the inside of a third world prison cell, with exposed rough brick and block-work, broken plaster and paint all around the outside of the window frame, and a new thick layer of dust over everything in the room. I am sure this will be repaired and re-plastered shortly. In the meantime this now only leaves the one remaining shabby window in Sian's room as the last vestige and relic of what the house used to be, the one lingering pitiful symbol of the grot that was Holly House before all of this started. I think if this is gone when I get home tomorrow night, I may suggest to Sharon, we open the half bottle of Champagne I bought her for Valentine's Day – a little perverse tribute to the hatred we had for the house's previous identity.

In the meantime and much later in the evening, I am swearing, and in fairly colourful terms at that. It's my old friend the boiler again, or more particularly, the lump of plastic with a digital display that hangs off the wall by the boiler and purports to control its every move, but seems to have as much control over the boiler as I do over the weather, but at least the weather knows not to keep providing searing heat twenty four hours a day. I go through the programming cycle, even though this seems to be a task of such scientific complexity that I feel like Spock sat on the bridge of the Enterprise (only I don't have the rather shapely and sultry Uhuru sitting just across the way, twiddling with something strange in her ear), and set the evening 'OFF' time for 10.30pm. The time is by now 11.30pm, the boiler is in a silent phase. Have I cracked it? I close the door quietly, and creep out as if any sudden movement will awaken it, but just as I head upstairs, it fires back into life.

"Fucking boiler!" I shout in a strange loud whisper.

I go back in, with some intensity and anger, and promptly burn my forehead on the flue pipe, which is extremely hot.

"Fucking, fucking boiler!" as if swearing at it in doubles will have some effect.

After some more Spock like, if rather ham fisted, punching of buttons, I give up

"Sod you!" I shout, as if dealing with a surly and uncooperative human and turn the whole thing off.

I know doing this means I will have to get up at about 5.00am in order to turn it back on again to enable us to have some reasonable temperature in the morning, but right now I have to rest my brain and its singed outer layer.

Wednesday 26 February 2003

It's gone – the one remaining window, the last link to the house that was, has been ripped out and lays broken in the skip. It should be a joyous occasion, but before that I know time will be ever so short over the next few days as we try and press on to create a finished interior from a rough but perfectly formed shell. My particular concern is the woodwork and the huge array of nail and screw holes that litter the skirting board and architraves like a plague of woodworm, although judging by some of the holes, any woodworm associated with these would be alarmingly big and in urgent need of a diet. My answer to these is the old favourite, a small trowel, a tin of plastic wood and lots of generous slopping about and stuffing into and smearing across said gaps and fissures. The only problem is, this stuff has the consistency of old, very stodgy and very cold semolina. It smelt better than I remember during some of my most horrible days in primary school, when I had to eat the stuff, even though it looked and smelt foul and tasted even worse – to this day, even the word conjures up images that are capable of giving me nightmares. Now, try splurging this into holes big and small, then realise as soon as it hits the air, it starts to dry and the end result is woodwork that looks like it has been target practice for school boys throwing mud, or, more likely, semolina.

Nevertheless, we still break open the small bottle of champagne and drink a modest little toast to the fact that the old house has been banished. We hope the work I am going to start tomorrow will (eventually) magically transform the place into a highly respectable house, but most importantly, a comfortable and inviting home.

Thursday 27 February 2003

I have little doubt, if it were not for parents and grandparents, the tea industry would be on its knees, probably the Indian sub-continent would be destitute, the whole world economy would be thrown into chaos and anarchy would very shortly reign. Indeed, you might reasonably surmise, if it were not for the tea industry, the same fate would befall elderly parents and grandparents, as it seems they are unable to function without an infusion of tea at least every half hour, but better still every five minutes. In fact there is a secondary industry in the form of digestive biscuit production that is also inextricably linked to this economic chain, but only if the biscuits are of sufficient quality to withstand a damn good dunking without falling off and drowning in the bottom of one's cup.

I have imported both parents from this morning in order to assist with the humungous workload of getting as much decoration done as humanly possible, rather deluding myself that we can substantially complete the kitchen/diner, the bathroom and Cara's bedroom. I realise after a few hours, I am more likely to win Wimbledon in 2003 and I don't even play tennis. Of course, the speed of progress could be improved if we were to limit the consumption of tea. But to be fair, I think this would be like removing an intravenous drip and I would rather both parents stayed intact and productive, neither do I want to be the cause of a huge drop in the share price of Typhoo or PG.

My original plan today was to start and complete the tiling and get on with some painting perhaps half way through the day. My underestimation of timescales and the size of the task reminded me that as a rather naïve twelve year old, I thought it would be a doddle to cycle to Cambridge and back on a pretty basic child's bike – in the middle of February – and it started to snow half way. That rather basic error was rescued by getting the train back, but this time, we can do nothing more than plough on and on and on and on, until nine thirty this evening, by which time we had achieved putting all the tiles on the wall, and half a bucket load of tile fixer on the worktop and floors and we hadn't even started to grout yet. Was I disheartened? Yes. Thankfully, parents are made of stronger stuff and in any event, they have the sustenance of yet another cup of tea, which clearly is the elixir of youth, while I merely reach for the bottle of whisky.

I love my parents dearly, but in the space of a day of being in frequent and close communication, I do wonder how I managed to live with them for so long and remain reasonably sane and stable. Ably assisted by the radio being on all day, to each other, we appear as parodies. My mother, the eternal doom merchant, absolute in her conviction that it *really* wasn't like this in her day and the country is 'going to the dogs', although which dogs, I am not too sure. Certainly, she is not referring to a trip to Walthamstow Dog Track. I, on the other hand, am the forty-something and intolerant cynic, telling my mother not be so silly (I always try and avoid the word stupid, none of my family are stupid, but they can be plenty silly) vilifying all politicians, celebrities and my mother's simplistic view. My father usually thinks the answer is another cup of tea.

This is going to be a very long five days

Friday 28 February 2003

Today is scheduled to be the builders last, but they have much to do, including plastering of the lounge ceiling. In view of this, they had indicated they might be fairly early in the morning, and in consequence had suggested they take the key to the new side door in case we weren't quite up and about by the time they arrived. Not a problem, I said, expecting them to turn up at sometime between 7.30 and 8.0 o'clock.

At 6.15 this morning, I emerged from a rather deep sleep, in that twilight zone of being neither awake or asleep imagined a deaf burglar had infiltrated the house. Certainly, if he had all his aural faculties intact, he would be aware that all the racket he was making would probably have alerted the nearest police station five miles away, let alone provoked me from my slumber. Hang on though, unless he is demolishing part of the house (and it could be he has taken a shine to some of the fitments recently put into place) I could not fathom why burglary would entail lots of banging and hammering. Some semblance of consciousness was returning. I now wondered if my father had become particularly restless and was starting rather early although since the noise seemed to be coming from the bottom of the stairs, that would seem rather odd, unless he had decided that tiling the hallway was the next big thing in trendy décor. A particularly loud series of constant hammerings then brought me round in the same way that a bucket of cold water might have done (only in a lot less messy fashion), and looking at the clock again in disbelief, I realised that when Steve said they could be early, he really did mean *early*.

I then become aware that other sounds are coming from other parts of the house, and as surreal as it seems, I am in bed in the middle of a building site before 6.30 in the morning. I now realise that sleep, or any other restful pastime amidst this growing cacophony is not a realistic proposition. I therefore arise, although slightly disgruntled, but can hardly blame the builders for wanting to start early. And in any event, it is a beautiful crisp morning, with the sun just beginning to blast through the windows at the front and flooding the house with a brilliant, crystal glow. I amble down the stairs to find Steve at the bottom, fiddling about with the final new door to go in place.

"Morning," I groan through an instinctive yawn.

"Morning," he chimes back, without a glance, apparently oblivious to the slight disquiet I feel that the time of day does not quite equate to this level of activity.

"You weren't joking when you said you could be early, were you?" I am not seeking an apology, just a small recognition that this is not normal behaviour

"Naah," he says, with only the merest look in my direction. I fear it is I who is out of step this morning.

To complete the strangeness of the morning, it appears that my father, who verges on the edge of being an insomniac, has slept, and continues to sleep, through the whole thing.

At a more reasonable hour, work for the dynamic tea drinking father and son duo begins again in earnest, and we are back on the tiling trail again. This is the part that creates so much mess, but is strangely appealing to men who have probably never got out of the satisfaction of playing around with, and in, mucky, gooey substances. Tile grout is nothing more than white, sloppy, grainy, sticky mud, only messier. We have found there is no point in being careful and precise with something that has all the stability and firmness of a bowl of jelly and ice cream, *after* Cara has been let loose on it for at least one minute. The best policy is to slap and smear it on the tiles and into the joints with gusto and purpose, thereby creating the desired complete coverage, but with the disadvantage of the excess mess having to be cleaned off rather rapidly, unless you want a tiled wall that will look like an untidy rock face. So, we develop a system whereby my father slaps it on and I do my best to wipe it all off again, but taking care not to be so thorough that I simply take off precisely the amount that has gone on in the first place, leaving enough to fill all the joints in a reasonably uniform fashion. This requires a constant supply of clean water and sponge and the amount of excess grout being washed down the sink does make me wonder if I am inadvertently creating a grout damn somewhere deep in the bowels of my drainage system.

This turns into almost another full day job, but by the end of it, I am gratified by the result. Although the tiles still do have a thin film of dry, white grout all over their surface, I am reliably informed this will take just a bit of good old 'elbow grease' to remove. Be warned – when you hear this phrase from parents, don't be fooled into thinking this will be a minor little task. Be prepared for a lot of hard work.

In the meantime, a whole troop of workers, many of whom I have never seen before, have piled in. I walk out of the kitchen to the front door, to be confronted with a crowd of people, inside and out, busy doing…well, everything really. Some man who looks like he has just walked off the terraces at Chelsea, appears to be doing some woodwork in the hall, but I dare not ask for fear of a headbut. An older gentleman in glasses is shovelling sand into the back of a trailer, dressed like someone's granddad, he looks as if he has just got up from his armchair in front of the television. Others mill about and are moving and shifting stuff, presumably as the closing moments of this particular contract get nearer and nearer.

In the lounge, Eddie, Andy and Steve are plastering at a pace making it all a bit of a blur. But clearly they have a deadline to get this complete by this afternoon, as do I. By mid afternoon, we have managed to switch to painting and as the wood is bare and untreated, it all must be primed before being painted. In order to give ourselves enough room, we have had to move all the furniture into a big pile just outside the French windows of the lounge. While the day started clear and bright, it has now become rather dark and threatening and what it is threatening to do is rain. Now, while it is true that the lounge furniture has had so much abuse, it has probably established a national furniture protection phone line ('Hello, I am a 12 year old armchair from Hertfordshire, and I don't think I can take any more of this treatment. Do you know of a safe warehouse I can go to?') I would not wish rain upon it, if only for the fact that it would not mix too well with ingrained dust. At about 4.00 pm, it started, ever so gently, to drizzle. Solution? Panic! While we grabbed cushions to shove back inside the kitchen, thankfully progress in the lounge was sufficient for some of the furniture to be squeezed in and we were spared the prospect of soggy seating.

By the end of the day, Steve had admitted partial defeat and accepted he would have to make one final return trip on Monday, at which point the railway carriage like trailer would go and new shingle would be placed over the drive that looked as if someone had dug a route for a major oil pipeline and reinstated rather badly. However, we could at last re-occupy the lounge, albeit under an obviously still wet plastered ceiling and standing on scrappy underlay, the carpet having now been consigned to the skip. It wasn't palatial, but at least we had some room.

Saturday 1 March 2003
We are missing a friend today, as for the first time in weeks, Wally is not in residence. It all seems rather quiet, civilised and spacious. With the lounge furniture heap now gone from the kitchen, or rather the dining area, we can appreciate the size and openness of this room. And we are going to need all the space we can get, as we pile into the painting today.

On one level, painting is a messy and literally painful exercise, particularly painting the ceiling. I have no problem with rollers, for large flat surfaces, they are truly a Ferrari of the paint world, compared to my battered old mini of a paint brush, but like all apparently good things, they have their drawbacks. For one thing, constantly rolling backwards and forwards can play havoc with your arm, and after a couple of hours, it feels like I have been trying to hold down Mike Tyson. For another, it splashes and speckles paint over everything, but in such small spots that I don't notice until much later, by which time I am trying to scratch and pick the little particles off the worktop, the radio, the floor and my own face that looks as if it has a strange white contagion. Rollers are also crap for edges and corners, where the Ferrari turns into an ill-handling twenty ton articulated lorry, with an unstable load and probable MOT failure. Finally, while the first coat is not a problem to identify, putting on a second coat and spotting where you have been and where you haven't is frankly one of life's great impossibilities. The only partial solution I have is to keep getting down from the step ladders, standing in a particular spot in the kitchen and trying to catch the light shining on the newly painted surface. This is fine as long as you can keep your eyes transfixed on this area while you try and navigate your way back across the room and on to the step ladders. If you are like me, you will trip and fall over several objects (usually the large tin of paint in the middle of the room), miss the bottom step on the ladder, fly the rest of the way across the room, inadvertently stuff the roller half way up your nose and along your arm, thereby placing far more paint on yourself than the ceiling.

On another level, I can find painting relaxing, even cathartic. This is particularly true of gloss painting, although strangely there is a point where catharsis becomes mind-numbingly boring. I had just about reached the latter stage in the process when I finished, after some five hours, painting the large triple sash window in the kitchen. Sash windows are not simple square chunks of wood, but have nooks, crannies, runners, guides, gullies and moving parts that all have to be carefully painted in order. Slowly and bit by bit, moving from the inside-out, being *ever so careful* and particular when painting alongside the glass, in order to avoid the sort of slapdash mess, I had inherited within so much of the rest of the house. The concentration needed to do this is consuming, but not exclusive, so while it is possible to do the job in a competent manner, while listening to the radio and having the odd conversation, you cannot allow yourself to drift into deep intellectual thought on a totally unrelated subject. So, don't go trying to figure out Pythagoras's theorem, ponder quadratic equations, or even the plot of Eastenders (there isn't one) while doing this. For me, it mercifully meant there was not quite the mental capacity to worry about all things work-related, and hence, for a while at least, I found it quite calming.

The calmness disappears when I realise that the 'One Coat' paint is a fraud and it will not be the first time I have discovered this. Paradoxically, it has no trouble in covering my hands in one very tough coat I have difficulty even scrubbing off, but is unable to do so with the wood, where I can clearly see beneath and as such it will require a clear second coat. I know this tin has a pretty meaningless guarantee, I am hardly going to call in the fraud squad. I am not going through the painful process of going back into B&Q to complain, for a £10 tin of paint. It simply is not worth the aggravation – and I cannot face the prospect of a very unproductive and frustrating conversation with yet another 'Customer Service' department living in the Twilight Zone.

Monday 3 March 2003

We are at it again. Paint, brushes and rollers to the fore, this time it's the wall that has the benefit of our attention, coupled with yet more gloss on the wood, including the second coat which, our friends who produce the paint with the famous dog tell me, should not be necessary. Come to think of it, using the dog as a roller or very large brush could be an option, maybe that's how they come to the conclusion that one coat would be enough. If you loaded up one of those with a tin of paint and splurged him on the wall, I dare say another coat really would be superfluous.

Later on (this time at a more reasonable morning hour) the builders return for their final push, generally a number of small finishing touches, but particularly to include some remedial measures on some of the gaps and cracks that have appeared over the last few weeks. While you might expect some areas where new skirting didn't quite meet the wall, in one or two places, some of the errors and distances were a bit surprising. One particular mitre and join in the kitchen were so far apart, they could not possibly have been related to each other, while a gap along the skirting in Cara's bedroom was almost big enough to be used as a handy magazine rack. Some of the cracks had opened up were also fairly sizeable, although not quite big enough that I could lose a child if it were necessary, shame. By the time I had to depart for the airport to pick up the returning dance troop, they were casting new shingle on the drive and beginning to hook up the trailer that had served as their office, store and bolt-hole for the last five months. I had a feeling of both relief and sadness, but in truth had not really thought in any depth about the day they were actually going to depart and in the meantime, I had a flight arrival to catch.

On returning home, I was gratifyingly able, for the first time in more than 150 days, to park properly and fully on my own drive, away from the house. In fact, precisely where the aforementioned trailer had been, so this was a place where we had not stood since before all the works began, back in September last year. As such, it was a vantage point we had not utilised to view the house, yet it was the one place to stand where you could view the whole of the front and side of the house and for the very first time take in the complete transformation. While we had seen the changes take place bit by bit, it was all a gradual process. The change was a form of metamorphosis, the impact being that much less than if we had disappeared for the whole period and then returned to see the revolution all in one hit.

Being able finally to look at the house now from this perspective was the next best alternative to that and it made us all stop in our tracks and stare. I cannot say that it is magnificent, as that would be rather foolish exaggeration, neither can I hail it as an architectural masterpiece, as it would be a blatant lie. I can however say that in the context of what stood before, this is Helena Christiansen as compared to Bella Emberg, or perhaps more appropriately more Victoria Beckham than Victoria Wood. It is reasonably handsome and well proportioned, without being devastatingly gorgeous, but so many miles better than the previous Holly House, it is in another continent.

While we could have done more and we might have wanted a different design, that would have meant more time and money, not to mention more angst with planners and parish council, but this was our acceptable compromise, and in the circumstances, it was good, maybe even very good.

Wednesday 5 March 2003
Two little, but telling events today. Firstly, I have a request to let Richard know of any problems remaining, or any work that seems still to be outstanding. I furnish him with a list of fairly minor issues and feel slightly petty in doing so. However, it brings home to me that while the builders may well pop back to do some tidying up, they are indisputably gone and finished. Secondly, a friend comes around and is genuinely gobsmacked by the change, and profers the view, the house now has character. I had not thought about this, as I generally only think houses have character if they have *acquired* it over time, rather than *purchased* it as part of a build process, but I think she

may be right. Perhaps by not trying too hard, we have given the house some character, albeit modest and muted, which can't be a bad thing.

Friday 7 March 2003

True to their word, Steve and his men have been back on site today and fixed most of the outstanding problems and omissions, although word has it the final, *final* snagging will be done on Monday, after which time, they will not be back.

One of the pieces of corrective action had been to do something with the rather large holes they had drilled through from the hall, under the stairs, into the boiler cupboard. Apparently, the heat in this particular cranny of the house was at times building to rival an equatorial rainforest, or at least get to such a stage the programmer couldn't take it and expired in a pool of melted wire and plastic, metaphorically fainting in the heat. This was why on more than one occasion all my button pushing and swearing had been completely in vain, as the poor bloody thing was effectively in a coma. Hence the suggestion to release some of this heat into the wider environment and perhaps provide the hall with a bit of a temperature boost, as well as helping to maintain a reasonable working environment for all the electronic bits and pieces. That was fine, but the holes drilled through for this exercise were like someone was re-enacting journey to the centre of the earth. I also noted they were low enough and sufficiently close together, you could, if you were so inclined, sit on the floor with your legs through them, like an upside down stock. This could be turned into a particularly heinous punishment, but I have to confess, the only candidate that crossed my mind was my old friend the conservation officer.

The missing bit from all of this effort, was the requirement to put some grilles over the holes, rather than have all my guests stare alarmingly at them in their raw state and wonder as to whether our sanity had been compromised by the previous six months stress. What I had not expected were large white louvred squares that look like they had come off a gloomy industrial estate from the former East Germany. You might reasonably have expected steam to have been issuing from them and people walking backwards and forwards in white protection suits and breathing apparatus, such were their size and starkness. Okay, I exaggerate, but they did look rather incongruous in the context of our new hall, even if its salubriousness was currently rather compromised by bare plaster walls, unfinished wood, half stripped wallpaper and the remains of a carpet to give a landfill site a bad name. Still, I am sure, somewhere we can find something better, even though it is rather difficult to make a vent look anything other than just that.

The remaining item that continued to cause angst was the control unit for the under floor heating in the Kitchen. This was not a simple thermostat on the wall, which would have seemed to me to be the most straightforward option, but consisted of a modest little box screwed to the wall with two little

LED's, but more problematic was another unit that was not fixed to anywhere. This was a remote programmer, which apparently connects to our little box on the wall, and tells it when to turn the heating on and off, what temperature you would like, what day of the week you would like it and how many sugars you take in your tea. Its peculiarity extends beyond its whole range of weird and wonderful functions, as it communicates this information by radio waves, presumably so you can wander about the kitchen at your leisure, with unit in hand, pondering just how you would like your floor. Warm, well toasted or scorching hot – and then sending the information to the said wall unit, located all of three metres away at maximum. The words 'pointless' and 'completely' spring to mind, but the words 'useless' and 'bloody' were those that issued from my mouth.

I had now tried no less than five times to get the remote to hold a meaningful conversation with the blank little box on the wall, but apart from some hopeful flashing of a red LED for a few seconds, they failed to hit it off. In order to get them even to this stage I had read and attempted to translate instructions that seemed to have been written originally in Russian, then subsequently translated and then sanitised into a language that bore only a passing resemblance to understandable English. It wasn't as though the words did not hang together, it was just they were so stilted and tight, they were positively anally retentive. It was no wonder that with such poor encouragement, the remote unit was not able to get it on with the shy little box on the wall. Needless to say I gave up and it appears the builders have had the same experience, as the remote sits again alongside its box and the now rather grubby and repeatedly folded and abused instructions. Sounds like another job for a member of the Star-ship Enterprise.

Sunday 9 March 2003
I have been painting again this weekend like my whole life depended upon it, as I am determined all such activity will be complete come Sunday night. On Saturday, this had consisted of acres of more gloss work on wood and I have to confess I am now getting a bit sick of the sight of pure brilliant white. Despite already knowing the stuff does not cover in one coat, I still murmur obscenities under my breath and curse even louder when one particular area looks as if it may even need a third coat. It was a good job Sharon and the girls were out, as both the volume and extent of this profanity were not for the young or faint-hearted.

Today, we got around to finishing the walls, including one tricky section that ran straight up to meet the roof at an apex, leaving very little room to manoeuvre within the forty five degree angle between wall and ceiling. Painting a straight line along the very top of this wall was a task to which I could not be said to be ideally suited. To do it justice, it would have been beneficial to be seven foot tall, especially thin at the top, an incredibly steady hand, razor sharp vision and the ability to hold your breath for minutes at a time. Alright, if you had all the previous faculties, the last one would not have been necessary, but I found it the only way I could keep sufficiently steady and concentrate for the appropriate length of time.

By mid afternoon, it was all done and having been cooped up in the house for most of the weekend, I agreed to take the girls down to the local park, if only for a bit of fresh air and a change of scene. I was pleasantly surprised at the almost spring like feel to the air, still chilly, but without the keenness that so characterises winter. Daffodils were bursting out of almost every bank and verge and a healthy smattering of crocuses hid shyly beneath many. Snowdrops are also resplendent in this part of the world and were providing there own finale along the fringes of the churchyard and the grounds of the grand Anstey House. Emerging buds and the odd bloom were now becoming evident on many of the trees and bushes and I felt uplifted by the thought that spring was not far away. My spirits were also lifted by the ridiculous, though inevitable, antics of Cara.

Once at the park, we played around on the swings and climbing frame and personally I never tire of a good swing. We played a little 'It!' and some general chasing around and silliness, but the climax was a game suggested by Cara – scissors, paper, stone. That this will be known to all is not in doubt, but not in the Cara format, as this is 'Whole-Self' scissors, paper, stone. None of this namby hands-behind-your-back stuff, in this ludicrous, but delightfully enjoyable, version, you each stand at a distance from each other, and on the count of 'three' undertake a complete impersonation of your chosen item. Paper entails you stretching your arms out above your head, while scissors requires you to stretch your arms out alongside you in 'vee' formation in the style of a pair of scissors. For the rock, you put your hands joined over your head. Okay, you could be mistaken as a complete bunch of loonies doing YMCA, and in a kids playground that will probably have the Police in close attendance in double quick time, but who cares? On revealing your chosen article, you must then perform the usual action, running towards your opponent to either cut their paper, blunt their scissors or cover their rock. This necessitates pincering your opponent in your arms repeatedly as scissors, bumping your backside into your opponent as the act of blunting them and physically smothering them as a means of demonstrating the properties of paper. The end result is always much the same, a cascade of giggling and running around, ending in a joyous heap on the floor. If you are ever feeling a bit down, I can recommend this game as an anti-depressant.

Monday 10 March 2003
Steve and crew have indeed been back again today and all seems to be as it should, other than they have clearly failed to be able to mate the programmer on the kitchen wall, the remote unit remaining disconsolately on the worktop. So, there will be another visit from someone, but I am told that matters are

now in train to render me with a final account and relieve me of the last payment in return for nearly six months of trial and turbulence.

There is no doubt a degree of normality has returned to Holly House. But it still remains a fundamentally bizarre place to live and will continue to be so until we have finished all the decoration and other internal tweaking that will finally establish it as the home, rather than the house. And when we have done this, we have the garden to look forward to, but I can't yet face the prospect of that.

So where are we? Well, we have space, light and a basic design of which I am no longer ashamed. On a guided tour, I can finally take you in through the front door, admiring the handsome, if slightly over large, canopy as you enter. Unfortunately, you will then have to avert your eyes from the bare chipboard on the floor, the unfinished plaster walls, and the windows only finished in primer, but at least there is sufficient room, I can actually call it a hall. Also within which not only could you just about swing a cat, but you could also invite in your dog and hamster as well, if you were so inclined. The stairs are now opened and looking up, natural light is for the first time evident from the landing. I confess the carpet that remains is from the house's previous incarnation, but at present, it acts usefully for us all to wipe our feet on, it blends perfectly with its dirty brown colour.

Off to the right is the study, but more accurately described at present as the dust depository. It remains the main storage room, and to that end has been largely undisturbed for some months, or at least it had until we removed the old dining table and chairs on Sunday. Doing so revealed a layer of dust and dirt so thick, I wondered if a blow torch might have been in order. For some of the books I discovered underneath one of the chairs, I genuinely could not tell what they were, the text on the front cover of the top two were completely obscured, like some ghostly novels with no name or title. The cretinous carpet theme from the hall continued, as did the combination of plaster, walls with semi-stripped paper and unfinished windows, but in truth it would not take too long to redecorate in something approaching reasonable.

The downstairs toilet is now a rather windowless hovel, with a collection of not one but two types of horrific cheap and nasty plastic floor covering, obviously repaired walls where the old internal door had been removed. And there is some pretty naff boxing supposed to hide all the pipe work and pump paraphernalia for the under floor heating that ran into the kitchen, but in fact at present did the opposite by attracting attention. This is truly a dreadful room, especially as it retains some of the worst horrors of the past, most particularly the door into the boiler cupboard, painted a strange deep sea type green, but only, I suspect, if it were a particularly deep and polluted sea. In addition the burgundy toilet and basin remains, but again only burgundy in the sense of it being a bottle that would be more likely to resemble Sarson's Vinegar when opened, I feel. Shame that the extractor cannot take away nasty vision as well as smell.

The kitchen and dining room are of course complete, although it is true that we need to do a little tidying up. No matter how steady I try and make my hand, inevitably my straight lines, especially around the edges of windows and skirting boards are never entirely as they might be. Those particularly bad can be put down to mid-job distractions, sneezing, or Whitney Houston on the radio, all of which are generally avoidable, but completely understandable. I have to confess though, I am pretty pleased with the final result here, it has turned out to be the light, airy and useable space we wanted, even G the Geezers little contribution looks pretty good.

The lounge is a blank canvas, even if it is currently a rather tatty and grubby one, of a predominantly dusty pink colour, owing to the profusion of unfinished plasterwork. With the large bay window at one end and the French windows at the other, again it is light and open, although the light reveals a floor that has in part no covering at all, while the remainder is repeatedly emblazoned with either 'Treadaire' or 'Carpet Right'. This seems a little peculiar to me – putting what amounts to an advert on underlay ranks with the time and effort that must go into designing the finish of a mattress, as for the vast majority of its life no one is going to see it. I swear some people buy a mattress because it has a funky design, completely oblivious to the fact, in usage thereafter, it will be covered. Unless you are likely to have some really strange, not to mention frighteningly inquisitive guests who lift up your bed sheet and say 'Oh, groovy mattress design, where *did* you get it?' it really is the height of pointlessness. While it may be true in current context in the Holly House lounge, the ads are shouting out of the floor, I really don't think the companies concerned would necessarily want to be associated with this environment.

The remaining scar in the lounge is the fireplace, although it is a positive joy compared to the rock-faced monstrosity there originally. We are left currently with a fairly large, square hole for the fire opening, but the fireback rather protrudes and is propped up on a shabby pile of bricks, which were used to bring the whole fireplace up to the level of the large in-your-face hearth that sat in front. Thankfully, it has now gone, but it has revealed, for reasons that entirely escape me, that the previous occupants had gouged out a big hole in the floor. (Gouge being the appropriate word here, as clearly no finesse or precision had come within sniffing distance of this exercise). They had then stuffed in a pile of cement and rubble, which stands just proud of the floor and looks like something nasty has begun oozing out of the floor, solidifying just as it emerged. I have no idea what these people were up to here, perhaps it is better I do not know.

If I take you now up the stairs, the amount of space on the landing and the fact we have a window giving natural light, is a revelation. It is so spacious, I feel I ought to burst into song, but apart from looking stupid, it would be an unpleasant experience for all. Again, walls are all plastered, as is the ceiling, which has banished a piece of comic artex repair undertaken by the previous owners. While I would not pretend I could have done much of a better job, I am fairly sure, had I attempted this, it would not have looked as if they had got a large bowl of rice pudding (sufficiently cold and stodgy) and thrown it hard up against the offending area that required repair and then left it to dry in situ, in all its dripping, turgid state. Having then assured themselves it had become suitably hard and crusty, it was then treated to a quick lick of paint, and hey presto, instant ceiling repair. The only remaining mildly disturbing item on the landing concerned the new boxing around the extract pipe that ran up from the downstairs toilet. They had unfortunately used a piece of board, which clearly had been walked across. And each time I saw it, I envisaged we had been visited by some mystic builder, who could walk up walls, leaving some very obvious size 10 boot prints leading all the way up to the ceiling.

Cara's bedroom is in the same state as it has been now for a couple of months, other than some of the cracks that had opened up have been rapidly filled with white filler, giving a strange pock marked appearance over walls and ceiling. However, the main event is that Cara is now back in residence which can mean only one thing – chaos. Until such time as we can decorate, all her personal bits and pieces continue to be housed in boxes on one side of the room. Initially these were fairly neatly stacked and ordered, but now the contents have gradually found their way onto the floor and are threatening to occupy most of the floor space, as they inexorably creep their way towards her bed. On the other side of the room, some of her clothes are doing the same, and a pincer movement is clearly developing, these apparently inanimate objects not being satisfied until the whole floor is covered. Of course, pink and lilac continue to dominate the overall effect.

Sian's room is of course largely untouched, although we need to fill the gap left by the eviction of the glass thing above the door, at least on her side of the room, as on the landing this has all been repaired and plastered. Her new window is now in, but until such time as we can find both time and money to fund a blind, her old curtain sits in place, but is of insufficient length to cover the entire depth of the window. This does look a little strange and funny, like a mini skirt that is not quite long enough to cover someone's arse, although I have to admit, I have yet to see someone's arse that resembles the bottom of a sash window and an unfinished shelf. Underneath the window, a new double radiator sits in place, but unfortunately, its depth is such, we now cannot put her chest of drawers back in their original place, although why we should concern ourselves with any sense of order in Sian's room, remains a mystery. Indeed, Sian's room is a mystery in itself, it always looks like the aftermath of a burglary, or murder (without the blood) or possibly both. It would make a good setting or opening scene for an Inspector Frost episode, but even he could not solve the riddle on why it is constantly in the state it is. Perhaps her room is the eighth wonder of the world.

The spare room is just that and has been returned in part to the position of general dumping ground and toy and game emporium. Again, all surfaces are finished and ready for the attack of the paint brush, although once again, the floor contains remnants of some of the nasty brown floor tiles that were in existence before. Some of these seemed to have a particularly strong will to survive, as it had proved almost impossible to prise them away from the floor, indeed one poor metal wall paper scraper had bent in submission, so there were small parts of the old house clearly still set on revenge. No doubt other little surprises and pockets of stubborn persistence would be encountered as we continue our quest to transform and entirely condemn the old into oblivion. At least the new window looks nice.

The master bedroom was in a similar raw state of readiness and was proving lighter than we had expected courtesy of our large single sash window, facing almost due south, benefiting from full sunlight, as and when the British weather chooses to give out its meagre rations of this ingredient. True, the act of running a bath now gave the impression of something being locked up in the new airing cupboard and was pleading to be let out, but hopefully, once we had stuffed this full of the usual towels, sheets and other linen, it might calm the creature down. The en-suite could now be used, or at least the toilet and basin. The former was a bit of a giveaway, as its flushing action was almost a match for the airing cupboard cacophony, but the basin provided no such aural assault. The shower remains out of bounds, as doing so without the walls being tiled will have serious consequences for the bare plasterboard. I am pleased to say the shower itself works fine, producing a spray to beat the previous impression of a light drizzle that issued from the old system in the old bathroom. I am also pleased to say standing up and moving around in the en-suite presents no problem, unless you try and make rapid progress towards the radiator on the farthest wall without remembering that without stooping, your head will be on a serious collision course with the ceiling. Suffice to say, I only made this mistake once.

The bathroom is perfectly usable, providing you don't splash water anywhere, which is always a little tricky in a bathroom environment. All walls and floors, together with the rather scruffy plywood boxing around the water and waste piping, is unfinished and in such a state is only too willing to soak up even the merest hint of moisture. Unfortunately, in doing so, it will hasten the breakdown of its very structure and before you know it, plaster will be running off the walls, we will be trudging through MDF mud and the boxing will be a disintegrating mess. Still, we do now once again have a nice big sash window, this time facing south east, and at this time of year is the main morning portal for dazzling shafts of low sunlight as the dawn breaks over the fields of East Hertfordshire.

Outside is much as it should and was meant to be, as long as you don't look at the garden and immediate area. The house is reasonably handsome and has that vertical emphasis and proportion I was so anxious to impart, the windows bringing some much needed style and muted character. All in all, I am pretty pleased with what has been achieved. Even the large grey concrete slab that has been laid for the conservatory to be constructed when we can finally find a chunk more dosh, looks fine and hardly detracts from what was a rather untidy part of the garden in the first place. The same cannot be said for the fencing which is now looking tired and precarious, particularly along the western side bordering onto the road, and I fear any repeat of the winds we experienced in October will forcibly remove any boundary definition and dump it in a neighbours' garden. The gardens overall are looking very tired, drab and unkempt, not helped by the great scar that runs the length of the front garden, by which the water now carries on through the site, rather than stopping for a 3 day party.

I think I can clearly see the focus of the next project.

ARE WE FINISHED?

Wednesday 12 March 2003
Well..yes and no. Other than possibly beaming down Mr Spock to sort out the programmer in the kitchen, the builders have all packed and left for their next job. They have done their bit and while we genuinely suffered on occasion, there was little roll-the-sleeves up effort required, other than the constant movement of stuff from one room to another.... and then there was the constant cleaning as well....not to mention the ripping up of floor coverings...okay, so there has, but not of the creative variety. But now it is my turn, and the kitchen decoration is only the beginning of it, there is so much more that needs to be done, and all of us impatient to get it finished. However, there is no doubt, the *really* hard and *really* expensive bit is done.

Builders attract some pretty bad press and I know from my own constant experiences that finding a service worthy of the name and cost is one of life's lotteries. While we might have had some small gripes, there is no doubt we have been truly blessed by a company and a group of individuals, who believes in the principle that if a job is worth doing, it is worth doing well. We may have had our sanity tested while we lived amidst the works, but what a pain in the builders' bum it must have been to do it all around our constant occupation, much better for them if they could have created as much shit and mayhem as they wanted, wherever they needed, in order to push on as quickly as possible. That, of course, is not possible when you have a family of four coming back to the place every night in order to do the usual family things of eating, drinking, home-working, relaxing and sleeping, interspersed with the not infrequent shouting, swearing and occasional crisis management.

All of this has been done during possibly the worst time of year you could feasibly choose to do such things, from the dawn of winter in October, through its coldest and wettest depths and only emerging to finish as the spring starts to shake itself into life. We have appeared to endure winds of hurricane force, rain of monsoon proportions and biblical length, arctic temperatures and periods of constant gloom and grey that merely reflected our mood. We have had power cuts, water leaks, blocked drains, blocked windows and enough dust and dirt to fill the Albert Hall. There has been sickness (umpteen times), diarrhoea (ditto), aches, colds and the odd physical injury, more arguments and tense silent stand offs than an Oprah Winfrey show, and a constant sense of frustration. We have been the victims of some of the crassest service known to man, but with the odd smattering of genuine commitment and honest human endeavour. Through it all there have been personal failures and a few serious triumphs, deep depression and periods of intoxicating elation and calm. I have seen the countryside and the scenery develop and reflect an astonishing array of guises and appearance, and witnessed flora and fauna in abundance. And I have seen some real sense of place and depth of spirit, while knowing truly the value of family and friends.

If I had a hat, I would take it off to the builders and thanks must clearly go to Steve and his brother Andy, Eddie, Pete, Wally and Arthur, all of whom showed humour and commitment in the face of what must at times have seemed the house and family from hell.

It has been a strange, interesting, difficult and not particularly wonderful experience and like all experiences, there is much of long standing value that can be extracted. We have achieved what we wanted and with a bit of luck, quite a bit more money, a fair bit of effort and a frequently imported father, within six months, the inside of the house should be done. So, through all of this, given what we have got, would I do it all again? Not on your life!

Printed in the United Kingdom
by Lightning Source UK Ltd.
100606UKS00001B/161-222